H. W. Smith. Sc.

Yours ever Emmy W. York

R. Andrews, Pr.

MEMOIR

OF

MRS. SARAH EMILY YORK,

FORMERLY

MISS S. E. WALDO;

MISSIONARY IN GREECE.

BY

MRS. R. B. MEDBERY,

AUTHOR OF MEMOIR OF WILLIAM G. CROCKER.

BOSTON:

PHILLIPS, SAMPSON AND COMPANY,

110 WASHINGTON STREET.

1853.

Wright & Hasty, Printers,
3 Water st., Boston.

DEDICATION.

To the members of the Charlestown Female Seminary, those who preceded the subject of this Memoir in their course of study, those who were associated with her, and those who have succeeded or who may succeed her in enjoying its privileges, this tribute to the grace of God as illustrated in the life and writings of one of the early graduates, is affectionately inscribed by a former teacher of that Institution.

Newburyport, Oct. 22, 1852.

PREFACE.

In attempting to present in the following pages a faithful portrait of her whose life and character are here delineated, the compiler has endeavored to make her as far as possible her own Biographer. In doing this she has sometimes taken the liberty to blend two letters in one, and, as Mrs. York left no journal, has frequently taken extracts from her correspondence without any mention of the person to whom she was writing. It is in this way that most letters addressed to herself have been used as well as many to other friends.

The death of Mrs. Waldo, soon after this work was commenced, was deeply felt by the compiler, as her judgment in many cases would have been invaluable. She has, however, been greatly indebted to the kindness of other friends, and has especially esteemed it a great privilege to be able to avail herself of the advice of Mr. York, in preparing that part of the work which relates to her life in Greece.

Should the work prove instrumental of stimulating any to more self-denying efforts, or more entire consecration of their whole being to God, the principal object for which it was undertaken will be secured.

Newburyport, Oct. 22, 1852.

CONTENTS.

CHAPTER I.

CHAPTER II.

CHAPTER III.

CHAPTER IV.

CHAPTER V.

CHAPTER VI.

CHAPTER VII.

CHAPTER VIII.

CHAPTER IX.

CHAPTER X.

CHAPTER XI.

CHAPTER XII.

CHAPTER XIII.

CHAPTER XIV.

CHAPTER XV.

CHAPTER XVI.

CHAPTER XVII.

CHAPTER XVIII.

CHAPTER XIX.

CHAPTER XX.

CHAPTER XXI.

CHAPTER XXII.

CHAPTER XXIII.

CHAPTER XXIV.

CHAPTER XXV.

CHAPTER XXVI.

CHAPTER XXVII.

CHAPTER XXVIII.

MEMOIR OF MRS. YORK.

CHAPTER I.

Her parentage—Early childhood—Connection with the C. F. Seminary—Character as a scholar—Conversion and religious views.

MRS. SARAH EMILY YORK was the eldest daughter of Mr. Charles F. Waldo, for many years an officer in the United States navy. In 1812, while performing his duty as sailing master on board the Constitution, then under the command of Commodore Bainbridge, he lost his left leg in the conflict between that vessel and the English frigate Java, off Rio Janeiro. Having by this misfortune become disabled for more active service, he was stationed at the Charlestown Navy Yard from that time till his death, which occurred August 30, 1838. In 1817 he was united in marriage with Miss Sarah V., daughter of Mr. Jacob Foster, of Charlestown, by whom he had an interesting family of two sons and five daughters.

Mr. Waldo was a man of strong mind and great decision of character, ardently attached to the Unitarian faith, and ever ready to vindicate his favorite doctrine. He was not, however, illiberal towards Christians of other denominations, but, possessing a mind naturally clear and discriminating, he was fond of argumentation, and always seemed happy to engage in friendly controversy, either by conversation or correspondence, with those of opposite sentiments. He endeavored at an early age to imbue the minds of his children with the same belief; yet he seemed mainly anxious to train them to habits of virtue and morality, and to impress their hearts with religious principle, as the only right motive to action.

In September 1833, his physical system suffered a severe shock from an apoplectic fit, followed by paralysis, which rendered him ever after an object of deep solicitude to his devoted family, and secured from them the most careful and prompt compliance with his wishes. During the remaining five years of his life, he devoted most of his leisure hours to the study of the Bible, and various commentaries upon it. And in his last sickness, though his disease deprived him of the use of speech, and thus rendered him unable to communicate his religious feelings, yet his calmness and patience under intense suffering, his cheerful acquiescence in the will of God, and especially his meek and quiet spirit, gave pleasing evidence to his friends that his soul had been renewed by divine grace, and that death was but the messenger to introduce him to that rest which remains for the people of God.

Mrs. Waldo was a lady of great refinement of feeling, polished and engaging manners, warm affections, and remarkable sweetness of temper. She was naturally frank and generous, kind and benevolent to all; but to her family and a large circle of friends she was a perfect pattern of devotedness, seeming wholly forgetful of herself in her sympathy with the joys and sorrows of others. Her powers of endurance were remarkable,—never mur-

muring under trials of any kind, but in the spirit of true piety, meekly bowing her will to that of her heavenly Father. During the last few years of her life, her religious exercises were very decidedly evangelical. With a hope of salvation resting entirely on the grace of God through Christ Jesus, she calmly and trustingly submitted all to God, and, hastening to join the dear ones who had gone before, sweetly slept in Jesus, June 8, 1851.

Sarah Emily, their eldest daughter, was born at Charlestown, November 30, 1819. She possessed the amiable and affectionate disposition of her mother, blended with the ardent temperament, strong feelings, and decision of character, which were so strikingly manifest in her father. From her earliest childhood she was fond of retirement, devoting much attention to reading, and beginning to employ her pen as a regular correspondent at the early age of ten. The basis of her education was thoroughly laid in the public schools of her native town, where her scholarship was always good and her conduct irreproachable.

At the age of fourteen she was placed in a small private school; but her parents, dissatisfied with her proficiency, had her removed in the autumn of 1834 to the Female Seminary at Charlestown. This Institution, which was organized in 1831, was then under the care of five Associate Principals, assisted by several under teachers. Finding herself associated here with some whose minds were of a high order, and whose attainments were in many cases far in advance of her own, her active mind at once received a new impulse, and her latent powers began to unfold and expand themselves.

About this time also she suffered a very severe affliction in the death of her younger brother, Henry, to whom she was devotedly attached. Her mind had been for some months previous seriously impressed, but this heavy bereavement was blessed of God to the deepening and strengthening of her piety. She said but little to any one respecting her feelings at the time, but a pleasing change was noticeable in her character, manifesting itself in an humble, subdued spirit, an increased effort to promote the happiness of others, and a conscientious improvement of her time, particularly of the opportunities furnished her by her parents for the cultivation of her intellectual powers.

As a scholar, she soon distinguished herself by her quickness of perception, clearness of thought, and readiness to communicate her ideas to others. Her countenance always brightened at the proposal of any question which opened a new avenue to thought. She loved to grapple with difficulties; nor was she ever satisfied till she could understand a subject sufficiently to explain it to others. The most prominent defects in her character at this time, were such as resulted from her natural independence of mind. Accustomed to rely upon the deductions of her own reason, she was slow to admit any thing on the mere authority of either teacher or text book. Her own mind must be brought clearly to apprehend a truth, before she could fully admit it; but, having grasped a subject herself, she did not always manifest a proper degree of patience towards those whose perceptions were more obtuse, or whose mental operations were more sluggish than her own. She had also such a love of simplicity of character, such a contempt for artificiality, as led her not only to despise every thing like affectation, but also to neglect some of those little courtesies which others had a right to expect from her.

Perceiving that these defects were becoming quite an annoyance to some of her teachers, one of their number held a long conversation with Emily, in which she succeeded in bringing her to view the subject in the same light in which it was viewed by others. From that moment she not only set herself in earnest to overcome these faults, but also sought the aid of the same teacher in discovering and correcting any other defects in her character; and almost every week brought from her a note expressive of some sentiment like the following:

"I feel greatly honored that you should have noticed me so much as to have labored to correct my errors. I know there is enough of wrong in me to be rooted out, and I feel truly grateful to any one who will take enough interest in me to correct my faults, especially so kindly as yourself. If your kind admonitions have had but little influence upon my conduct, it is not because I have not felt their weight. Do not think that they are useless. The soil doubtless is sterile, but many dews may soften and fertilize it."

These and similar expressions were not heartless, nor complimentary. But having been made to feel the impropriety of a certain course, the whole energy of her character was at once brought to bear against it. Her affectionate heart attached itself to the person through whom she felt she had been assisted, and gradually she began to confide to her some things which had hitherto been known only to Him who searcheth the heart, and knoweth our most secret thoughts.

Gratified by the confiding trust which Emily reposed in her, yet deeply conscious of her own weakness, her teacher addressed to her a note in which she endeavored to direct her mind to God, as the proper Centre of the soul, the Fount of all true blessedness, particularly as the only being on whom we can safely depend for guidance, and whose will should be our only rule of conduct.

To this Emily replied as follows :

"*March* 8, 1835.

"Judge not, my dear Mrs. ——, either from my former notes, or from my actions, that I have not tasted the sweet mercies of Him who is able to save,—that I have not drank of those living waters which quench every thirst. Think not that I am what perhaps I appear to be; I have taken the yoke of the blessed Saviour and have found it light; I have laid myself before his feet, and humbly trust that he will not cast me off."

A few days after, she again addressed the same friend as follows :

"In your last note you requested me to tell you what grounds I had for my hope in Christ. It was about a year ago that my mind was first awakened to a sense of my sinfulness. I had often read, 'Except a man be born again he cannot see the kingdom of God;' yet I had never thought of its peculiar application to myself. About the time I have mentioned, I was in great distress of mind; I could not but remember how often I had broken the commands of God,—how often I had crucified my Saviour anew. It seemed as if there was no hope for me. There was an internal load that I could not shake off. I often conversed with my dear grandfather about my feelings; and though I at first almost despaired, not seeing how so great a sinner could possibly be forgiven, he led me to those comforting passages of Scripture which I shall never forget. My mind was relieved; and though since then I have frequently had to weep that I had yielded to temptation, and have at times almost given up my hope, yet that dreadful load I have never since felt."

This was the first time she had ventured to make known her feelings on the subject of religion; but the way having been thus opened, she freely unbosomed her sentiments, both in respect to what she trusted the Spirit of God had wrought within her, and also in regard to those views of Scripture truth on which she felt constrained to differ from her parents.

It has no doubt been thought strange by some, that she did not at once communicate to her parents the happy change which she fully believed had been wrought within her by the Spirit of God. Her strong affection for them must certainly have prompted the desire to make them partakers of her joy. Her reasons for not doing it, as given in repeated conversations and notes on this subject, were briefly these:

When oppressed with a sense of her deep sinfulness, her principal anxiety was on account of those inward corruptions, that entire destitution of heart-holiness, which as no human eye could see, she felt that none but a divine power could reach. She was therefore, at this time, fearful of making her feelings known lest others might not apprehend her true state. It was Scripture truth which had opened the wound, and she wanted nothing but the same truth to heal it. She studied her Bible as she would have listened to her Maker's voice and there she found Christ presented, as she thought, in a different manner from that in which she had been taught to regard him. Her faith laid hold on Jesus as "the way, the truth, and the life." She saw in him a fullness of which she had never before had a conception, and was led to exclaim with Thomas, "My Lord and my God."

From this time it seemed to her impossible to make known her feelings to her father without expressing some views from which she well knew he must dissent. She had always been accustomed to yield implicitly to his authority; and now, though duty to a higher Power impelled her to differ from him, she dreaded to inform him of the fact. Her heart shrunk instinctively from the bare thought of giving him pain. "My dear father's life," said she, "hangs by so brittle a thread that I fear the effect of any agitation. I often leave home in the morning feeling that it is very uncertain whether I shall have a father on my return." Her great desire was to make the little remnant of his days happy. And though she panted after communion with those whose experience and sentiments accorded with her own, yet she was willing to make any personal sacrifice rather than do any thing which would expose her dear father to a degree of suffering he seemed so ill able to bear. The following extract is from a note dated

"*August* 14*th*, 1835.

"My own mind is now made up on the course I ought to pursue. I do not expect that a statement of my opinions will change my parents' views, even should they permit me to follow the dictates of my conscience, though with God all things are possible. With him I can cheerfully leave all; knowing and feeling that whatever he orders, all will be for the best. The trial is to me great and heavy; but I know that he will not break the bruised reed, nor quench the smoking flax. My trust is in him. Be he but my guide, and I will not fear the most thorny road. May I but lean on the Rock of ages, and I will not fear the storms and sorrows of this world.

"Sweet indeed would it be to hold communion with his visible church; but if this be denied me, I can still hold sweet communion with the Father of my spirit. And it is my constant prayer that he will grant to each member of my loved family the same blessed privilege which I trust he has granted me, that, filled by the renewing influences of his grace, we may at last all meet, an unbroken family, forever to enjoy the bliss of heaven."

CHAPTER II.

Visit to Chester—Trying situation—Letter to her parents respecting her change of views—Their feelings and correspondence on the subject—Her own feelings.

In August 1835, during her school vacation, Emily spent a few weeks in Chester, N. H. Here she formed an acquaintance with several families, whose simple, unaffected piety made a deep impression on her mind, and under whose influence her own religious feelings were strengthened and increased. She regarded them at that time as the peculiar people of God, and oft referred to the season spent with them as a bright spot in her life. From this visit she returned home with a fixed determination to acquaint her parents with her true feelings; but, before performing so momentous a duty, she set apart some weeks for solemn reflection and prayer.

Her situation was at this time peculiarly trying. The very delicate state of her father's health, his keen sensibilities, rendered still more acute by disease, and his strong attachment to his own principles, added to the fact that she had never yet crossed his wishes nor allowed herself to express any dissent, however much her opinions might differ from his,—these, and similar reasons, caused her affectionate heart to shrink from a duty which she was fully aware every month's delay was rendering more painful.

At length, however, after much deliberation and prayer, she prepared the following letter, which, though without date, was presented to her father, December 4, 1835. The communication itself is a remarkable one, as she was then but sixteen years of age; and so determined was she that the thoughts and sentiments should be purely her own, that she would not allow, even to her most intimate friend, the privilege of knowing any thing either of its character or contents. It was left with her eldest sister, to be given to her father while she herself was spending vacation week with a friend in Brookline.

"My dear Parents:—I have long wished to address you as I now intend, but have preferred this time and opportunity. I wish, my dear parents, to speak to you concerning all-important things, which though on some accounts they may rejoice you, yet on others I fear may be painful.

"As Christians then, my beloved parents, it will doubtless bring you joy when I tell you that I trust, by the renewing grace of God, I have been led to see the enormity of my sins, and to look 'unto Jesus, the author and finisher of our faith,' as one through whose merits alone I can be pardoned. Perhaps I have done wrong in not communicating to you this happy change of mind before; but, my dear parents, if I have, forgive me. I said nothing to any one at the time, of the state of my feelings, except grandpa. In the earlier stage of my religious feelings, while I still doubted whether God would forgive so great a sinner, he asked me one day if I had ever thought any thing about religion. I told him how I felt. He pointed me to some of those beautiful promises addressed to penitent sinners, and showed me that God was mighty to save; and I, as I trust, submitted myself to him.

"As I said before, I was led, I trust, to see that if my sins were pardoned, it must be wholly owing to the merits of Christ. But though I believed it must be by his merits, because the Bible teaches that whosoever believeth in Christ shall be saved, yet, my dear parents, I could not understand how a *man*, in the common sense of that term, could bear the sins of a world sunk in sin. I was afraid it was because I had not faith, but thought if I could be sure of what the Bible stated, I need not fear. I examined the Bible; and, my dear parents, as I studied its sacred pages, it seemed as though it must be God, and God alone, who could bear the sins of the world. The Bible seemed to say it, and my own conscience gave witness to it.

"But as the thought first struck my mind that I was believing other things than I had been taught, other than my parents believed, I stood aghast at the thought, and tried to think I was giving credence to a lie. But the Bible seemed to present still stronger proofs. The same attributes were ascribed to Christ as to God. For instance, *Omnipotence*, ('All power is given unto me in heaven and in earth.'[a] 'Which is the head of all principality and power.'[b] 'Angels, and authorities, and powers being made subject unto him.'[c] &c.)—*Eternity*, ('Whose goings forth have been from of old, from everlasting.'[d] 'Jesus Christ the same yesterday, and to-day, and forever.'[e] 'I am Alpha and Omega, the first and the last.'[f] &c.)—*Omniscience*, ('I am he which searcheth the reins and hearts.'[g] 'He knew what was in man.'[h] 'No man knoweth the Son but the Father, neither knoweth any man the Father save the Son, and he to whomsoever the

[a] Matt. 28: 18. [b] Col. 2: 10. [c] 1 Peter, 3: 22. [d] Micah, 5: 2. [e] Heb. 3: 8. [f] Rev. 1: 11. [g] Rev. 2: 23. [h] John, 2: 25.

Son will reveal him."[i])—*Omnipresence*, ('Lo I am with you always even unto the end of the world.'[j] 'For where two or three are gathered together in my name there am I in the midst of them.'[k] &c.)—*Holiness*, ('That Holy thing that shall be born of thee shall be called the Son of God.'[l] 'These things saith he that is holy, he that is true.'[m] 'For such a high priest became us, who is holy, harmless, undefiled, separate from sinners, and made higher than the heavens.'[n] &c.)

"Again I saw the works of God ascribed to Christ. For instance, *Creation*, ('All things were made by him, and without him was not any thing made that was made.'[o] 'For by him were all things created that are in heaven, and that are in earth, visible and invisible, whether they be thrones, or dominions, or principalities, or powers; all things were created by him and for him.'[p]) —*Raising the dead*, ('For as the Father raiseth up the dead, and quickeneth them; even so the Son quickeneth whom he will.' 'The hour is coming, and now is, when the dead shall hear the voice of the Son of God; and they that hear shall live.' 'All that are in their graves shall hear his voice, and shall come forth; they that have done good, unto the resurrection of life; and they that have done evil, unto the resurrection of damnation.'[q] 'Who shall change our vile body that it may be fashioned like unto his glorious body.'[r])—*Judging the world*, ('When the Son of man shall come in his glory, and all his holy angels with him, then shall he sit upon the throne of his glory; and before him shall be gathered all nations; and he shall separate them one from another,

[i] Matt. 11: 27. [j] Matt. 28: 20. [k] Matt. 18: 20. [l] Luke, 1: 35. [m] Rev. 3: 7. [n] Heb. 7: 26. [o] John, 1: 3. [p] Col. 1: 16. [q] John 5: 21, 25, 28, 29. [r] Phil. 3: 21.

as a shepherd divideth his sheep from the goats; and he shall set the sheep on his right hand, but the goats on his left.' 'And these shall go away into everlasting punishment; but the righteous into life eternal."[s] 'And he commanded us to preach unto the people, and to testify that it is he which was ordained of God to be the judge of quick and dead."[t] 'For we shall all stand before the judgment-seat of Christ.'[u] 'The Son of man shall send forth his angels, and they shall gather out of his kingdom all things that offend, and them that do iniquity; and shall cast them into a furnace of fire.'[v] &c. 'The Lord Jesus shall be revealed from heaven with his mighty angels, in flaming fire taking vengeance on them that know not God.'[w] I take, my dear parents, but a limited number of passages, but you may add to each of them.

"Notwithstanding so many proofs, I still sought to stumble; but so fully and plainly did the word of God declare to me that Christ was God, that I dared not contradict it. What else could the Bible mean in the verse, 'God was manifest in the flesh'?* And since God expressly declares we shall worship none else but him, what else can mean those glorious descriptions in Revelations, nor in them alone, where Christ receives the highest honors as God? What else did Christ himself mean when he said, 'I and my Father are one'?† What else mean the thousand passages in the Prophecies, Gospels, Epistles, and Revelations, which testify to the supreme divinity of Christ?

---

[s] Matt. 25: 31, 32, 33, 46. [t] Acts 10: 42. [u] Rom. 14: 10. [v] Matt. 13: 41, 42. [w] 2 Thess. 1· 7, 8.

* 1 Tim. 3: 16. † John 10 : 30.

"These, my dear parents, I could not reconcile with the idea that Christ was only a man. I was overpowered, and could no longer withstand the weighty arguments the Bible itself offered. I prayed earnestly that God would not leave me to believe a lie, and I think my prayer was heard. My dear father will perhaps ask me why, if Christ was God, he should pray. But, dear father, Christ had a human, as well as a divine nature. As he took upon himself our nature, he took it wholly; and therefore it was no more strange that he should pray, than that he should eat. How these natures are united, I cannot presume to tell. Shall I, who know not how these few thoughts of an immortal mind are transferred to you, attempt to show the union of the natures of God? O presumption!

"But I would not simply tell you, my dear parents, what I cannot believe; I will endeavor to tell you what I do believe. I would not prescribe to any one, but only say what the Scriptures prayerfully read seem to teach me. I believe in God the Father, God the Son, and God the Holy Ghost; that is, one Being acting in these three different capacities. Nor do I, dear father, think that in this there is necessarily implied a superiority in one; for when the Jews said that Christ blasphemed because he called himself the Son of God, thus making himself equal with God, he did not rebuke them, nor deny it. And the apostle himself says he 'thought it no robbery to be equal with God.' I believe also, my dear parents, as Christ hath expressly told us, that a change of heart is necessary; and that our salvation depends not on our own merits, but on those of a crucified Saviour,—that by him we are made free; and that the grace which quickeneth us is free;—that we ourselves are by nature sinful; as the Bible says, '*There is none that doeth good, no not one.*' I believe in man's free will, and God's fore-knowledge, and that we should follow the example of our Saviour when he was baptized in Jordan.

"This belief, my dear parents, I do solemnly assure you, was given me by no living being. I have embraced it as taught by the Bible. No interested motive could lead me to embrace it, for ridicule and scorn will doubtless be my lot. As this is my firm, unalterable belief, I cannot of course attend our church with proper feelings. And, my dear parents, I feel it to be my duty, and at the same time my most ardent desire, to unite with the church of Christ below. For this reason I have written to you to beseech you to permit me to do so. I know that I ask great, very great things of you. I know it is very painful, both to you and to me; but I feel it to be necessary for my spiritual good.

"O my dear parents, no one can tell the trials I have mentally undergone on this account,—how many prayers I have raised to the throne of grace for guidance,—how many tears I have shed before I could bring myself to the performance of this most painful duty,—and how many fears now agonize me lest you should deny my request. But, whether you are willing to grant it or not, I trust that God will give me grace to bear either, and to show that his Spirit can do all things, even in one so unworthy.

"But, my beloved parents, as you value my eternal interests, as you value the future welfare of this immortal soul, as you consider the shortness of life, and the length of eternity, do grant my request. My dear father, greatly as I know that you are opposed to this belief, firmly as you rest on your own, I come to you as your child, given you by God to prepare for eternity,—I come to you as one on whom my future welfare depends, to give me your assent. And, my dear mother, to whom I am united by the tenderest ties, to you I come, as to one whom, next to my God, I most devotedly love,—to you, the dearest of all earthly beings, that you will give me your permission. Think that perhaps I soon may be called to leave all that is earthly, and think then what an incomputable happiness you will bestow upon my death-bed, or on the contrary, how unhappy I should feel should my request be denied. But I leave all to yourselves and my God; may he guide you.

"I have written, my dear parents, for I dared not trust myself to converse on the subject. And now do consider that my future happiness depends greatly upon you. You know how much I *have* loved you, but a new, a stronger tie will then bind me to you, a love stronger than ever before, if for the spiritual welfare of your child you can sacrifice so much. May God in his wisdom guide you, and give me grace to bear all.

"Emily."

This communication took her parents entirely by surprise; for though there had been a very noticeable change in her character, which they had supposed attributable to an increased spirit of piety, they had never before had the least intimation of any change in her views of religious truth. Her father replied to the letter in a manner worthy of himself. He expressed his joy that she had been seriously impressed with religious truth, his disappointment that she should have embraced sentiments so unlike his own, his fear that she had not properly considered the full scope of that faith which she had adopted, and his hope that her own good sense and clear mind would yet lead her to discard it, particularly after she should have read some books which he wished her to examine. "All that we ask of you my dear child," says he, "is to consider and investigate before you decide upon so momentous a question."

In a letter to the teacher to whom Emily had so long confided her feelings, under date of December 8, 1835, Mr. Waldo thus writes:

"To say that disappointment, that feelings of deep and bitter disappointment are mingled with our sensations on this subject, is but to admit our common participation of humanity. It is hard to part with long cherished expectations. But I trust we have too just a sense of what is due, both to ourselves, and to our child, to have but one thought upon the course to be pursued. We would have her feel herself free, free as air, to worship the God of her fathers after the dictates of her own conscience.

"To yourself, my dear madam, we cannot but feel that we are under the highest, the deepest obligations. If you have not made our child all that we could wish, we believe that a conscientious sense of duty to a Higher Power has constrained and governed your motives and actions. Under your guardian care and attention, our dear child has expanded and improved to the delight and gratification of her parents and relatives. We feel that we owe much to you for the improvement of her mind, her morals, and her manners—that to you, under God, we are indebted for what she is; and never was child loved by earthly parents with fonder and truer affection.

Under all the circumstances of the case, we know not that you could have done otherwise than you have.

"God forbid that a child of ours, a descendant of the Pilgrims of New England, in this blessed land of civil and religious liberty, should not feel that she had full liberty to call her soul her own, in the fullest extent and meaning of that phrase. We have only to regret that any motive should have induced our child so long to have withheld her trust and confidence from us, her parents,—we trust her ever kind parents. It is the first trait of disingenuousness we have known in her character, and bitterly, as unnecessarily has she suffered in its indulgence.

"Believe me, madam, that for yourself we entertain only feelings of respect and gratitude, and will endeavor to bury our own feelings of disappointment and sorrow deep in our bosoms,—trusting and believing in that beneficent Power who from disappointment and sorrow, can elicit joy and gladness; and who hath promised that all things shall work together for good to them that love and put their trust in him.

"Very respectfully,

"Charles F. Waldo."

Many persons situated as was Mr. Waldo's family at this time, would have charged upon the Seminary with which Emily was connected, the act of proselyting her; but they had too high a respect, both for the character of their daughter, and of her teachers, to harbor any such thought. Addressing the same teacher some months afterwards in reference to a report of this character, Mrs. Waldo thus expresses herself:

"My consciousness of never giving foundation for the report, is matter of rejoicing with me. On first reading Emily's communication relative to the change in her views, this idea did arise in my mind; but I now rejoice that my lips never gave utterance to it. I very soon discarded it as injustice, both to you and myself, and gave the surest proof of my confidence in you by immediately placing under your care another daughter. Your indirect influence was perfectly natural, and had effect I have no doubt, when Emily's very strong affection for you is taken into consideration. But I should as soon think of attaching blame to one for their personal beauty, as to blame such an influence under such circumstances. The first is the gift of heaven, and the last might be heaven-directed.

"I feel that I am blessed indeed in being the mother of such a child as Emily. May God in his infinite mercy long spare her. May she be a burning and a shining light, and may her example induce her brother and sisters early to dedicate themselves to the Lord, and drink of the fountain of living waters, of which whosoever drinketh shall live forever. I cannot sufficiently thank you for the kind interest you take in our welfare, but assure you that it is warmly returned by

"Your very affectionate friend,

"SARAH V. WALDO."

Having seen how her parents wrote on the subject, we will now turn to Emily, whose affectionate attachment to them led her to magnify every expression of sorrow on their part, and to charge upon herself the crime of having interrupted that domestic harmony which had hitherto invariably blessed them. In a note addressed to the same friend she remarks:

"I feel more sure than ever, that neither you nor any one else can realize my present feelings. You may have passed through a trial somewhat similar, but your situation was widely different. No sick father's hopes, no mother's burning love were centered in you. My parents, who love me with all the affection which parents can feel, and yet, I believe, not more devotedly than I love them, have seen all their fond hopes blasted. They have seen their fondest and brightest hopes all crushed, and the fair fabric which they trusted to have reared has disappeared in empty air. And it is I who have done all this. It is I who have withered their hopes and wounded their hearts. The thought is dreadful to me. A word, a look, overcomes me. I fear I do not feel so willing to live and suffer as I ought. It seems sometimes as if my only wish was to lie down under the green sod and be at rest.

"But I know, and at times sweetly feel, that it is God who rules; and that he is a God 'too wise to err, too good to be unkind.' At such times I feel perfectly resigned to suffer all his will. But again it seems as though Satan desired to have me, that he might sift me as wheat. My father mourns, my mother weeps, my pastor intreats, yet my prayers rise up continually before the throne of Him who is the hearer of prayer, that he may give me grace to go through this fiery trial, that like gold in the furnace, I may be seven times purified. Pray for me, for I need prayer. My parents do not know, and I pray they never may know, all that I undergo on this account. I feel that I cannot long endure this conflict. One way or other I must pursue; and O may grace be given me to tread the strait and narrow way that leadeth to eternal life."

CHAPTER III.

Her parents consent to her joining the Baptist church—Her religious feelings—Her baptism—Desire for the conversion of her friends—Removal of her pastor—Close of her connection with the Seminary.

As Emily often spoke in strong terms of her trials at this time, it seems proper to remark here that these trials were not on account of any opposition from her parents. They ever treated her with all possible tenderness, showing every attention to her friends, and omitting nothing on their part, which could possibly tend to render her home happy. But from a mind sensitive as hers, it was impossible to conceal the fact that her present views and feelings were a source of grief to those whom it was her greatest bliss to make happy. And to her affectionate heart, the thought of giving them pain was a much more severe trial than some would experience from the strongest opposition. She was also often in doubt how far she ought, on minor points, to yield her own sense of right to the plain duty of honoring and obeying her parents; a doubt which her peculiar tenderness of conscience sometimes rendered quite painful.

With her duty of professing her faith in Christ, her parents never interfered; they only wished her to delay long enough to examine more fully those points on which her present views differed from theirs. This she willingly did. And, having satisfied them that the sentiments which she had adopted were her deliberate and conscientious views of divine truth, and that it was from a sense of her duty to God, that she desired to separate herself from the denomination in which she had been brought up, she received their full permission to follow the dictates of her own conscience. From that time she became a constant attendant at the First Baptist Church in Charlestown, then under the pastoral charge of Rev. H. Jackson. This was about the first of March, 1836.

For two or three months after this, a cloud seemed to rest on her mind. "I can hardly believe," said she, "that it is only the darkness to which Christians in this imperfect state are exposed; it seems too much like the darkness of a mind still under the dominion of sin. Yet, though often on the brink of despair, I can never bring my heart to confess that I am without God and without hope in the world. I feel no desire to return again to earth's lying vanities, or to enjoy again its empty pleasures. I feel that there is no true happiness except in religion.

"I trust you never forget me at the throne of grace, but it is sweet and solemn at our consecrated hour to feel that I am specially remembered in your prayers. For myself I find my chief delight in secret prayer. There is but one Being to whom I can wholly unfold the secrets of my heart; and, blessed be his holy name, in him I can trust. Prayer is my only refuge. Here I can pour out my soul unto God. I can tell him my wants, and be relieved. I do not believe there is one who enjoys the company of Christians more than I do, yet when I would speak, a seal is on my lips, and my tongue is still."

A few weeks later she thus writes: "I feel to thank God that he has again, as I humbly trust, lifted up the light of his countenance upon me. O may he grant of his sovereign grace that I may not be deceived. May his renewed goodness lead me to sincere repentance and devotedness to his cause. Pray for me that I may have strength to come out from the world and be separate,—to follow my dear Saviour beneath the liquid grave, and never disgrace the high calling of the Christian."

In the latter part of May, she offered herself to the church as a candidate for baptism; and though heretofore she had shrunk from speaking of her religious feelings except to one or two confidential friends, she was enabled to speak on this occasion with great freedom; giving a clear and very satisfactory account of her conversion, dwelling particularly on the atonement of Christ as her only ground of hope, and ascribing the blessed change which she trusted had been wrought in her, entirely to the abounding grace of God, through the operation of the Holy Spirit. She thus writes to a friend:

"*June* 9, 1836.

"Within a few days past I have enjoyed a very, very happy frame of mind. I find a sweeter peace, a holier joy, a more longing desire to be a faithful laborer for the Lord than I ever felt before. Especially does my soul look forward with uncommon joy to the coming Sabbath. May God grant that, as I hope to be buried with Christ in baptism, I may rise to newness of life—that when this mortal flesh shall lie in the cold tomb, my spirit may rise to God who gave it, to dwell forever with him.

'O glorious hour! O blest abode!
I shall be near and like my God.'

Shall I, a sinful worm of the dust, enjoy this blessed rest? Dear Redeemer, blessed Saviour, thou art worthy. Fix my wandering affections on thee, and may my soul constantly aspire after thee.

"I rejoice that the church of Christ will permit me, unworthy as I am, to become one of their number, to enjoy their privileges, their joys, their triumphs, and, as Mr. J. says, their trials too. Pray that I may never disgrace the Christian profession,—that I may ever be a faithful laborer, enduring unto the end. Pray that the Lord will strengthen me for the ordinance of baptism, as I trust he did strengthen me to declare unto the church what he had done for my soul. Not that I have any fears in regard to the administration of the ordinance, but that I may thus be enabled to glorify my dear Redeemer."

On the second Sabbath, which was the twelfth of June, she was baptized by her pastor, Rev. H. Jackson, in a beautiful little cove in Charles River. It was to her a delightful season; and the more so because she was accompanied to the water side by her beloved mother, who was always happy to do every thing in her power for the gratification of her daughter's wishes. To this season she often referred as one of the most precious means of grace she had ever enjoyed. Its anniversary was always hailed with gladness, and generally spent as a season of special prayer. Her cousin, E. A. D., who received the ordinance of baptism with her, she was ever afterwards accustomed to call her *Jordan twin*. The following little note, addressed to her a year afterwards, beautifully illustrates her feelings in reference to this season.

"*June* 12.

"Does my dear Ella remember the blessed day of which this is the anniversary? If she has not forgotten the love to Christ, and to each other, which then fired our bosoms, will she go with me this afternoon to those blessed waters, and there with me renew our covenant vows, and give ourselves anew to God and to each other?"

In connecting herself with the church of Christ, she felt that she was assuming important and weighty responsibilities, and her covenant vows were ever after regarded as solemnly binding upon her. Never, except from unavoidable circumstances, was she willing to absent herself from any meeting of the church. She loved the church because it was dear to Christ. Yet we often find her at this time mourning the weakness of her love to Jesus. "My dear Saviour," says she, "how little does my daily conduct evince of love to thee. Yet thou knowest that I love thee, though that love be comparatively faint and feeble. How blissful the thought that in heaven we shall all love without interruption, or interfering affection, that blessed Saviour who has died for us. How I long for my blessed home! As the penitent criminal longs for the moment of release to visit his own dear home, and with tears of penitence to seek his father's blessing, so does the soul, imprisoned in this world of death, long for the moment when it shall be released from its prison-house and seek a heavenly Father's home. *So*, did I say? O, far more. As much more as that blessed home is better than any earthly abode, or as our Father above is better than any earthly parent; as much more as the chains of sin are more galling than the heaviest chains of iron."

Her desires for the salvation of her kindred were at times intense. During the summer of this year she frequently expressed herself in language like the following:

"How can I look on those who are bound to me by nature's strongest ties, and see them unpardoned, and unsanctified, and yet say nothing to warn them of their danger. While thinking of the possibility of their at last falling short of heaven, how can I say, '*Thy will be done*'? I could bear to see them enduring scorn, poverty, sickness, or suffering of any kind, yes, death itself, if they were Christ's. But how can I see them as they are now, without lifting the agonizing prayer, Save, Lord, or they perish? O save in thy rich mercy and thou shalt have all the glory. What should I do without a Saviour, an Almighty Friend to whom I can unbosom all my sorrows. He is my only hope for myself and my dear family. Pray that I may so live as to win them to Christ—that I may be a burning and shining light; and pray much for this dear family, that we may all meet, an unbroken circle, in the paradise above. Blessed Redeemer, O save these souls, and enable me to *walk* if I may not *speak*."

The removal of her beloved pastor in the following September was a great trial to her. Her feelings on this subject are expressed in the following extract from a letter.

TO MISS A. C. HILL, NOW MRS. KELLY.

"*Oct.* 5, 1836.

"You have doubtless heard of our great and heavy affliction in the departure of our beloved pastor. He went in obedience to the call of God, and we have now, we trust, given him up to Him who gave him. But, O sister, it was hard; it was trying. Though I had been acquainted with him but ten short months, yet it was to me a most severe trial. He was my guide, my guardian, my under shepherd. I looked up to him in sorrow and in joy, and found him a constant friend.

"But though the trial is great, I trust I have been enabled to bow to the will of our heavenly Father; and while I mourn for him who is gone, I rejoice that God has answered his and our prayers, in granting us that sweet love and union which is the type of heaven. If you could be here and see how brotherly love doth abound and continue, how union marks every meeting, and peace every countenance, you too would praise the Lord. The church have extended a unanimous call to Rev. William Phillips of Providence. He is now considering the question, and we trust will come, if it be the Lord's will."

TO REV. H. JACKSON.

"*Charlestown Navy Yard, Dec.* 15, 1836.

"Beloved Father in Christ:—Although but few weeks have passed since I received the parting blessing, yet they seem like months, and the events in them like a dream. To see a stranger fill the long accustomed seat, to hear a stranger's voice at every meeting, to look in vain for the loved countenance, to hear no more the accustomed welcome, seems dream-like and sad. But doubtless God has ordered all for the best, and we will praise his holy name.

"Let all the church praise him for his great goodness to us in not leaving us alone, but sending us so holy, so faithful, so affectionate a pastor. Though I feel a love more strong and endearing than I can express, for the dear servant of God who buried me beneath the baptismal wave, yet I love this servant of the Lord also. He is a faithful preacher of God's blessed gospel. There seems to be some waking up among the dear people here. Our meetings are well attended, interesting, and solemn.

"As to my own feelings, through the grace of God, I feel in some degree quickened in holy love. It is my anxious desire to grow in grace, to live wholly for the glory of God and the good of souls. I have had during the last three weeks, such wrestling with God in prayer, as leads me to ask of you, dear father, if you think any one can be so earnest for the salvation of others as to sin in pleading for them, and feeling that they must be saved. Should there not be more of submission? O I fear that sin is mixed with all I do. I am sure the great blessedness of heaven will consist, not so much in freedom from toil, sorrow, and suffering, as in exemption from sin. 'I shall be satisfied, when I awake with thy likeness.'"

Her connection with the Seminary closed in the spring of 1837. This she regarded as quite an important event in her life. In anticipation of it she thus wrote:

TO MISS A. C. HILL.

"*March* 7, 1837.

"Time has fled swifter than an eagle's wings; for it is my last term, Abby, really my last. A father's ill health, a mother's infirmities, and my own increasing years, call for me at home. I do feel sad to think how much precious time I have wasted, how many opportunities neglected, and how little, very little, I have done for Christ. But, dear Abby, how much has he done for me. During this time, this heart, if ever it was, has been changed; these blind eyes have been opened to see in some faint degree, not only the loveliness and fullness of Christ, but also the error of my former belief. I have within this time been permitted the precious privilege of being buried with Christ in baptism, uniting with his dear church, commemorating his dying love, and enjoying some sweet hours of communion with him. O Abby! what has he not done for me? and yet I cannot feel that I am making any returns. Pray that I may improve the remaining few weeks to the glory of God.

"I had a letter from dear Mrs. J. two weeks ago, a beautiful letter; and last week a dear good letter from Mr. J., my beloved pastor. I wonder if you feel towards him as I do. Dear, blessed man! Whom can I love on earth more than him who led me in the sweet steps of Christ? I hope, God willing, to visit them in Hartford next summer. The state of things here is very interesting. Dear Mr. Phillips is, if possible, more engaged and devoted than ever. Harriet and Mary, with five others, are to be baptized next Sabbath. Don't you want to come and witness the sweet ordinance? Will you not be here to attend our examination? How I wish our '*old set*' could meet together once more. Maria and Joanna, Abby and Elvira, Ellen and myself. O happy days! fled and gone. Yet why should I regret? Let me live henceforward for God, that whether my life be happy or not, it may be for Christ's glory."

A few weeks later she addressed the same friend as follows:

"Your last was joyfully received in the midst of the hurry and bustle of Examination, while my heart was yet trembling with the dread anticipation of more dreaded events. Yet even then the sweet and humble spirit of heavenly devotion which it breathed, soothed, and calmed, and elevated in some degree my troubled mind. That was my last school day, Abby, and of course a sad, sad day to me. Recollections of the past three years, of the abounding goodness of God towards me, since first I entered these dear walls, bringing me, as I trust, from 'Nature's darkness into his marvelous light,' and strengthening me to declare to the world the change,— these, and other kindred subjects, rushed into my mind; the forms of dear loved friends with whom I had been here associated, passed in imagination before me, and my only relief was in gushing tears.

"Your letter, my dear Abby, you must allow me to say, was excellent. Our own unworthiness, the love of Christ, and the free grace of God, afford abundant themes for the Christian; themes too, which we cannot dwell upon too long, or consider in too exalted a light. O if Christ and his cross were all our theme, how much more good might we do; how much more holy and extensive would be our influence; how much nearer should we approach Him of whom we talk. I feel to mourn and lament before God my past unfaithfulness in this respect. How often, even with the professed followers of Christ, have I talked of the things of this present life rather than of the crucified One. 'What manner of persons ought we to be in all holy conversation and godliness.' May I henceforth live wholly for the glory of God."

The three years and a half which she spent in connection with the Seminary, were valued by her, not more for the knowledge she there acquired, than for the endearing friendships she then formed. Speaking of her schoolmates, she remarked :

"A band of sisters, we have shared each other's joys, borne each other's sorrows, and assisted each other up the steep ascent of the 'hill of science ;' but the parting hand must be given, the sad farewell uttered, and we shall be scattered to the four corners of the earth. Yet when the knowledge we have together acquired shall come to our aid, when we bow before Him whom we have together supplicated, though wide lands, or wider waters may separate us, our prayers shall not only ascend for each other, but for this beloved spot, that the richest blessings of Heaven may ever fall upon it, and that from this fountain many streams may go forth to 'make glad the city of our God.'"

How highly she prized the instruction she there received, may be seen from the following note addressed to one of her teachers.

"*Charlestown Navy Yard, March* 27, 1837.

"MY DEAREST, BEST-BELOVED FRIEND,—who watched over me with a mother's care, and loved me with a sister's love, who bore with all my waywardness, and gently, but firmly, reproved my many faults, must I, must I part with one so dear? Must I leave my mother, counsellor, and friend? Yet I will not murmur; the remembrance of past happy moments shall assist me to bear the troubles of the present. The most ardent professions, or the most grateful acknowledgments, would be no return for all your love and kindness. I know that, should they be all, you would have reason to think that I loved the person only, and not her instructions. No, dearest Mrs. ——, it shall be my aim so to live that you may feel that your labors for my good have not been lost. May that sobriety, that thoughtfulness, and that self-respect, which you have so earnestly labored to inculcate, adorn my future life. May your past and future prayers for me be answered. And be assured that never, while memory holds her seat, will I cease to pray for your happiness, usefulness, and piety. One blissful hope strengthens me to bear this parting, even the hope of our eternal home. Till there we meet, pray for

"Your own

"EMILY."

During the following summer, her time was mostly spent at home, fitting herself, as she often remarked, for the duties peculiar to woman. In reference to leaving the walls of the school-room for the duties of domestic life, she observed:

"Though woman's mind is as worthy of cultivation, and often as capable of it as that of the other sex, she has another and a sweeter sphere in which to move. Man may cultivate the head, but it is woman's prerogative to rule and form the heart. Woman is not intended to be the statesman, the physician, or the clergyman, and therefore needs not the education requisite for such duties. Not but that she can fill these stations, for she has done it; but it is not her place, and she who seeks for it, steps aside from the path in which her sex should tread. She has other duties to perform, and therefore needs other schools and other teachers."

The character of her duties at home may be seen from the following brief extract.

"I know not but you have thought that Emmy had forgotten you, but, dearest, had you been in my situation, you must have owned it was impossible for me to write sooner. Father and sister have been sick, and mother is never well at the best. Beside the overplus labor thus brought upon me, in addition to my new domestic employment, I have quite a little school, most of them to be sure sisters, but a school nevertheless, which confines me every afternoon, except Wednesday. Will you accept, dear sister, this excuse, and believe that your own Emmy loves you as deeply, as devotedly as ever, and that nothing but necessity prevented her from demonstrating it?"

CHAPTER IV.

Religious interest in Charlestown—Sickness and death of her father—Decides upon taking a School in Boston—Efforts for the good of others.

The year 1838 was a season which will long be remembered by the churches in Boston and vicinity, as one of special religious interest. The following extracts give some account of the work of grace in Charlestown at this time.

TO MRS. M. T. JACKSON.

"*Charlestown Navy Yard, Feb.* 7, 1838.

"My own dear Mrs. J:—You cannot tell how rejoiced our hearts were to hear of the glorious doings of the Lord among you. We know there is no blessing comparable to the Spirit; and if you are enjoying its outpouring, you are happy indeed. I know that your hearts are rejoiced. The knowledge that souls around you have been, and are being brought to God, must fill you with unearthly joy. While your souls are wrestling for the salvation of your own dear people, and your hearts are filled with mingled gladness and anxiety, one could hardly expect you to feel so deep an interest for us. But, dearest mother, when you feel that you cannot be denied, offer one plea for this dear people.

"Perhaps you ask what is the prospect among us. There is a sense of our deep necessity, a spirit of great solemnity and prayer, and some inquiry. Last Monday was observed as a day of prayer, and was very solemn. We have had meetings every evening except Thursday; most of the time is spent in prayer. There was one case of deep, and interesting conviction Monday night, several others are openly serious, and I believe many are secretly inquiring. There have also been a few hopeful conversions. But O, we want to be more earnest and believing, desiring only the glory of God. The Sabbath school is in an interesting state, but we need quickening. Will God pass us by, while he is pouring out his Spirit around us? The young sisters have established a semi-monthly prayer meeting, which is very interesting. Do remember us and entreat that our prayer, specially offered for brothers and sisters, may be heard."

TO MISS A. C. HILL.

" *April* 24, 1838.

"The state of things here is still interesting, but for some reasons the Lord seems to hold back the blessing. The church feel it much; for ardent hopes, and longing desires have been cherished for those dear ones who are yet unreconciled to God. It must be something in us. God is the same unchangeable, compassionate One. He will bless us. He cannot, he will not leave us.

"Unless greatly deceived, I have enjoyed for the last four or five weeks, sweet communion with God. Eternity never seemed so near, heaven so sweet, or souls so precious. O I long to be delivered from self and sin,—'to be clothed upon with my house which is from heaven.' What is there in this wilderness world on which the soul can rest? What can fill its deep void but the fullness of

God? I feel, Abby, as if I wanted a larger heart; mine is so narrow in its conceptions, so limited in its love. O, I long to know the height, and depth, the length and breadth of Jesus' love, My soul pants to praise him without sin,—to sit at his feet, and never, never wander. How can it be that Jesus can love a creature so far removed from him, so unlike his spotless purity? To be without sin, without one unholy thought, would be the highest happiness I can conceive of. May I soon be prepared to enter that kingdom where sin cannot come. How long, O Lord, come quickly."

TO MISS M. B. CARROLL, NOW MRS. BROWN.

"*May* 4, 1838.

"The work of the Lord here has been great, not so much in the numbers who have passed from death unto life, as in the character of the persons, and the manner of their conversion. They have been, generally speaking, the last persons we should have expected. The first Monday in February was observed by the church as a day of prayer. Such desires for the conversion of children, I never before heard expressed. Mr. H——, especially, felt deeply for his son at college, and requested special prayers that his increasing influence might be given to God. And, Maria, if it required faith to pray for a Saul of Tarsus, it is no exaggeration to say it required more to pray for him. He had been from the age of thirteen, a deist,—firmly, decidedly so; and, being naturally gifted with strong argumentative powers, he generally '*wound up*' all who argued with him. While a deist, he was strictly moral; but about a year ago, he gave up his deistical opinions, and with them his hope and his morality. He has since said, that he knew he should be lost whether or no, and therefore determined to do just as he chose. His Sabbaths were spent in reading novels, and playing cards. There was but one hopeful thing about him. His mother had so thoroughly taught him the Bible that he could not get rid of it, though he often vainly wished he could shake it off. But for such a son, prayer was requested, and contrite, agonizing hearts pleaded for his salvation.

"A few weeks only had elapsed when his youngest sister, a lively girl, full of the bitterest enmity to religion, received a letter from him, and opened it to read the story of his conversion,—to read from him whose pen had hitherto written only witty jokes, cutting sarcasms, and proud opposition to religion,—from him to read the entreaty to make her peace with God. The Mighty Spirit bowed that proud heart, and in weeping and anguish she laid her head that night on her pillow. The next day brought up all her sins in black review; she cried for mercy, and the following afternoon was enabled to rejoice in hope. Such a change in those two hearts! But they could not be alone. Many a heart felt, and many a tongue said, 'If S. and A. can become Christians, any one can.' And two days after, another brother and sister, the gayest of the gay, the last ones we could have expected, were made glad in the same Saviour. The next week a young man who had not entered a meeting house for years, whose constant scenes of amusement were the ball-room and the theatre, was awakened in his shop, and found no rest till he found it in Jesus. The same week, two brothers, who had been in the habit of making the Sabbath a holiday, and God's name a jest, cried in earnest for mercy, and obtained it. Indeed almost every case has been of this kind; so that I begin to look around at the most hardened and thoughtless, as those who may be expected to be snatched from perdition. There are many who feel deeply, yet cannot believe; but God can make them willing in the day of his power."

On the 25th of June, 1838, Mr. Waldo had a second attack of paralysis, which terminated his life on the 30th of the following August. Emily, who was then on a visit to Watertown, hastened immediately home, and took her mother's place in the family, that her father might have the best possible attention. A few days before his death she wrote as follows:

TO MISS S. T. BOSWORTH.

" *August* 23, 1838.

" Most glad am I to be able to snatch a few moments from almost distracting cares and duties, to write to you once more. We are at present, and have been during all father's illness, destitute of help. My mother has been unable to leave his sick room to do any household work; so that all the unaccustomed, and heavily responsible cares of a large family have devolved upon me. And, dear Sarah, the confusion of sickness, the tedious and laborious routine of household affairs, the care of two little sisters, and the general supervision of the wants of the family, have hardly allowed me time to attend upon a sick and dying father, to comfort a beloved mother, to point an afflicted family to a Father above, and to look to my own state and standing before God. Alas, I fear these duties have all been but poorly done. But God has always dealt with me in love, and I know it is so now.

Yet I fear I do not feel that penitence of spirit, that brokenness of heart, that entire submission to his will, which I desire and pray for. O this endless conflict with sin, this constant struggle, so often ending in defeat, because we have forgotten some of the perfect armor; when will it cease? When shall grace reign through righteousness? How beautifully expressive and comforting that blessed, thrice blessed promise, 'As we have borne the image of the earthy, we shall also bare the image of the heavenly.' How thoroughly have we borne the impress of the *former;* and, blessed be God, we shall as entirely bear the image of the *latter.* Will heaven, dear Sarah, be our home? 'Every man that hath this hope in him, purifieth himself, even as he is pure.' We need not be uncertain on this subject. The time must come when we can say, 'I know that my Redeemer liveth,' or be strangers to peace. Why not know it now?

"I see from your letter to J., that you are indulging unfounded hopes of my dear father's recovery. No, it cannot be. His time, his long-delayed time has come. That weary, suffering frame, will soon be laid to rest, and we shall be fatherless. His disease is not of a nature that admits recovery. He may linger awhile, but that weak and wasted form cannot be with us long. He is patient, gentle, quiet, calm, says that his trust is alone in Jesus, and that he is ready, happy, desirous to go. He is only understood by signs, as he cannot talk. Do pray for him that he may rest on no other foundation but the Rock, Christ Jesus.

"God has been gracious in the midst of affliction. He has granted me the conversion of one of my dear class, a dear girl of fourteen, who witnesses to all that she has learned of Jesus. There is no special interest here now, but an encouraging state of feeling, particularly in the Sabbath school."

About three weeks after the death of her father she thus writes:

"*Charlestown Navy Yard, Sept.* 20, 1838.

"DEAR, DEAR SISTER:—Every week since I was so suddenly, and sadly called from your dear house, have I longed to write to you. But it was impossible. New and constant cares have called for even more than I could give. To take the management of a somewhat large family, to smooth a father's dying pillow, to comfort a mother's aching heart, to walk so as to glorify God in the day of visitation, in the eyes of a dear brother, sisters, and friends, seemed to allow no time to seek the sympathy, or ask the guidance of the dearest earthly friend. At such times there was but one friend to whom I could unbosom my sorrows, for whose direction I could pray, on whose arm I could lean. And yet, my own dear mother, sister, friend, the thought of you was comfort in many an hour of spiritual despondency, and filial sorrow. You of all others, I was confident, knew how to pray for me; and O I felt that you did pray for me, and that God would hear. My loving Father has indeed tried me. Without were troubles, and within were fears. His awful nearness seemed only to unvail the deep corruption of my heart. In the light of his holiness I was ready to cry out, 'Wo is me, for I am undone, for my eyes have seen the King, the Lord of hosts.' When I turn my eyes from Calvary all is dark, but in Jesus I find righteousness and wisdom, sanctification and plenteous redemption. Now I can say, Welcome trouble, affliction, bereavement, if I may but be humbled and sanctified. Will you, dear sister, pray for me; not so much that I may be comforted or sustained, as sanctified. Pray that I be not hardened under prosperity. I begin to feel that trouble of some kind is the only element which can sustain my spiritual life. My heart is not humble enough to bear prosperity.

"But, sister, I have lost a father. He is gone, gone. My dear, kind, indulgent father, shall I see him no more? Shall I never hear his voice again? Shall I no more give him the kiss of love? O, am I fatherless? Alas, the silent house, the empty room, the garment of mourning, tell too true a tale. He has gone the way of all the earth. His weary, wasted body rests in the silent tomb; his immortal spirit is in the hands of God. We are alone. How desolate! The pleasant scenes we have loved so well, the quiet security we have enjoyed, the sources of comfort and happiness from which we have drank so freely, are but so many monitors to remind us of our bereavement. Our heavenly Father hath done it; even He who doth not afflict willingly. His stroke hath made the tear to flow, the heart to bleed; and yet his rod is used in love. Forever shall I have reason to say, 'Bless the Lord, O my soul.'

"While God permits me to call him Abba, Father, am I then fatherless or alone? If he gives me promises I never had before, and in his sure word, 'As thy days, so shall thy strength be,' now supplies my larger wants, and ever increasing needs, shall I mourn? If he thus brings me nearer to himself, shall I weep that he has removed farther one so dear? O, no. If I am an heir of God, I can never want. Having but an evidence of my adoption, I can rejoice in tribulation. How sweet is every word of the 121st Psalm! What a precious portion to the faithful, humble believer!

" Indeed, dear sister, I am not without joys. In communion with God, in learning of Jesus, in worshiping him in the assembly of his saints, and in hope of a sinless home, I must, I do rejoice. Yet when I have the clearest evidence of my adoption, when I feel the strongest assurance that my sins are forgiven, then are they the most loathsome and intolerable. Then do I most sincerely say,

' To Jesus, the crown of my hope,
  My soul is in haste to be borne;
O bear me ye cherubim up,
  And waft me away to his throne.
When that happy era begins,
  When arrayed in thy glories I shine,
I shall grieve then no more by my sins,
  The bosom on which I recline.'

" Remember my dear, precious mother in your prayers. You know something of her trials; but you cannot know all the void she feels, the utter loneliness of her widowed heart. Father was all her care; always in a measure dependent, but for the last five years requiring every minute want to be supplied by another; and no hand so dear as hers. Do pray for her, and for all this dear family; don't forget one. You know how I want you to pray for them. The recollection of your supplications for me in sweet, by-gone days, brings warm tears from eyes that ought indeed to flow. But, my own best friend, I trust they went not up in vain. The seed sown in patience and love, watered full oft with tears, and nurtured with unwearied care, is, I humbly hope, now springing up. You have not labored in vain. Bitterly do I mourn that you are so ill repaid; but God, my God will bless you. And when, sister, this weary pilgrimage is ended, and we go home to Jesus, one star in your future crown of rejoicing will be

"Your own

"EMMY."

Soon after the death of her father, Emily's thoughts were turned upon teaching. This was an employment to which her natural taste had always led her. And now that the family had been deprived in some measure of their former means of support, she felt it due to them, no less than herself, that her talents and education should be turned to some profitable account.

Addressing a friend, she says, "I have long expected to teach somewhere, but had supposed I should leave home. I now think I shall not, as I am expecting to take a school in Boston, and should prefer the walk from there to Charlestown rather than board in the city. Aunt C. is very much interested for me, and has very kindly engaged to procure me a small school in Boston, which I expect to commence in December. On many accounts I dread it. Not that teaching is any less captivating to me than ever. I love the young, and should delight in devoting myself to their instruction. But a school in the city will have many trials and temptations which a country school would not. The increased expense, the tripled responsibilities, the diminished hope of success, all conspire to damp my spirits, and daunt my courage. But then, if my expectations are realized, I can do more for mother so than in any other way; and besides, I should not lose the religious influence which God has given me at home. I feel that God has placed me here, and here I wish to stay. Of course my time will be much taken up, and I cannot give to friends present, or absent, the time that once was mine."

During the time that intervened between the death of her father and the opening of her school, her pen was employed in various works of love; now seeking to reconcile friends who had become estranged from each other, now comforting one whose heart had been stricken by the unfaithfulness of those from whom better things might have been expected, and again endeavoring to reclaim some wanderer. Most of these letters are of too personal a character to be given to the public; but they evince a heart full of the tenderest sympathy, as well as a mind ever active, and steadily set upon benefiting her fellow men.

The following was addressed to one for whose salvation she never ceased to labor, till she saw her rejoicing in hope:

"*Friday evening*, 10 *o'clock*.

"MY DEAR C.—I cannot even at this late hour retire, without first writing a few words to you on the all important subject of religion. I love your soul, and must be faithful to it. Is it, can it be true, dear C., that you are still indifferent to the salvation of your soul? Are you still rejecting the offers of love, and treasuring up wrath against the day of wrath? O say, shall it be in vain to you that Christ has lived, suffered, and died? Just think, for you, yes, for you he died. He is holding out his arms of love, and in the sweetest tones bidding you turn to him. Long has he said, 'Daughter, give me thine heart.' Can you from that precious Saviour any longer withhold it? Never by a whole life of sacrifice can you repay his infinite love. And will you live on in sin, grieving that dear Saviour, and resisting that Spirit which may soon cease to strive?

"O my dear C., by the worth of your soul, by your hopes of heaven, and your desire for salvation, by the agony and suffering of the blessed Jesus, by all in heaven, in earth, or in hell, I beseech you to repent. Have you not enough of which to repent? Is it not time to repent? O come, and Christ and heaven are yours. Be assured you have the prayers of Your own

"EMMY."

To one who was about to enter the married state she thus writes:

"I rejoice that the Lord has raised up one to be the partner of your joys, the soother of your sorrows, your instructor in holiness, your helper in grace. Yet while you cannot but thank the Giver of every good gift for this new proof that he careth for you, the solemnity, the responsibility, the eternal consequences of the connection you are about to form, must, I think, lead you to exclaim with deep feeling, 'Who is sufficient for these things?' Now, if ever, you must feel your need of directing, strengthening grace; now, if ever, must the throne of grace be precious, and you be found often there. No doubt you feel your proneness to love the gift above the Giver, to look to the reflection rather than the source of light, and to idolize the chosen object of your affections. You will need to 'watch and pray lest you enter into temptation.'

"You may think it strange that a child like myself should offer advice on a subject where your own wisdom and piety would best direct you; but I love you, and tell you all my heart. May the Lord do better for you than I can ask or think."

CHAPTER V.

Commences her School—Sketches from her Memorandum—Extracts from her Letters—Visit to Northampton—A Thunder Storm—Letter to a Member of her Sabbath school Class.

In December, 1838, she commenced a private School in Somerset Place, Boston, which she continued till February, 1843. To this School she devoted all her energies, endeavoring to refine the manners, and mould the heart, as well as cultivate the intellect of her pupils. In order to adapt her instructions to the peculiar wants of each, she always made it a point to study their individual characters. In her memorandum book we find against the name of each scholar, some note like the following, which, for the sake of avoiding any personality, are here appended to the letters of the alphabet instead of the names with which they were originally connected.

" A.—Tolerably studious,—very timid,—gentle,—professedly religious.

" B.—Rendered backward by sickness,—needs constant encouragement,—willing and affectionate; but thoughtless and talkative.

" C.—Very good student,—ambitious and energetic,—naturally petulant,—but I think converted.

" D.—Conscientiously studious, but excessively timid, —requires a very gentle hand.

"E.—Indolent scholar, but of active temperament,—needs constant watchfulness.

"F.—Can copy, not originate, yet anxious to learn,—lady-like and quiet.

"G.—Diligent, but not a genius,—very nervous, but loveable.

"H.—Good abilities, but needs the spur of praise,—frolicksome.

"I.—Backward from sickness,—anxious to learn,—gentle and truly pious.

"J.—A compound of oddities,—great observation,—no application,—made to try one's patience, and yet one I dearly love,—a great wit.

"K.—Superficial,—willing to learn,—needs much encouragement,—thoughtless."

&c., &c.

It was to this minute observation of character, and careful adaptation of her mode of instruction to meet the peculiar wants of each, that she owed much of her success as a teacher. Her School was the chief object of her thoughts, and no time nor expense were spared to render herself in the highest degree useful to those under her care. "I leave home," said she, "as early at least as half-past eight; spend my intermission in the School-room, and am seldom quietly settled at home again till six o'clock, our hour for tea. Two or three evenings I generally attend meeting, and feel obliged to spend the time in study till eleven or twelve o'clock, in order to meet the demands of my School; of course I have but little time to devote to friends."

TO MISS S. T. BOSWORTH.

"*March* 21*st*, 1839.

"How little did I think a year ago that I should now be engaged in a School in the heart of Boston. I should hardly have admitted the idea of my instructing thirty young minds as being within the bounds of possibility. But so it is. God hath led me in a way I knew not. All his ways have been mercy and goodness towards me. His favors have been new every morning, and fresh every evening. He hath remembered his promises to the widow and the fatherless, and hath been an all-sufficient Helper. Kind, devoted, faithful friends hath he given me, especially so in my dear, kind uncle and aunt. Yes, in a word, he hath been far better than my fears, aye, than my hopes. I find School and its duties stern, yet pleasant realities; and I bless God that he has made me a teacher.

"And now what have been God's gracious dealings with you, sister dear? When you last wrote me, you mourned the hidings of your Saviour's face, and deplored the withering effects of the world on your soul's inward life. But now, when a Father's kind hand hath removed a little in the distance the allurements of earth, and left your soul unbiassed by its maxims, and freed from its unhealthy atmosphere, I trust the Saviour hath beamed on you in light and love. May he make all your bed in your sickness, and so sanctify you thereby that you may come forth, dearest, like gold seven times tried.

"I have just been reading Philip's 'Love of the Spirit.' Have been very deeply interested in it. The subject is so novel, and so delightfully treated, that it seemed to give me new life and vigor. We hear much of the love of the Father, and of the Son, but who speaks of the love of the Spirit? We make mention of his power, and of our entire dependence on his aid, but who adores his love? Yet was it not love which led our despairing souls to the cross, and bade us live? Was it not love which, witnessing with our Spirits that we were born of God, enabled us to say, Abba, Father? And whose assisting love but his hath restored our backslidings, strengthened our trembling faith, and enabled us to pour out our souls 'with groanings which cannot be uttered?' The love of the Spirit,—blessed theme! Reason indeed have we to adore alike the Father who chose us, the Saviour who died for us, and the Spirit who renewed us."

During the summer, the cares of school bore heavily upon her health and spirits, and her religious exercises seem less cheerful than formerly. Addressing an intimate friend, she says:

"My aching heart has long desired to unbosom itself to some praying soul, for thick clouds hang between me and my soul's Helper. A name to live I have, but fear I am dead. Pride, and self, and worldly cares have shut out the light of God's countenance. Happiness is not the main thing I want, but holiness. O to be right, I need to be converted anew. My desultory life breaks up my religious hours and habits. And so ready am I to wander, that I have made this an excuse for the neglect of my accustomed seasons of prayer, and of reading God's blessed word. Of course I am away from my Father's embrace. And as day after day calls for new confessions of the same ingratitude and forgetfulness, shame fills my soul. But it is not true repentance, for it has to be repented of."

A few weeks later, she wrote to the same friend, "We are going to try our 'Young Sisters' Meeting' again, on Wednesday afternoons, will you not meet us at a throne of grace? Do not forget me. I am still roving, wish I could be more equal, more stayed on God. But I vary with every circumstance; Chameleon-like, I change with every atmosphere I breathe. Is there no way for me to escape this soul-enthralling influence? If I would but gird myself in the blessed panoply of Jesus, I know I should not be thus vulnerable."

Her summer vacation was mostly spent in Watertown, soon after which she wrote as follows:

"*September* 21*st*, 1834.

"Three weeks of this new term have passed. I commenced with earnest prayer that God would help me to overcome my besetting sin, and give me grace so to act in reference to my dear flock as to glorify his name. I have tried to watch over myself, to repress my hasty spirit, to be gentle, kind, and forbearing, and I have been blessed,—blessed in my own spirit, in the love and confidence of dear friends, and the affection of the little ones. Not that I feel satisfied with myself, or think that I have already attained. O no, no. But I should be ungrateful to that grace which I am conscious has assisted me, if I should say that I had made no progress. Yet do not think me proud, or self-complacent. If I know my own heart, I do feel humble, that with all the gracious assistance so freely offered me, I still so often come short, still so often fail. I feel no more secure, if not every moment watchful, than ever before. If I ever felt delight in prayer it has been when casting myself on God for divine direction and keeping.

"Sometimes I think that I am too much absorbed in school. My prayers are principally that I may have grace to glorify God as a teacher, and fulfill my duties to my little flock, as intellectual and immortal beings. My meditations and feelings run in the same channel. What I hear affects me chiefly as it has a bearing on the same point. Even my very affections are mainly bestowed on the same object. Do you think there is danger of my becoming too much bound up in school? Or is it not my duty to give myself to my calling? School is very full and I have much to do; am busy from morning till night, and even in dreams am still hearing classes. But I love it more and more, and mean to make it the aim of my life to be a good and useful teacher."

"*Sabbath evening.*

"How sweet, dear sister, are the bonds of Christian fellowship. I have been thinking as I sat in the solitude of my little chamber, how delightful the communion of kindred spirits on the engrossing theme of religion. I have not felt alone; no, God has been with me, and my little room is bright with his presence. Yet I never realized before how perfectly alone we feel even in the midst of a multitude, with not one of whom we have a kindred emotion.

* * * * * *

But enough! God sees it to be best; yet how strange. Why this difference of taste and interest? The time is not out of memory when I was wilder than the wildest. I can only say, '*Even so Father, for so it seemed good in thy sight.*' Truly '*He leadeth the blind in a way they know not.*'

"I have been struck lately at discovering how superficial is our knowledge of God's word, and especially of the teachings of Christ. There are beauties indeed on the surface, but the deeper you go, the richer the ore. They are an inexhaustible mine. Their first contemplation, especially the application of them, fills the mind with wonder and delight. But when we study into them, when we unfold the germ which they enclose, what new beauties ever offer themselves to the view. And yet the last, leaves the impression that much more remains undiscovered. This is true of no other science, at least in any thing like a comparative degree. And if it seem thus here, with our limited conceptions, and darkened minds, how dwarfish will all our views appear, when with the giant capacities of heaven, we begin to learn the height and depth, the length and breadth of that which passeth perfect knowledge.

"Do we, dear Sister, live enough of heaven below? If the world must talk of its interests and concerns, ought not the ransomed of Christ, the heirs of heaven, to have some higher, holier themes than the passing concerns of the day? May Jesus bless our friendship, may he sanctify it, and prepare us, dearest, for mutual converse where we shall sit at his feet and see him face to face."

In the early part of 1840, her heart was cheered by the hopeful conversion of two or three of her day scholars, and one or more of her class in the Sabbath school. Her own mind had been previously quickened as is seen by the following extract.

"*February* 26*th*, 1840.

"I was glad to hear such interesting accounts from W. The Lord is indeed blessing you. He is graciously refreshing his weary heritage all around. And, dear sister, I trust he has blessed me, even *me*. The last month has been one of the happiest months I have ever spent. I had passed a season of great mental conflict; but, despairing of my own strength, I cast myself on that strong arm which I felt could alone uphold my wavering feet. The Lord heard my despairing cry, and has been ever since a present God. O it has been long, since a throne of Grace was so precious, communion with God so delightful, religious duties so inviting, and Christian converse so sweet. God has done great things for me and I will praise him. I have found that no cares nor circumstances, can keep the soul from God, if it really desires communion with him. Not that I have become *dead* to the temptations of the world; O no, no. They are still strong, very strong. But his grace *can* keep me. O that it ever may.

"I am beginning to lose my liking for a city again. It is so much more difficult to lead a religious life there, so hard to tell what the mass of professors consider religion to be. Not that that should be the standard, at which the devoted servant of God should aim. No, religion is always the same; city, or country. But it weakens that fellowship and confidence which ought to spring up with the very name of Christian. I am too warm and excitable for a city. It imposes too much restraint upon the feelings. It begets so much art, so many smooth-tongued expressions of friendship, while the heart does not feel one emotion of interest; so much of religious cant where vital piety is a stranger. But this is the dark side. Yes, after all, a years' residence has endeared Boston to me, and formed a thousand tender associations never to be forgotten. Its intellectual privileges and its refinement are sources of real pleasure to me; and then there are some dear good people here to whom I am strongly attached, in whose company I find, not only 'a feast of reason and a flow of soul,' but sweet communion on holy themes.

"Yet I think we worship mind too much. I know that intellect is a precious gift, and its cultivation highly important. But the conviction is forcing itself upon me that the most intellectual are not the most happy Christians, that they do not enjoy as much of the love and favor of God, as many of more humble pretensions. I long for intercourse with such plain, but loving Christians as I met with in Chester years ago. And, weary of the influence of city life, I often heartily exclaim, 'O for the pinions of a dove,' for then would I fly to different scenes.

"How cold the happiness which intellectual pursuits and acquisitions afford, compared with the life and glow of affection. We love to feel that we are loved,—that other hearts throb in unison with ours,—joy when we joy, and sorrow when we sorrow. But how little in this gross, earthly state do we know of the sweetness, the intensity, the purity, the bliss, of perfect love. When immortal life shall flow through our veins, and the love of sin be destroyed, then, and not till then, shall we know its deep meaning. I think that I am too exclusive, that I have too little of that enlarged benevolence which beats with the great heart of mankind. I need more of that love which moved Jesus, and I believe that God means to make me feel this."

"*March 25th.*

"I have latterly found a great deal of comfort and happiness from the conviction that in every event, however minute, God is concerned,—that he ever designs our best good as well as his own glory. I have found it far easier to bear with the volatility and waywardness of my pupils, when I have thought of them as sent in love to try the sincerity of my faith, than when I regarded them as merely the outbreaks of youthful folly and sin. The little crosses and disappointments which life daily brings with it are far less difficult to submit to, when viewed in this consoling light."

During the summer, her health became much impaired from excessive labor, so that she gladly embraced the opportunity of spending her August vacation in Northampton. From this place she wrote several letters of which the following are brief extracts.

"I am very much better already; my strength is every day increasing; and well it might when fortified by so good an appetite as this fresh air creates. Northampton is in all its beauty now. We have had delightful showers every day since our arrival, and the country wears all the freshness and verdure of mid-summer. From my chamber windows may be seen one of the most beautiful views on which the eye ever rested. The horizon on the right is bounded by the noble Holyoke, covered with dense woods, and, ever and anon, lost in the misty clouds, which for the last three days have hung over its summit. At its foot lies the beautiful village in all its quiet loveliness, adorned with most tasteful and romantic dwellings, which, peeping through the thick foliage, gives to this place its peculiar beauty. Far on the left, lie, here and there, the picturesque towns which environ this Eden-like spot, and a dim line of distant hills terminates the view.

"Would you could sit, and see and feel with me the ten thousand ever varying beauties of this gem of nature. Would I could spend in sweet communings with you my many leisure hours. The pleasures of life are doubled by being shared with a friend. Brighter is the sunshine, greener the verdure, lovelier the scene, when, in a congenial bosom, kindred emotions and pleasures are awakened. In many things, Sarah dear, we are unlike, very unlike, yet there is a sympathy of heart, a oneness of taste in many things, which form golden links to bind us together; above all, those feelings and hopes which are connected with our eternal well-being, awaken an interest in each other's weal or woe compared with which all other interests are worthless."

TO HER COUSIN, MISS E. A. DAMON, NOW MRS. BOWERS.

"*Northampton, August 18th,* 1840.

"I wish my dear Ellen could see some of the fine sights, the beautiful scenes I am daily witnessing here. Somehow we have of late seen but little of each other. Yet I love you dearly, and your affection is dear to me. My school of course occupies most of my attention when at home. It is indeed with me an all-engrossing subject. To that I would bend every energy, and for it employ every faculty. The only thing with which I am dissatisfied is myself. Could I feel conscious that I was perfectly fitted, thoroughly educated, my every earthly wish would be gratified. To improve my few attainments, enlarge my sphere of knowledge, and fit myself to benefit to the highest possible degree the dear ones committed to my care, is the single object at which I aim, subservient alone to the glory of God.

" Teaching appears to me the most exalted of all vocations,—the most noble of all pursuits,—the most encouraging of all employments,—containing in itself its own reward. Woman can in no way, so benefit her species. This broad arena challenges her to action, invites her to gird herself with the panoply of religion and of science, and fight and toil manfully while strength and life are hers. She has the young heart in its freshness, tainted indeed by sin, but with more simple affections, and tender feelings than in any other period of life. I begin, Ellen, to be an enthusiast in teaching."

TO HER MOTHER.

" I wish you could have been here yesterday. Such glorious sights and sounds I never saw or heard before. For more than a week the sun had shone with intense heat, and not a drop of rain had fallen to quench the thirst of the parched earth. Day after day, we had watched the clouds and seen them gather and scatter without the reviving shower. Yesterday between eleven and twelve, dark, black clouds were seen hurrying from every quarter in the direction of Amherst ; seemingly at the impulse of half a dozen different currents. Vivid flashes of lightning were followed by peals of thunder, which seemed to shake the very earth beneath us. We all stood gazing at the gathering clouds. We could distinctly see the torrents of rain pouring upon Amherst, while no other place was yet watered. From our high, and commanding situation, with a landscape before us, having a radius of twelve or sixteen miles, we could see all the apparatus of the tempest. The rain-clouds spread to the north; you could distinctly see the line of the falling shower. Amherst was at last visible. The clouds which had retired to the left, began to move in a rapid current towards the right, shutting in our horizon, till we seemed to be in the midst of the clouds, and the sheets of water poured down upon us. For nearly an hour, the hoarse roar of thunder echoed round the hills, and lightning of the most dazzling brilliancy flashed before us.

"Just about five o'clock, the cloud retired a little from Northampton, the sun shone out in its splendor, and the most brilliant rainbow I ever beheld spanned the broad heavens. It was no pale, broken, disjointed arch, but perfect and radiant, it rested its broad base on the neighboring hills, as beautiful as when it first met the wondering eyes of Noah, telling him of God's long-suffering goodness. The evening was, if possible, still more grand; the brilliancy of the lightning being increased by the surrounding darkness. Wrapt in thought, I gazed, and gazed. It was a Sabbath I shall never forget."

TO A MEMBER OF HER SABBATH SCHOOL CLASS.

"*Northampton, August 24th,* 1840.

"MY VERY DEAR HARRIET:—Very glad was I to find that you remembered your absent teacher. I have had many letters from my friends, but have read none with more delight than yours; for I feel as if you were in some sense my child, that is in a spiritual sense. God has in a measure committed you to my care, and I must feel great solicitude and anxiety on your account. I do not feel anxious that you should be rich or prosperous in the world, but I do feel anxious that you should grow in grace,—that you should love God more and more,—that you should look to Christ, feeling still more deeply your constant need of his grace,—that you should hate sin more and more, and love holiness with increased desire. I feel desirous that the Bible should be studied daily, with a clearer understanding,—a greater love for its commands, its promises, and its warnings. I want that you should pray more in faith, be always praying in spirit.

"I feel very anxious, dearest Harriet, that you should never cast a reproach on religion,—never grow cold in God's service,—never backslide from him in heart,—that your example, your conversation, and all about you, should make your young companions feel that you have something which they have not. My dear child, you are looking forward to a most solemn hour. If God permit, you hope soon to make a public profession of your love to him,—in the presence of God the Father, Son, and Holy Spirit, of the holy angels, the church, and a scoffing world, to be buried in the flowing waters as an emblem of your death and burial to sin. You will thereby promise, from that moment to live only for God,—to care no more for the vanities, or pleasures of this world; but to employ your time, your example, and all you have for Jesus' cause. Dear Harriet, think well of all these solemn things. Ask yourself whether you are willing to spend your days for God,—to take up your cross daily and follow Christ. Unless you are, do not enter the church of God. I trust and believe you are, dear Harriet, but you must examine yourself.

"You say you have some trials. So has every Christian. You know the Bible says, '*Whom the Lord loveth he chasteneth, and scourgeth every son whom he receiveth.'* It is best for us to have trials, for they show us how much our faith is worth. When you are tempted look to Christ for help. Remember that he will be grieved if you yield to temptation, but will help you if you sincerely ask his assistance. Be patient, be submissive, return not evil for evil. Be gentle, be industrious. Endeavor to be an example in all that is good. Do not cease to labor and pray for your young friends. Their souls are as precious now as when you first wept over them. Do not rest while they are not safe. In a few days I hope to see you. May the Lord keep and bless you, and make you a bright star in his crown of rejoicing is the prayer of

"Your fond teacher,

"EMILY W."

CHAPTER VI.

Letter to Miss S. P. C., on the Death of a near friend—Grateful recollections of her School days—Letter to Miss S. T. B.—Letters from Watertown—Effects of her vacation—Resignation of her Pastor, Rev. W. P.

THOUGH Emily always had a large circle of friends towards whom her affections and sympathies freely flowed, yet she generally had one with whom she was more particularly intimate, to whom she could breathe her inmost feelings, and whose sympathy was her dearest earthly blessing. The removal of an intimate friend in 1837, left her for a while without any particular associate; but at length she was led by some peculiar providence, to select Miss S. P. C. of Charlestown, as her special confidant; and a friendship like that between David and Jonathan knit their hearts together in a most tender attachment, which continued unshaken till death.

The following letter, written in reference to the death of Mr. Francis Cole, September, 1840, was addressed

TO MISS S. P. CARTER.

"MY OWN LOVED SISTER:—It is the blessedness of Christian fellowship that it comes to our aid, not only when all is bright and happy, when our cup runs over with blessings, and we bask in the sunshine of prosperity; but the believer rejoices to find the sympathetic heart beat as warmly in the bosom of his brother or sister in Christ, when trouble or sorrow comes. Dearest S., I have shared your joys, and participated in your blessings, let me now partake of your griefs. The blow that wounds your heart, and awakens there a sister's anguish, strikes through you to me, and I would weep with you over the departed. Yes, he is gone, the brother, friend, and Christian. We shall no more hear his cheerful voice, nor look on his happy countenance. We shall miss him from the house of God, the church, the prayer meeting, the family circle.

" But while the aching void thus left in your heart will cause the tears to flow, and the spirit to sigh, yet my Sarah will not forget the hand of love that has dealt the chastising blow. It is no stern, arbitrary decree of a Sovereign Ruler, who has no regard for the feelings and affections of his creatures; but it is the gracious ordering of a Father, who '*knoweth our frame, who remembereth that we are dust.*' He who formed the heart with its keen capacities for enjoyment and sorrow, its exquisite sensibilities, and its strong affections, he hath done it. Dear Sarah, while you weep, kiss the rod. Bless Him who gave, and who hath taken away. Still each repining feeling, while with the saint of old you exclaim, '*It is the Lord, let him do what seemeth him good.*'

"Was it not needed to teach you more forcibly that every thing here is unstable? Was it not to wean affections too strongly wedded to earth, and form a new link to heaven? Was it not to teach the necessity of being ready, ever ready to depart, to be up and doing, diligent in the Master's service? Did not the blessed Refiner see some dross, that could only be purged away in this furnace of affliction, and did he not therefore send it in love?

"You are my elder, and superior, I would neither dictate, nor reprove, but only ask you, dearest, if it is not in some such light, that you view this mysterious providence. Dark as it is, the kind voice of our merciful High Priest, who can be, and who is, touched with the feeling of our infirmities, may be heard from the clouds and darkness, saying, '*What I do thou knowest not now; but thou shalt know hereafter.*' What a comfort at such times is the Christian's hope. It makes us feel that the sufferings of this present time are not worthy to be compared with the glory which shall be revealed in us hereafter. Dearest S., if Christ's, soon you will lay aside this earthly tabernacle. The departed, and the loved, may then be the first to welcome you to the bright abodes, where he now reigns with Jesus. Blessed be God, we sorrow not as those without hope.

"Give my love and sympathy to dear Abby. I have written this for her as well as yourself. The Lord bind up her broken heart, heal her wounded spirit, and enable her, who by this affliction must say, '*Lover and friend hast thou put far from me, and mine acquaintance into darkness,*' to add, '*It is good for me that I have been afflicted.*' To Him who tempers the wind to the shorn lamb, you are both most fervently commended by

"Your fond, EMILY."

The more she realized of the cares and duties of a teacher, the more she felt to prize the labors of her own instructors. The following extract from a letter addressed to one of her teachers, will illustrate not only the warm gushings of her affectionate heart, but also the workings of that sanctified nature, which finds God in every thing, and makes every thing the occasion of new gratitude and praise to him.

" *November 9th*, 1840.

"When reason deserts her throne, when consciousness is lost, and memory destroyed, then only can I forget my more than mother. No, though the stream may flow less noisily now than once, time has but deepened its channel. Each day as it passes, makes me more fully realize how much I owe to your unwearied, faithful instructions. All my success as a teacher, my usefulness to my family, my own self-improvement, under God I owe to you. And when, in the wear and tear of every day life, I feel the importance of the principles you so carefully inculcated, I feel to bless God, that he ever led you to take an interest in me, and bear with me, in spite of my constant waywardness.

"The more I think of it, the more I feel that God awoke the interest in your heart. It certainly was not natural, for there was nothing in me to interest one like yourself. My tastes, habits, feelings, were all so unlike yours, that I feel convinced, if God had not interposed, and directed your attention to one so wholly unlikely to awaken it, I should never have experienced the fostering care, so long my rich portion. It is not then, I trust, with idolatrous affection for a mortal being, that I look upon you. It is not, I think, a sinful excess of love, that awakens so many deep and inexpressible emotions, that sends the hot tears down my cheeks, that makes me so often repeat your name with feelings no other can awaken. But it is that in you I see one of the dearest proofs of that Saviour's love which alone has made me what I am. O how often have I wished that I might live over the last five years of my life. Not as I have lived them, O no. But alas, I fear I should still have to mourn over abused privileges, neglected opportunities, and misimproved blessings. The same evil heart of unbelief would still, I fear, lead me from God. Did I not at times catch a glimpse of Jesus' full atonement, did not I realize the preciousness of that soul-reviving promise, '*Though your sins be as scarlet, they shall be white as snow, though they be red as crimson, they shall be as wool,*' I should not dare to hope.

"I think I have enjoyed religion this fall more than for a long time. In the spring I was the subject of deep excitement. I think, however, I needed it to break up the apathy into which I had fallen. But it was not a healthy state of mind to remain in, and indeed was conducive to my indisposition in the summer. I have of late known more of calm, uniform enjoyment of God's presence, than ever before. Never did I so much enjoy the reading of the Bible. Yet I often feel constrained to ask if it is possible that one so vile can be the object of God's love, can ever enter a heaven of spotless holiness. Surely none will have such reason to sing of sovereign grace."

TO MISS S. T. BOSWORTH.

"*Charlestown, July* 29, 1841.

"MY OWN DEAR SARAH:—School has at length closed, my labors for a while are over, and I improve the first opportunity vacation offers to write my much-loved, absent friend. Your name, dear one, has been often on my tongue, and yourself most present to my mind, since we parted; nor shall I ever forget this eventful visit. I have learned to know and appreciate you more than in all my previous acquaintance, and shall ever feel grateful to God for the privilege of ministering to you in your weakness. God in his mercy grant that on the heavenly hills, we may together talk of all the wondrous way in which our God hath led us, together sit at Jesus' feet, and, laying there the crowns he hath purchased, forever gaze on his beauties and learn of him.

"O what a precious balm it is to the aching heart, to know, that the hand of God is in every thing,—to realize that the most minute event cannot occur without his will, —that he takes cognizance of all our weakness, and remembers that we are but dust. When severed hearts throb with anguish, how sweet the thought that He, who knows in a fuller sense than man has ever known what it is to love, hath parted us. When we sigh for a kindred spirit to be present with us, how soothing to remember that He, who knows the cravings of the human heart, hath denied the boon, and offered himself a glorious substitute to fill every void in the heart.

"Does the good Shepherd, dear sister, lead you into the green pastures, beside the still waters, carrying the feeble lamb in his bosom? Do your views of God enlarge, and seem more and more like blessed realities? Dear Sarah, at the foot of the cross we found mercy, there let us abide, thence never remove. There alone will the world fade into its real insignificance, and eternity roll upon us in all its solemn, sweet reality. There shall we see down deep into the blackness of our hearts, and feel our constant dependence on the dear Redeemer. There will love, strong and ardent, fill our souls. O Saviour, fix us there.

"God bless you, Sarah, and let me see your face again in joy. Till then,

"Fondly yours,

"EMILY."

A part of her summer vacation was spent in Watertown from which place she wrote to a number of friends.

TO HER SABBATH SCHOOL CLASS.

"*Watertown, Aug.* 19, 1841.

"MY DEAR CLASS:—It always grieves me to be absent from you, and I never should, did I not feel that duty required it. You are not absent from my thoughts, though I cannot be with you personally. I need not tell you how dear you all are to me, how deep an interest I feel in each of you, how earnestly I desire you to be truly happy. And yet, my dear girls, you often make me very sad. Do you ask, what you can do to grieve me. I will tell you. You are very kind and affectionate; many of you who have been long with me, I know, love me much. I do not doubt your affection. You are generally very attentive too, and willing to do many things to please me. But, dear girls, suppose one of you had a friend whom you loved very dearly, and esteemed above all others; suppose too that I, knowing you had this high regard for her, should meet the person, and treat her with indifference and coldness, and even show contempt. Though I might treat you with all possible kindness, should you not feel unhappy, should I thus conduct towards your friend? I think you would.

"Well, dear girls, I have a very dear friend whom you always treat in this manner. I love him very much, more than all the world beside. I have often talked to you about him, and told you how good he was, but you always treat him very coldly. He would love to be your friend and do as much for you as I think he has done for me. But you will not love him; and do you wonder that I feel sad? Beside, this dear Friend of mine, my Saviour I mean, alone can save you. You are each of you lost, guilty sinners; and you know there is no other name whereby we may be saved. It is for your interest, my beloved class, that I wish you now to seek that precious Redeemer, who has so long been calling you to turn unto him and live. However you may doubt, I can say, from most thorough experience, there is no true happiness aside from trust in Jesus. I have tried a great many pleasures, but have never found any to compare with God's forgiveness and blessing. When I can feel that God loves me, that for Christ's sake he has forgiven my sins, I am perfectly happy. Nothing can trouble me much. And do not you think you should be happy in the same confidence?

"Beside, my dear girls, God has commanded you to love and serve him; and you should not dare to disobey, even if you can be so ungrateful as to wish it. O then decide this day, this hour, that you will give yourselves to God. The Lord bless and save you, is the prayer of

"Your fond teacher,

"S. E. Waldo."

TO MISS A. C. HILL.

"*Watertown, Aug.* 25, 1841.

"Dearest Abby:—I have been quite disappointed in not seeing you in W. during my long visit here. The world is accustomed, dear sister, to congratulate the maiden whose hand is plighted, and whose heart is given; but not with its cold formality, not because custom requires it, but because my own heart bids it, do I congratulate you on your present happiness and your future prospects. The gift of a loving, manly, virtuous heart, is doubtless a precious boon, and though I cannot speak in the eloquence of sympathy, I can imagine that you receive it as such, from the Giver of all your mercies. May God's choicest blessings, dearest Abby, here and hereafter, rest on you and yours ; may he hallow your mutual affection, guide you below, and unite you above.

"I have had a delightful visit here. You cannot tell how good it is to be away from the shackles of the city. I am glad to find, as I was almost afraid I should not, that if I once breathe the free air of the country, I love it better far than a city life. Last winter when almost surfeited with intellectual privileges, with constant opportunities of hearing scientific lectures, with avenues to knowledge opened wide on every side, beginning to form acquaintances with many highly cultivated and refined minds, I almost turned away in thought from the quiet retirement of country life ; but I see more clearly now, and still feel not quite corrupted from my early tastes.

"Dear Abby, I have felt more than ever of late the mutability of all things earthly. Friend after friend has been separated from me, till I feel quite alone. Sarah C., who has long been my most intimate friend, leaves Charlestown next week, and then I shall feel almost forsaken. Yet how sweet is the thought, God never changes. Time, distance, circumstances, death, cannot affect him. '*The same yesterday, to-day, and for ever.*' This thought is sometimes unspeakably precious. O, to be absorbed in love to God, to have my affections most intensely fixed on him. We need these changes to detach us from a world too fondly loved—to make us feel that here we have no continuing city."

TO MISS S. P. CARTER.

"My dearest Sister:—'Blessings brighten as they take their flight;' and your affection seems inexpressibly dear, as I think of parting with you for a season. I have long thought that I loved you, but I did not know the strength of the cords that bound our hearts together, till the thought of absence tried them. I did not know the depths of affection in my own heart which I had given you. * * * * * *

"O, I have loved your own true heart, the soul that loved me in return. *Have* loved did I say, I do, shall ever love. Yes, sister Sarah, blessed be the abounding grace of God for the hope that we shall love forever, that in our common hope, our common Saviour, we have a bond of union durable as eternity. Differing widely as we do on many points, this offers so broad a base for friendship that it must stand firm. If then we hope for a dwelling above, what shall our love be in heaven?

"Here, there is, there must be, something of a vail, even between hearts most united. There are feelings within, which we would not unvail to mortal eye. But then, with naught to conceal, our souls transparent as the light, the vail shall be withdrawn, and in a high and holy sense, we shall see each other face to face, soul to soul. Then will our communions be sweet, while we review the whole way through which our God has led us; while we look upon our exalted Saviour, and with voices tuned to celestial harmony, join the song of Moses and the Lamb forever; while we hasten with joyful alacrity on errands of mercy, commissioned of Jesus, then, then alone shall we know what it is to love. What manner of persons ought we to be, seeing we cherish such hopes?

"Ah, Sarah, we are far short of the goal of Christian perfection. Let us pray for more rapid progress in the race set before us. Gladly would we have traveled together through this wilderness, but it could not be. Still the same Guide attends both, and he will lead us by a right way, for this is our assurance, 'The Lord shall preserve thy going out and thy coming in from this time forth, and even forevermore.

"Fondly yours,

"EMMA."

TO MRS. M. C. BROWN.

"*Sept.* 13, 1841.

"I cannot thank God enough, my dear Maria, for enabling me to walk in so pleasant a path. I do not believe that any one has a more quiet, diligent, docile, and affectionate class than I am privileged to teach. I think there is no earthly pleasure more pure, more exalted, more exquisite, than that offered to a teacher. No occupation is more worthy the noblest powers of the mind, the highest attainments, the warmest affections, the most ardent piety. I bless God that I may serve him as a teacher,—that he has led me to engage in a pursuit taxing constantly the whole soul. When I can enjoy religion in teaching, there cannot be a more happy, contented being than I am. I can take my every want, duty, care, or desire to him, and he is so sweetly near. O may he ever keep me in the dust at his feet.

"I do feel profited by my vacation. I was living so much within myself, and loved so exclusively, that I needed to learn the lesson my visit to my friends has taught me,—the blessedness of expanded sympathies, and universal interest. I feel that God has taken Sarah away that I might not be absorbed in one, but love the whole church more deeply. Still this will be against nature, and must be the work of grace. For two or three years I have been much away from home, and now feel that I have not filled my place as a member of this dear household; but by the influence of my vacation, my eyes have been opened to the fact that here, just here, and nowhere else, is my place,—that just as I am, and just as they are, God has brought us together and made us one household, where I may find my own greatest happiness and do the greatest good. This is a very simple conclusion, but one to which, as a practical thing, I have but recently arrived.

"Dear Maria, God has been most gracious to me of late. He always has been; but he has just added to all the rest, the conversion of one of my dear Sabbath school class. I can hardly realize that the blessing so often implored is mine. I feel so unworthy to have been made in any way instrumental of a soul's conversion. Free grace, free grace, is my constant cry. If not deceived, God has given me of late some of that yearning for souls which I would desire ever to feel."

On the third Sabbath in September, Rev. Mr. Phillips resigned his pastoral charge of the church with which she was connected. Her feelings on the occasion are expressed in the following note.

TO MISS S. P. CARTER.

"We have been taught by another most painful lesson that nothing here is sure. Our beloved Mr. Phillips has resigned his pastoral care of us, and that so decidedly and fully, that no persuasion, argument, or entreaty can move him. It is a dreadful, a most unexpected blow. Your father informed me of his intentions on Saturday afternoon. I could hardly believe it, for I had never thought of such a thing. At our little prayer meeting in the evening, tears fell fast,—all felt sad; for, with the exception of myself, he had been made the instrument of the awakening and conversion of each, and had baptized them in the name of the Holy Three. Sabbath morning came, and still many were ignorant of his intentions; though the news had spread with some rapidity. Mr. P. made not the slightest allusion to the subject in his prayer, sermon, or elsewhere, but was evidently ill at ease. At the close of the morning service he simply remarked, 'I have a particular reason for wishing all the congregation to attend this afternoon.' Through the afternoon service no reference of any kind was made to the anticipated change, unless it might have been in his prayer that we might be prepared for trial, and to part with those we loved. After the singing of the closing hymn, he arose and read a concise statement of what he was resolved to do. Twice he faltered, and his quivering lips could hardly articulate his words; but in general he seemed to be wonderfully self-possessed. Every thing had been done, and no room was left for argument or entreaty. He must go. It was an impressive moment. The crowded house was still as death, except where sobs from sad hearts could not be suppressed. Yes, we are again without an under shepherd. The Lord have mercy on us. Dearest sister, you will think much of us, and your prayers will go up with ours for guidance. Early Monday morning Mr. P. left for Providence, and will probably remove his family there within a month. It still seems a dream."

CHAPTER VII.

Important era in her Christian experience—Season of deep depression—Efforts for the conversion of others—Consecration of her whole being to Christ—Steps by which her mind had been led—Nature and effects of that consecration—Letter to her sister M. J.—To Miss S. T. B.—To Miss S. P. C.

The year 1842 was on many accounts a most important year to Miss Waldo. She was not only permitted to witness the blessed effusions of the Spirit both at home and abroad, but her own mind became the seat of its deep and powerful workings. From a combination of various circumstances, she was led to examine more particularly than ever before, what the Scriptures require and expect of the followers of Jesus. One of the most obvious results of this inquiry was the adoption of a new, and far more elevated standard of piety; not a mere theory, the contemplation of which might inspire self-complacency at the discoveries she had made in divine things, but a full and hearty conviction that her own religious life fell far, very far short of what Christ requires of his disciples. The deep heart searching, the keen remorse, the distressing doubts and fears, which this conviction awakened within her, were at the time confined, for the most part, to her own breast. Occasionally, however, she expressed herself to intimate friends in language like the following.

"*January* 6, 1842.

"I feel all too vile to expect that heaven will be my home. And yet I do not love to say so; not because unwilling to make the confession, but because it gives me in your esteem an undeserved title to humility. *Undeserved*, because you do not know the depth of meaning I attach to the expression. 'Vilest of the vile' should be no cant term on my lips. Yet I think I do love Jesus, and wish to live henceforth for him. O would I *had* done so. Pray for me; pray only for my sanctification."

"How suited to my case is the 51st Psalm. Truly '*I was shapen in iniquity; and in sin did my mother conceive me.*' Against God have I sinned and done sore evil in his sight. Yet would I cry, '*Hide thy face from my sins, and blot out all my transgressions. Create in me a clean heart. Cast me not away from thy presence, and take not thy Holy Spirit from me. Deliver me, O God, deliver me from blood-guiltiness, and my tongue shall sing aloud of thy righteousness.*' This is truly the sinner's Psalm."

But while her own hopes of heaven were beclouded, she labored untiringly for the good of others. Though hardly willing to believe herself a child of God, she writes to a friend: "This I can say, that, if I ever pray for any thing, it is that *you* may be sanctified, and conformed wholly to God; that he may ever delight in you, dearest, and that he will glorify himself in all his dear people. But as to myself I have dreadful doubts."

The following notes, written at this time, are a specimen of the manner in which she labored with the unconverted, while still in a state of great inward conflict.

"DEAR C.—For some reason, I can hardly tell why, you have been in my thoughts for several days past, and I have felt, day and night, that I must be constantly pleading with God for your conversion. I have felt that I could not rest till you were made a child of God; and last night, when at my request our little praying circle entreated the Lord for you, I felt almost assured that you would be now reconciled to God.

"Say, my dear C., do you feel no corresponding interest nor anxiety for yourself? Does no sense of danger, no consciousness of guilt, awaken in you some alarm for your salvation? With all your knowledge of divine things, is your heart unaffected by them? Do you see no loveliness in Jesus that you should desire him as your Saviour? Do you not feel the condemnation of the law resting upon you, and justly sentencing you to death eternal? Do you feel, dear C., no need of Jesus' most precious atonement, no inclination to come wash in the fountain he hath opened for sin and uncleanness? Can you refuse to give yourself to him, soul and body, when he offers himself to you an all-sufficient Saviour?

"O that I had an angel's tongue to entreat you to come to Christ. O that I could so describe his inexpressible preciousness to the soul that trusts in him, that you too would cast your all on him. Dear C., what hinders your salvation? What can possibly hinder? Come, this blessed hour, on the bended knees of your soul, confess to a long-suffering Saviour your guilt and unworthiness, and throw yourself on his mercy. It will not be in vain. Your faintest desire will be regarded, your weakest prayer be heard. O will you not then, dear C., come now; yes, literally *now*, to a willing

Saviour and be at peace? You know full well the way. O will you not walk in it? Do I not hear you say, '*I will arise and go unto my Father, and will say unto him, Father, I have sinned against heaven and in thy sight and am no more worthy to be called thy child?*' This you can do, will you?

"Anxiously yours,
"S. E. W."

About a week after, she addressed the following to the same.

"Dear C.—If you can spare an hour this evening, will you make one in our little, *very little* prayer meeting at half-past seven, in my chamber? I have wished very much to see you this week, and have thought of you by night and by day, for I still feel as deeply desirous of your salvation. Do come if you can; but, if you cannot come, will you, dear C., remember that we are praying for you, and put up one heart-felt, earnest plea for yourself?

"Most truly yours,
"S. E. W."

The burden of her desire for herself at this time, was not simply the pardon of sin, but grace to be, and do all that the gospel requires. And God, whose blessing is always commensurate with our faith, was pleased to manifest himself to her to a degree that she had never before experienced. Had she kept a journal of her private religious experience, to which we could now have access, we should no doubt find much of a deeply interesting character at this stage of her history. But, in the absence of these, it is certainly great cause for gratitude that she was directed, as we trust by the Holy Spirit, to communicate, so fully as she has done in her correspondence, the effects of his gracious operations on her soul. The following letters are of no ordinary interest.

TO MISS S. P. CARTER.

"*Charlestown, March* 16, 1842.

"MY LOVED SISTER:—It is with no common feelings that I sit down to write to you to-night; for I trust, dearest, that God has made me a new creature,—that, in a measure at least, old things are passed away, and many things become new. Yes, he has, I hope, called me from all my wanderings and guilt, to cast myself a helpless sinner at the foot of the cross, and in that cleansing fountain wash away all my deep, dark stains. Sometimes I think that I have never before known the truth; but yet I think I have had some feelings which were not the fruit of the natural heart, though mingled with much which seems contrary to a renewed state. But I have been brought to feel that it was not my place to agitate the question whether or not I had been converted, but to decide whether I could now trust in Jesus and serve him with my whole heart. Let me tell you a little more particularly.

"There have been times when I felt, as I then thought, much engaged in religion, and desirous to live for Christ and the salvation of souls, but I think I was never before really willing to submit *every* thing to God, to choose him for my *Lord* and *King*, as well as my Saviour. Some duties I was willing to perform, to some extent would be separate from the world, but *complete devotedness* I have hitherto not known.

"I have felt lately very wretched, I could not satisfy myself, and I found so much pride and rebellion in my heart, such unwillingness to take up every cross, that I have been often in bitter anguish of spirit. Several times I have been on the point of saying to all the world that I never was converted, and begging the prayers of God's people for me. At length I came to feel that I must give up all to Christ, and cast myself now on his blood and righteousness, or else despair. I never doubted the fullness of his atonement, but I knew that I could not come and ask for pardon through his blood, and yet feel at the same time conscious that I was unwilling to obey him *wholly*. I prayed for submission, but every thing was dim and distant. Yet I pleaded for mercy, and at length thought I could surrender all. The words of this hymn had been for some time running through my mind,

'And must I part with all I have
My dearest Lord for thee?
It is but right since thou hast done
Much more than this for me.
Yes, let it go! One look from thee
Will more than make amends
For all the losses I sustain
Of credit, riches, friends.'

"O thought I, if I could only say, 'Let it go;' and at last, I trust, I could. With many doubts and fears, and a cloud still over my soul, I tried in God's grace to perform the long-delayed duty of confession, and to proceed at once to take up the many crosses which I had been so long trying to avoid. The right-eye sin of worldly conformity rose like a mountain in my way, but I felt it better to enterinto life with one eye, than having two to perish. Then came the duty of faithful warning which, as I once told you, I had felt unwilling to do. God strengthened me.

* * * * * * *

"O how sweet to feel that Jesus knows all my trials and anxieties, that he is all powerful, and can do the most impossible things. I do expect great things; I do expect our dear family all to be converted. And why not? If Christ has given the greater blessing he will not withhold the less. O, Sarah, I want to live on the word—to believe in the promises—to be dead to the world, and have my life hid with Christ in God. I do not yet feel that intensity of affection, that strength of faith, that deep humility and brokenness of spirit which I would, but I dare to hope for them through my adorable Redeemer. Pray, O pray that I may be kept.

"Do not imagine, love, that I expect to live without sin. No, I feel daily need of renewed application to the blood of Jesus, but I hope to live henceforth for him. I feel that I shall always look back with deep regret on abused influence, wasted spiritual strength, and neglected duty, I can only hope now for grace to spend the remnant of my days for God. Sometimes I fear lest I am deceived, but think I can sincerely pray, Lord, search thou me. My dearest Sarah, forgive all that you have seen in me which has grieved you, and be very faithful. Pray much for this dear family, and for

"Your own

"EMMY."

TO THE SAME.

"*Charlestown, March* 30, 1842.

"MY LOVED SARAH:—I see that you do not understand all that I feel, indeed that would be impossible, but I mean all that I wished to express to you. From your reference to my feelings some two years since, I infer that you suppose me only more than usually aroused to divine things, as Christians in times of revival often are. But, dear Sarah, unless deceived, this is, I trust, a deeper work than that,—a change for life, a *thorough* change. At the time referred to, and at many other times, I have been strongly excited, but I never was calmer than now. I have often before been moved upon by extraneous influence, but this work has been all within. My life, my heart, never seemed so sinful, so unholy as it now appears, and yet I never before felt a consciousness of justification springing so entirely from a single reliance on the word of God.

"I have sinned against great light, and wondrous love, have crucified the Son of God afresh, and put him to open shame. Yet I can personally believe that 'the blood of Jesus Christ cleanseth from all sin.' Christ never seemed so precious—so truly all in all—so able to meet my every necessity—to fill every void—to occupy my whole affections. I feel often that I would close my eyes to every object of sense that faith might take a stronger hold on spiritual things. I do now feel them to be more vivid realities than once they were; yet my constant prayer is, more faith, more faith. There seems to me such a depth of meaning in that text 'For ye are *dead*, and your life is hid with Christ in God.' Think how little effect the gayest or the saddest scene has upon the senseless corpse. Dead to the world! Yes more, buried; buried with Christ in baptism. That has ever been condemnatory, for I have been often most keenly alive to the pleasures, the maxims, the vanities of the world. That glorious world above sometimes dawns so brightly on my longing sight that earth seems a burden. Yet I do not wish to die, for I would live to honor that dear Redeemer I have so long dishonored,—to bear the cross from which I have so long shrunk, and to undo the evil influence ot the past.

"Twenty-two years of my brief life have gone forever, and they appear almost a blank—a constant cause of repentance and abasement before a long-suffering God. Dear Sarah, if even I may enjoy such peace, such hope, what is not reserved for you? O draw, my own sister, sweet draughts from the fountain of living waters. Hourly, yes, each moment, refresh your oft sad heart by a glance at the sweet fields beyond. We are separated now, and probably shall continue to be in this world; but I love to think of meeting in heaven, where, even my robe washed and made white in the blood of the Lamb, we shall together gaze on the Saviour's face, and never, never sin.

"How willing are we to have Christ for our Redeemer, while we refuse to own him as our King and Lord, whom alone we are to obey. How base to hope for the crown, yet withdraw from the cross; to wish for all the happiness, but perform none of the service of a Christian, to desire to be confessed of Christ at the last, yet fear to be denied by the world now. Religion must be every thing or nothing. I see no consistent halting place, between thorough atheism and complete consecration to God. Once admit the being of God and the truth of revelation, and where else can we stop? If we believe the declaration of Christ, '*If any man will come after me, let him deny himself and take up his cross daily and follow me*,' and make any practical application of it, should we not be alarmed to find one day pass during which we have had no cross to bear? The heaviest cross I meet with is faithfulness to the impenitent; yet even in this I often find the quaint remark true, that 'when we stoop down to take the cross it rises up to meet us.'

"And now, dearest, praise the Lord with me, that he has brought the wanderer home, and given peace to a long troubled soul. Pray that he will keep the weak one in the hollow of his hand, and fill her more and more with his own grace and spirit. So prays for you

"Your own fond

"EMMY."

The following to her sister M. J., was written about this time.

"*Home, Friday evening.*

"MY LOVED SISTER:—I live within a little world in which I find many sources of enjoyment, though I hope that, with the spirit of my Master, my sympathies and prayers go far beyond it. A few hours in my beloved home at morn and eve, almost nine busy hours in my little school-room, and a few brief moments occasionally in the room of prayer, form the routine of my fast flying days. Refreshed by sweet interviews with my reconciled, and gracious Father, allured and sustained by the unmerited, but glorious hope of a blessed immortality, life is pleasant though death is sweet. Nature is beautiful as it bears his glorious impress,—friends are dear as the gift of his hand,—home most refreshing as a sweet stream by the way. O God is so good, is it not strange that we do not love him more? I feel that since he has forgiven me so very much I must love him greatly.

"What a treasure is committed to you, love; a loan bestowed by an indulgent Father to be trained for him. No doubt to your fond gaze, its tiny limbs and bright blue eyes, and cherub face, are all full of beauty. But this is only the mortal. The gem of richest worth, lies hidden, its beauties yet all undeveloped, its powers unknown. Yes, you are the mother, sister, of an immortal. Your babe can never die. True, its curiously fashioned frame may decay, but, if redeemed, it shall shine a gem of dazzling beauty in the Saviour's crown forever.

"Ah, dearest, who is sufficient for these things? What divine teachings do you need to be its teacher? What gracious influences should distill upon your soul, that your instructions might be like the soft dew to her young spirit. May God guide you, darling, to himself, teach you from on high, and make you the child of his adoption, that you may say at the last, Here am I, Lord, and the child thou hast given me."

TO MISS S. T. BOSWORTH.

"*Charlestown, April* 9, 1842.

"MY MUCH LOVED SARAH:—Let me thank you for your most interesting account of dear Fanny; we were all deeply affected by it, and would renewedly express our heart-felt sympathy for you all. These are sorrows, dearest sister, that none but Jesus can heal; and though I gladly would comfort you, and bring the sweet consolations of the word of life to your memory, yet your wound can be healed alone by personal application to the balm of Gilead. And how does my heart rejoice that there you have hourly access, and that it is not an unmeaning thing to tell you how his love fills every void, or to speak of the fullness there is in him.

"O it is sweet to feel that those we love, love Jesus too; that the language of Canaan is not strange to them; but full of sweet, deep meaning, learned by blessed experience. How true it is that the carnal mind understandeth not the things of the Spirit, because they are spiritually discerned. Most painfully do I often feel this in my daily intercourse with those I love most fondly.

"Dear Sarah, I trust I have been made a new, a changed being since I last wrote you. I have experienced feelings which were never mine before, and trust I shall ever bless the grace of God for all he has done for my soul of late. Sometimes I think that I never before knew the truth, or experienced the regenerating influences of the Holy Spirit. Sure, at least, I am that I have never served God with a *whole heart*, or implicitly submitted my will to his before. Do not suppose I imagine myself to be entirely sanctified; Oh no; I daily need fresh application to the blood of Jesus. But I trust God has enabled me to surrender myself *wholly and forever* to him, to come *entirely* out from the world and be separate, and find in him my all-sufficient, my abounding joy. I had wandered very far from God, and as I looked back on occasions when I had denied my blessed Lord, and put him to an open shame, as I felt, even at the time, conscious of an unwillingness to bear the cross daily, deep darkness and almost despair filled my soul. I was for some months a most wretched creature, thinking I must first settle the question whether I had ever been converted, and often half resolved publicly to renounce all hope of interest in the great salvation.

"Unable longer to endure this constantly increasing distress, I was led at length to cast myself, a self-ruined, guilty, perishing sinner, on the blood of Christ, and lay at his feet my all for time and eternity. I have since felt a peace, a confidence, a joy of soul to which I have been a stranger heretofore; and which, I hope, and pray, and believe, will ever increase. This one thing would I do: forgetting the things which are behind, I would press forward to the mark for the prize of my high calling in Christ Jesus. It is all of grace; and you will, I trust, look above me to that blessed One, whose compassion hath abounded to the chief of sinners.

"Crosses daily present themselves, but, having taken for my motto, '*If any man will come after me, let him deny himself and take up his cross daily and follow me,*' I feel that I have occasion for alarm, when the passing day brings no cross with it. Yet few seem heavy except faithfulness to souls, though even in this God has greatly blessed me. * * * * *

"God has wrought a great and glorious work here. Ninety or a hundred in our society have, we trust, accepted of the great salvation, and the interest is now very deep. There have been some most striking conversions; and the change in the church has been almost as manifest as in the congregation. Dry bones have been made to live again, and the wilderness to bloom like the rose. In the Seminary the work has been powerful and interesting, and our Sabbath school never saw such days. Little children sweetly lisp the Saviour's praises, and even babes sing of his love. Out of my large class of twelve, eight are now, I trust, in the fold of Jesus; six of whom are recent converts, and the remaining four will, I believe, soon join them. Glory to God in the highest. In the Navy Yard, and in the state prison the same blessed work is going on. Two young sailors will tomorrow be baptized; indeed God is in our midst of a truth.

"At the throne of grace we still meet nightly, you know, and therefore we cannot forget each other; and you will not forget to pray much for

"Your ever fond

"EMMY."

TO MISS S. P. CARTER.

"*Boston, April* 14, 1842.

"MY BELOVED SARAH:—You cannot tell how sweet your last letter was to me. I never felt more ready to bless God for your affection. O it is sweet to be loved by those who love our souls,—who have learned the language of Canaan—to whom, indeed, it is full of precious meaning. Nothing, I think, tends more directly to give a reality to unseen and spiritual things than the converse of spiritual friendship. The communion of the world appertains so exclusively to earth, that the faith, which had just soared in secret prayer to the very presence of God, falters, and faints, and almost doubts whether eternity, and the soul, and God, are indeed realities, when rational beings heed them so very, very little. Often, when in the still solitude of my little chamber, my gracious Saviour has revealed to me his surpassing loveliness, and opened to my astonished sight the boundless eternity before me, when it has seemed as if all who were heirs of the same immortality must feel the nothingness of this world, my heart has been pained to find beloved ones talking, thinking, and living in the passing moment. Is it not strange, dearest? And yet when we remember what little practical influence these same solemn realities have exerted over us, who have professed to have felt their power, we can only hide our abashed heads in the dust, for shame and repentance.

"God grant that I may never again be alive to the world. Thanks to his wondrous grace that he has given me a deadness to it to which I had hitherto been a stranger. Yes, love, God has done great things for me; he has brought me out of a land of darkness and death into a large place; he has filled my mouth with praise, and my tongue with rejoicing.

'All my capacious powers can wish
In him doth richly meet;
Nor to my eyes is light so dear,
Nor *friendship* half so sweet.'

"I see in him a blessed fullness never before realized. I have enough in Christ; my soul can rest in his love, nor sigh for ought beside. O for an increase of love for him, intense, all-ruling, consuming every evil thing, that the heavenly guest may fix his dwelling in my heart, and never, never depart thence."

TO THE SAME.

"*May* 28.

"I have never felt more than to-day the impossibility of finding any happiness in the absence of my Saviour.

If but a cloud intervene for a moment between my soul and him, the world is all dark. Yet

> 'In *darkest* shades if *he* appear
> My dawning is begun.'

"The value of his love never seemed so priceless, so worthy of every sacrifice, so able to compensate for every loss. Some trying things have led me lately to see how easily a person might feel ecstatic raptures, as he supposed, and yet, at the very time, show in his daily life a great want of the Spirit of Christ. And I have felt to plead more earnestly than ever before, that religion might be with me a living, practical reality, moulding my whole being, and entering into all the minutiæ of life. I have borne a much stronger resemblance to the erratic comet than to the unwavering planet. May I never again feel any other change than an increase of faith, of penitence, of love, and of holy zeal for souls. So much has been lost and worse than lost in the past,—the day is so far spent, the night so near at hand, that I would do with my might the many things that my hand finds to do. I am of myself, weakness, sin, and folly; but Christ is made of God unto me 'wisdom, and righteousness, sanctification and redemption.'

"The candidates before the church last evening were peculiarly interesting, and none more so than ———. Hers was the most interesting relation I ever heard—not because it was a good story well told, for it was spoken in weakness and trembling, but because *it redounded to the praise of the Holy Ghost.* She is a most humble, conscientious Christian."

"*June* 1.

"It is Wednesday evening. I have just returned from the house of God. Have passed a pleasant hour; only it was sad to feel that the conversion of souls weighed less deeply on the hearts and desires of God's people. How do we carry the selfishness of our natures even into the kingdom of God; and, rejoicing in our own salvation, soon tire of efforts for the salvation of others. I think the reading of Harris on Mammon, or rather his introductory remarks, has been blest to the awakening in my soul of a constant, strong desire for the conversion of sinners, which I did not formerly feel. Still there is no one thing for which I feel to plead so earnestly as an increased love for souls.

"I rejoice in your increasing confidence and hope in God. The Lord hath done it, and I bless him. May he give you, dearest, to know the sweetness of *entire* submission to his will, and consecration to his service. May he enable you to die to the world, *even though that death be by crucifixion;* that you may every hour live by faith upon the Son of God, and with single reference to his approval and favor.

"I have had within a few days some new thoughts in connection with teaching, at least somewhat new to *me.* I was thinking a few days since, how anxious I was to have every thing just right in my class when I anticipated your visit to school. The thought flashed upon my mind, have you not a dear friend who visits your school daily, hears every recitation, notices every inadvertence, and is a far keener observer than Sarah could be? And should you not feel a stronger desire that he should find all right, than that she should approve? Do you wonder at my calling these *new* thoughts? I do not mean that the great principle involved in them had not often weighed with me, but the reality in this light never struck me so before. I feel now that I have always *company* in school. One is at my side whose smile on each moment's instruction is infinitely desirable, and gives a sacredness, a sweetness to common duties which would otherwise often weary.

"You spoke of the missionary meetings,—the very word excites my whole soul. Why have I never felt, why never acted before? Why never realized the claims of a perishing world on my sympathies, interests, prayers, and means? I feel as if just awakened from a long, a guilty sleep, and a thousand objects of thrilling interest crowd upon me, at times, with almost bewildering power. Each day I feel more deep and bitter regrets for the past; and while I wonder at the long-suffering and the compassion of God, I desire more and more to be up and doing, during the brief remnant of life.

"We are about forming two missionary societies; one in the Sabbath school, the other among the young members of the church and congregation. They are greatly needed and the prospect of success seems encouraging.

"God is pleased still to give me sweet peace in believing. He has graciously filled my heart with his love, and makes me to rejoice without ceasing in the riches of his grace. Pray much for

"Your fond

"Emmy."

CHAPTER VIII.

Her attention is directed to the subject of becoming a Missionary teacher—Document signed by herself and two others—Communication to Dr. Bolles—Anxiety to be guided aright—Letter to Miss S. P. C.—Answer to various objections.

MISS WALDO had long felt a general interest in the cause of Missions, and this interest was much increased by her forming, soon after she went to Boston, an acquaintance with the family of our former beloved Secretary, Rev. Dr. Bolles. In the early part of 1842, while visiting at his house, her attention was directed to a letter from Mrs. Buel, urgently soliciting an assistant to Mrs. Dickson, in her School at Corfu. With her characteristic warmth, Miss W. expressed an earnest wish that she was qualified to go. She was, however, greatly surprised, when Dr. B., a short time after, seriously proposed the subject of her going. This was in the month of February, when her mind, as we have already seen, was in a dark and tried state. Referring to it some time after, she writes, "I can truly say that the bare mention of it filled me with distress, for it was at a time when I had almost abandoned the idea that I was a Christian. In the strongest terms I utterly refused to bestow the least thought on a subject of such a nature, and though for a day or two distressed by the idea that any one could imagine me fit to become a Missionary, I soon forgot that it had been mentioned; being wholly engrossed in my personal feelings, and intently occupied with the pungent convictions which were driving me almost to despair. O the darkness, the wretchedness of that season, never can it be forgotten. On the very day when peace broke in upon my prostrate soul, ere I had hardly sealed a complete surrender of my being to God, having entirely forgotten that any thing had been said of the Greek mission, Mr. P., the foreign Secretary, called to urge upon me the consideration of the subject. I told him of my recent and present feelings, of my past life, and that indeed I could not, ought not to think of it. I had much, very much to do at home to undo the past, and years must pass ere I could engage in such a work without dishonor to it,—though resolved to be wholly the Lord's, it was too late to serve him as a Missionary. His reasonings did not change my purpose, though I consented to delay a formal negative."

The following document which was signed by herself and two others, illustrates the character of her Missionary zeal.

" *March* 12, 1842.

" Believing that he who loveth not his brother whom he hath seen, cannot love God whom he hath not seen, and knowing that millions of our brethren are continually sinking into perdition for want of the word of eternal life, acknowledging also, that we are not our own but His, ' *Who though he was rich, for our sake became poor, that we through his poverty might be made rich,*' we do hereby feel it our duty, in the fear of God, and in view of the judgment day, to make every effort, and every saving which we can, that we may do something more than we ever yet have done for those who are perishing. The question with us shall not be, What can we spare from our usual expenses for the spread of the gospel? but, consecrating all to God, will simply inquire, What ought we to take from the Lord's treasury for the actual supply of our own needs?

"And as the Karens seem to be peculiarly committed to the Baptist denomination, and call loudly for an increase of laborers to gather in those fields white for the harvest, we would like this year to raise for the Tavoy Mission the sum of one hundred dollars, in addition to our usual Missionary contribution.

"That we may not deceive ourselves in this matter, we do purpose to look to the Lord in the spending of every cent, and to bestow nothing on personal decoration, upon which our Lord and Master would frown. To this we are stimulated by the teachings of holy writ, that only he who calleth on the name of Lord shall be saved. '*How then shall they call on Him of whom they have not heard? And how shall they hear without a preacher? And how shall they preach except they be sent?*' And how can they be sent without means?"

A few weeks after her interview with Mr. Peck, having carefully weighed the subject, she addressed the following communication

TO REV. DR. BOLLES.

"*Charlestown, March* 29, 1842.

"VERY DEAR SIR:—I feel too deep an interest in the welfare of the Greek Mission, to delay unnecessarily some answer to your present expectations. I have fully and finally decided,—in the presence of the heart-searching God, and with a single eye to his glory, I have decided in the negative. I must not go to Greece! I write, dear Sir, because I dare not trust myself to an interview, lest my inclinations should beguile my judgment into further indecisions, and, relying too much on the indulgent esteem of dear Christian friends, I should look duty less boldly in the face.

" Do not imagine, dear sir, that I congratulate myself on having escaped from a heavy cross, by coming to this conclusion,—that I rejoice in the conviction that it is not my duty to go. O no! Deeply conscious of my utter unworthiness from the first, I dared to think of it only with the despairing hope with which a fond mother views the life of the little one on whom death has already laid his seal; and I relinquish it as painfully. It was a bright vision, all too glorious to be realized, which it seems presumption even to have looked upon, and which leaves one, as it disappears, in sadness. Yet I need not assure you, that never was mother dearer, sisters more loved, or home sweeter than mine. Cradled in the arms of doting affection from my earliest infancy, every want anticipated, every pain soothed, every comfort proffered, I should have every thing to learn. Relying much on the sympathy of others, a most dependant creature, my nature would shrink from such a trial. The grace of God, and love of souls alone could enable me, who like the weak vine, have ever been seeking something around which to twine, to tear myself from all such dear supports, and go alone to a land of unsympathizing strangers. To relinquish all the social, intellectual, and religious privileges I enjoy,—to bid a last farewell to all I hold most dear,—

to cut my very heart-strings, must be no common sacrifice.

"Yet if I were supported by the conviction that God, and duty, and dying souls called me,—that my Master would be honored thereby, I think I should not shrink. Though the heart might throb, the cheek blanch, and gushing tears flow, I would say, 'Here am I, Lord, send me'. But the deep, the settled, the prayerful conviction, that I should only wound the cause I would henceforward serve, should bring reproach on the Master whom, alas, I have too often crucified afresh,—should injure the holy cause of Missions, and cast a stumbling-block in the way of many dear unconverted friends,—should leave undone duties which ought indeed to have been long ago performed, but which none but myself can now perform,—all these and many similar motives oblige me thus to decide. I trust indeed that God's grace will enable me to live in the future wholly consecrated to that dear Redeemer, whose blood alone hath purchased my salvation. But I have much to undo, and much to perform at home, before I can honor God by leaving it. I cannot tell you all the reasons which force me, as I love my God, thus to decide. A discussion of the subject would only be painful, and ought not to change my decision.

"God bless the loved mission, and raise up one to fill this station, with the gentleness of a John, and the zeal of Peter, filled with the spirit of her blessed Master, and wise to win souls to Christ. Do not delay to seek immediately one thus qualified, that the dear girls of Corfu may not want her instructions, efforts and prayers. I shall ever feel the deepest interest in this mission, and will pledge myself to raise one hundred dollars, for the passage of a teacher to Corfu,—the sum I believe which you mentioned.

"For your kind but undeserved esteem, I shall be ever grateful, and trust a place in your remembrance and prayers, will ever be granted to your truly grateful, but most unworthy, young friend,

"S. E. W."

As her heart was so evidently in the work, and her unfitness the sole reason for her declining it, she was still requested to postpone her decision, if possibly the hand of Providence might yet point her steps thitherward. She had decided one way, God had designed another, and gradually her mind was brought to harmonize with the divine plans.

In a note to Rev. Mr. Peck, dated May 7, she says:

"Your brief suggestions on Saturday last, awakened new feelings, and led to some different views of the subject, which, however, are now too vague and unsettled to allow me to express them fully. Pray for me, dear sir, that I may not mistake the suggestions of my own heart, or the opinions of my brethren, for the guidings of the Spirit; or so misinterpret the leadings of Providence, as to bring only a reproach on the blessed cause, I would fain henceforth honor."

There seemed, at this time, to be but one question with Miss Waldo, viz., "Does the Lord call me to this work?" No question of self-interest was allowed a moment's consideration; she had given herself to Jesus, and was willing to work where he called her. Writing to a friend about this time, she says:

"You ask me, dearest, if I feel that I have consecrated my all to Christ? How could I do less, and hope at all in his mercy! Yet do not mistake me, love, I probably do not mean all that you do by the expression. I would by no means have you infer that I suppose myself perfect in the fulfillment of every duty; but I think I have so surrendered my all to God, that in each act I would have single reference to him. Would I read, I would select a book on which I can ask his blessing,—would I visit, I wish in that visit by words, looks and manners, to secure his approval. Would I hear a recitation, I would be so patient, so faithful, so gentle, so firm, that God shall be glorified.

"Yet I do not mean that I perfectly fulfill all these intentions, but that it is, as never before, my desire and aim so to do. This may seem to you self-complacent, but I think I never felt less so. I only wonder at the grace of God. One sentence expresses all I can say,—I am the vilest of sinners, saved by the richest grace.

"O the precious comfort of those texts, 'The blood of Jesus Christ his Son, cleanseth from all sin.' 'Though your sins be as scarlet, they shall be white as snow.' 'He is able to save unto the uttermost all that come unto God by him.' 'Jesus Christ came into the world to save sinners, of whom I am chief.' I believe these precious declarations,—I cast my soul upon them,—Jesus is my surety, my all-sufficient righteousness. As far as respects myself alone, I have nothing to mar my peace, but the sad, the embittering recollection, that I have worse than wasted the life, the talents, the influence, a gracious God has given me. Yet when I sin, I have 'an Advocate with the Father, Jesus Christ the righteous.'"

Knowing that Miss Waldo was accomplishing a great amount of good in the position where Providence had already placed her, the friends to whom she looked for advice were anxious that she should carefully weigh the subject before she exchanged her present sphere of usefulness for one of doubtful issue. The following extracts are from a reply to a letter of this description, dated June 22, 1842.

* * * * *

"That my happiness would seriously affect my usefulness, I admit as fully as yourself; and a life spent in unavailing regrets for disappointed expectations, would neither promote the glory of God, the salvation of souls, nor my own spiritual welfare. But would the life of a Missionary teacher in Greece be so unhappy? You say I must inquire what I may reasonably expect from past experience. That I have been a dependent being, ever ready to learn, you know as well as myself. The changes, the duties, the responsibilities of the last four years have indeed changed me somewhat, and compelled me to learn to stand alone, that is in reference to human support. My happiness I think does not depend on the many. I am perhaps, too indifferent to society. I never care to meet many except in religious meetings, social and public. To be deprived of these privileges would be certainly one of the greatest sacrifices I could make. In thinking of leaving my native land, the idea that I shall no more assemble with a glad multitude as they go to the house of God,—no more unite with joyful hundreds around the table of my Lord,—no more be surrounded by thousands, one in interest, hopes, views and aims,—that I shall meet so few who share my hopes and fears,—this is second only to the thought of leaving my mother's fond, sweet embrace.

"But I never should be quite alone, some few would sing from renewed hearts the high praises of God. A few would gather together around the mercy-seat. The gospel in its purity would be preached to a few hungry and thirsty souls. I should not like Mrs. Judson be destitute of Christian sympathy, nor so far away from home that almost a year would pass before the reception of intelligence therefrom. But I should leave a darling mother who has long watched over me with zealous care, afraid lest the winds of heaven should blow too roughly on me,—who anticipates every wish, and seeks to guard every avenue to pain and sorrow. Dear mother! she heard with heavy heart my mention of the subject, and a night of tears could hardly enable her to control her feelings. She does not say, 'You must not go;' but she cannot endure the thought. She does not speak of it now, but says very frequently, 'How thin you are Emmy. Don't you feel sick? Poor child, you cannot bear any thing. You are very delicate,' &c., &c. Can I leave her and be happy? But suppose God should take her this year from me, shall I say there is no more happiness for me, I am too wretched to do any thing in the world? Most certainly not. Might I not then hope to be happy, to be useful even in Greece?

"As to changes of feeling, I do not doubt that Christians are often moved by strong excitement, which, when passed, leaves no holy or marked impress on the character. But on the other hand, that Christians are the subjects of deep and vital changes, which powerfully, and lastingly affect the religious character, is to me equally unquestionable. I feel no security that the recent change in my feelings will continue, except in the promised grace of God; but I have more reason to believe in its permanency than in that of any previous change; and I hope it will continue forever.

"With regard to the other subject, that we are ever prone to believe a change of circumstances must produce a change of character, and that to be a missionary must of necessity make a man a saint, it is I know too true. But I do believe there is much in the nature of a missionary life to conduce to deep piety. Is not the influence of old, long cherished associations much weakened? And is not the tendency of the new relations and associations of a sacred character? With a fixed determination to live for God, may I not expect to find in Greece fewer temptations to wander from him, than I should at home? You compare my present field of labor with that offered me in Greece. I have read Mrs. Dickson's private letter, have seen Mrs. Buel's account of the School, and think it offers almost as many points of encouragement, certainly more of interest than my own.

"Your remark that God expects me to labor as earnestly and directly for the salvation of those now under my care, as if appointed by the Board as a missionary teacher, has awakened more misgivings than all you have said beside. Conscious of past unfaithfulness in this respect, and of the trial it still is, I have trembled lest in this most important particular I did not know myself. The subject is to me one of awful solemnity. I can hardly think of it without trembling. There are other phases of the subject equally momentous which I cannot now mention.

"The state of the case seems to me simply this: Providence has placed in my way an opportunity to labor for the cause of Christ in Greece; am I to infer that it is my duty to improve or decline it? This I must decide, under the Spirit's guidance, by my fitness, inclination, and prospect for usefulness. My fitness must be two-fold, of heart and mind. The latter I leave to my friends; if they are satisfied, I am decided. The former is the real ground of all demur on my part. My inclination, my hope of usefulness would encourage me to go, though not I hope self-complacent; but a daily increasing sense of the unholiness of my past life fills me with doubts and misgivings. 'Mature piety,' says the Board, 'is the primary qualification.' To be sure I have been a professor of religion six years, yet I look back upon those years with more keen regret, with more heart anguish than on my whole previous life of sin. Dear Mrs. M., you do not know how very far I have wandered; God has indeed, I trust, led me to deep, sincere repentance, has washed away my sins of crimson dye in the fountain opened in Judah,—has accepted the righteousness of Christ, in lieu of the obedience I should have rendered, and implanted in me a gracious, and intense desire to be wholly his. But this cannot undo the past in its influence on others, though I sometimes dare to hope that God will overrule all that is past, so as to permit me to glorify him in going.

"Do write me very soon, and tell me very frankly all your views and feelings on this momentous subject, every word will be highly prized. And do remember, at the throne of grace Your own

"EMMY."

CHAPTER IX.

Baptism of a particular friend—Letter to her Sabbath school class—Her feelings in reference to the Mission —Sympathy with a friend in affliction—Her decision to join the Greek Mission.

THE last Sabbath in June was one of special interest to Miss W., on account of the baptism of her particular friend Miss C. H., for whose salvation she had long labored, and who was ever after her intimate friend and correspondent. Of this baptismal season she thus writes to Miss S. P. C., under date of June 29th.

"It was seven o'clock; the sun which had poured his scorching rays upon us through the day, was vailed in sunset clouds, and refreshing coolness revived each languid frame. Not a ripple ruffled the glassy surface of the beautiful Mystic, on whose green, rising banks stood a numerous throng, hushed in unusual stillness. The boisterous laugh, and coarse joke were for once unheard, and no sound disturbed the soft air but the melody of Zion. The song was hushed; solemn words of warning and persuasion were addressed by the man of God to the gazing multitude; and then the blessing of the hovering Spirit was implored. Again all was still, and the quiet waters yielded to the minister of Jesus, as he led in his footsteps young F., and there, beneath the blue sky, buried him gently beneath the wave in the name of the blessed Trinity. Mr. S. was the same calm soul he ever is, and his dear wife never seemed so lovely as when she rose from the parted wave. But dear Caty! next to my own dear kindred nothing could have moved me more. I had looked, and looked so long for her coming, till I almost despaired. Yet there she was, meekly, happily following Jesus. O Sarah, what a Saviour is ours! Can we ever doubt him?

"Our covenant meeting on Saturday evening was very delightful. The room was crowded. There was good old Mrs. W., who gave us the experience of thirty years, and the kind advice of a warm heart; and dear tender-hearted nurse T., with all the simplicity of a child; and sister E., always so ready to sympathize with the young; and there too were a right good number of young converts, all of whom spoke in the most interesting manner."

"*July* 27.

"Wednesday eve has returned, and finds me with my loved sister, in Salem, enjoying my first week of vacation. I very much enjoy being with her. Her warm heart, her gentle spirit, her sweet disposition, chastened in its vivacity by the seriousness of new responsibilities, all unite to rivet closely the sweet link of sisterhood, which binds us. And added to all, a deepening interest in the welfare of her immortal spirit, gives a sacredness to precious affection.

"I have kept a record of all my Sabbath school scholars, and a brief outline of the character of each. It is an interesting document for reference. I have had in six and a half years, thirty scholars, thirteen of whom I trust from the evidence they have given me, are the disciples of Christ. I do not know the condition of all the rest, but hope all will be brought in."

From Salem she wrote the following letter:—

TO HER SABBATH SCHOOL CLASS.

" *Salem, July* 29, 1842.

" My much loved class:—When absent from you in former days, I have always loved to write to you, if it were only to repeat my anxious desire for your souls' welfare. But I write you now with very peculiar pleasure. I have known what it is to weep over an impenitent class. Often sick at heart, I have returned home ready to conclude that I should never be permitted to witness your conversion. But now, what hath the Lord wrought? What wonders of mercy hath he shown to our dear class! Whom hath he so richly blest? Yet who so sinful, so unworthy? It becomes us, teacher and class, to exclaim, 'Where sin *had* abounded, grace did much more abound.' Most of you I humbly hope are new creatures in Christ Jesus, and heirs of eternal life. Yet I have still many anxious moments on your account.

" You have each peculiarities of temper and disposition which make you liable to wander from God, and bring reproach on the cause of the dear Redeemer. From the first hour of your spiritual birth, until the present moment, my most earnest desire has been that you might live wholly to the glory of God, and never dishonor the Saviour who purchased you with his own precious blood. It seems to me it would almost break my heart should I see any of you turn back again to the world. No doubt you would start back from such a thought yourselves, and yet, if you are not increasingly watchful and prayerful you will soon do so. Then pray constantly, not only when on your knees in solitude, but pray at all times in your heart, whatever you may be doing. You cannot fall into sin at any time, if at that very moment your heart is rising in prayer to God.

"Sometimes I fear there are moments when you forget that Jesus is by your side, and will be grieved by one word, one look of sin. I fear you sometimes speak without remembering that that word, though whispered, was heard by God, who will remember it. Read more of the word of God; I want to see this still more precious, better understood, and more familiar to you. Accustom yourselves to talk when together, on your religious feelings, and not on trifling and worldly objects. Your conversation will do more to show what sort of Christians you are than any thing else. Be faithful to your impenitent friends. Do you not sometimes spend hours with them without saying a word about their souls? Always improve every opportunity to entreat them to be reconciled to God; and pray for the blessing of God upon your efforts. Especially pray much for the dear ones left in the class unconverted; never rest until they are saved."

Writing to a Christian friend about this time, she says:

"My narrow heart, so long contracted to the little circle of self, is slow to acquire that spiritual elasticity which will allow it to expand and fill with strong desires for dying souls. Eternity is at times delightfully near, and life a vapor soon to pass away, desirable only as it can be spent in rescuing others from perdition, and in being fitted myself for everlasting glory. What matter where I labor for God, if

'When life's toil is done,
  And spent I sink to die,
He'll take me to his throne
  On his dear breast to lie,
Upon his beaming face to gaze,
Among his sons to shout his praise.'"

TO MRS. R. B. MEDBERY.

"*Charlestown, Sept.* 28, 1842.

"MY DEAR MRS. M.:—What a long, long time has passed since I saw you; a year of events and feelings, though a few weeks in reality. I have lived longer than in months before. Intense excitement, agonizing feeling, self-distrust, and sinking of soul, have been no strangers to my bosom. The little world within has been stirred to its deepest depths, and nothing but the dear voice which midst the tempest said, 'It is I, be not afraid,' could calm the perturbed spirit. Do you smile, dear Mrs. M. at my missionary spirit? Yet I do want to go withal, yes, sometimes pant to be gone. Ah! were I but alone, unbound by sweet relations, did I alone suffer, could I act independently of my influence on others, then welcome the bark which would bear me away. But it is not so.

"Do you ask then, sister, if I am decided to go? I dare not refuse so to do. I am perfectly passive in the hands of God, if he lay any obstacle in the way, I have no wish to go,—and most earnestly do I pray that He, in whose hands are all events, will never let me go unless it will conduce in the highest degree to his glory. I would rather die at once, or languish out my life in wasting disease, rather suffer, do, or be any thing, than go uncalled. If I ever earnestly, sincerely prayed for any thing it is this. Can I be left to self-deception? Will God allow me to enter his service without his blessing? My deep sense of unfitness and unworthiness is often overwhelming. I never so fully realized the heinous nature of sin. The sins of my childhood, my girlhood, my Christian profession, gather like mountains, and seem to smile contemptuously on the desire to go abroad to labor for Christ. The fear of self-deception, by which I have often been so grossly duped, sometimes takes away all self-confidence, and I know not what to conclude. And then the soothing voice of my own Redeemer will say to me as to one of old, '*Thy iniquity is taken away, thy sin is purged.*' '*My grace is sufficient for thee.*' The consciousness of a changed heart, of new desires and motives, of an intense longing after holiness,—after perfect conformity to God,—a new and ever increasing love to souls, and deep, pungent, hearty sorrow for sin, together with the perfect righteousness of a justifying Saviour, revive my drooping spirit and I rejoice.

"But my sweet home, my sad mother, my weeping sisters, my distressed brother, how can I leave them? How distress them so keenly? On the other hand there is dear Mrs. Dickson sinking for want of help,—the school in the most interesting state possible,—the call for immediate help loudly sounding in my ears, and why should I not go,—I who profess to love the cause of Christ above all other things, and to have given all I have and am to God? Shall I not wonder at the grace that stoops so low, and takes from the dust a worm to exalt to such a glorious service? Am I not an expectant of eternal glory, professedly a pilgrim here, a warrior girded for constant battle? Shall I seek ease and comfort, while I leave to perish, souls for which Christ died? Shall I unbind the sacrifice laid upon the altar, because the touch of the knife is painful? Shall that admitted in theory, be too much for practice, and religion have nothing real in it? But you need none of these interrogatories, they are suggestions of my own weakness.

"You are probably aware that the whole matter is now generally known. This has been a bitter drop in my cup, as you may suppose, and places me before the public in a delicate situation. Do pray for me, dear Mrs. M., that *God's* blessed will, not *man's*, nor *mine* may be done. I would not wish that God should allow me to go, as he allowed the Jews to have a king. Pray too for our dear family, for precious mother, that God will comfort and support her, and bless all to the good of her precious soul;—and dear Charles, he is sadly unreconciled, and has implored me to give it up. I never knew him to manifest so much feeling on any subject. O pray for all."

The following letters show that the current of her piety was still steadily onward.

TO MISS S. P. CARTER.

"MY DEAR SARAH:—Most fully do I accord with your remarks on the love we should bear to Christ. Even love seems all too cold a term to express the deep, burning, all-ruling attachment, the ransomed soul should feel for its Redeemer. Feeling deeply the force of the sentiment, 'To whom much is forgiven, the same loveth much,' I have dared to hope that I felt something of this unutterable love. But when dear Christians, whose lives condemn mine, speak as you did in your last, I fear to confide in my supposed feelings. Yet 'one thing I know, that whereas I was blind now I see,'—see all things in a light wholly different from that in which I have before regarded them; and lament in agony of soul my past views and acts, which though forgiven, can never in their influence on others be obliterated. O how inexpressively sweet then to feel Christ to be 'the end of the law for righteousness.'

"But you can hardly conceive how mystical, or rather devoid of meaning, the subject of Christ's imputed righteousness was formerly to me. And O there is a freshness, a glory in it now which those who have always believed in it, can never fully comprehend. I love to dwell upon it, to repeat it over and over to myself in my solitary hours or walks, to try to sound the depths of those precious words, '*For he hath made him to be sin for us, who knew no sin; that we might be made the righteousness of God in him.*' What a depth of meaning in each dear word to the sin-burdened soul. Beneath the overwhelming load which would rest upon my soul, this blessed declaration is a refuge into which my desponding spirit gladly flies. Justification! 'tis the sweetest word that ever fell upon my ear; for who would believe that sinful man could be just with God. Sin never seemed so dark, so heinous, as now. Yet if God had not forgiven, if he did not accept me, should I be conscious, as I hope I am, of a desire to be wholly devoted to his service!

"How unworthy, how unfit am I to labor any where for the blessed Jesus! How blessed to suffer for him! I have thought much of that expression, '*Unto you it is given, in the behalf of Christ, not only to believe on him, but also to suffer for his sake.*' Is it not a privilege? O to love him more, to be filled with Christ, to be dead to all else, to live by faith on the dear Son of God. Pray for me.

"What a precious truth in this text, '*There is forgiveness with thee that thou mayest be feared.*' How I love to repeat it again and again, and to assure myself that it is even so. God can pardon and yet be glorified; for by the church shall yet be shown 'unto the principalities and powers in heavenly places, the manifold wisdom of God.' What unsearchable wisdom, what inexplicable love! How often does the thought present itself, How can God love us, so ignorant, feeble, polluted? What bond of sympathy, what cause of compassion could move him to our salvation? O the blood of atonement! This is our only hope. It seems to me that no other person can know as I the preciousness of that sweet promise, '*I will heal their backslidings, I will love them freely.*' Forgiven so much, I joyfully offer myself to the work of missions, not as *peculiarly pious*, but as peculiarly called upon to suffer and to toil. Welcome the hottest of the fight. Dear Sarah, pray for me, that I may be wholly, wholly Christ's without reserve, a living sacrifice."

TO MISS S. T. BOSWORTH.

"*Charlestown, Dec.* 20, 1842.

"MY BELOVED SARAH:—Your letter awakened all my sympathies, and I longed to reply immediately in words of consolation and of truth to its sad spirit. You have indeed, love, drank a bitter cup, the more so because before untasted; yet mingled by the same hand of love that had ever given you sweet waters of which to drink.

Your gentle Fanny is no more,—the comforts, the luxuries to which your father's fortune had accustomed you have been restricted,—life in its sterner, harsher realities has opened on your youthful soul, and the bright visions of hope, have vanished but too soon. You are sad, love, your heart aches almost to bitterness; but, sister dear, do you sorrow as those without hope? Has your Father forgotten his child,—left her to the tender mercies of relentless chance,—proved to her a barren wilderness, a faithless friend? 'Is there no balm in Gilead,' no ray of hope, no sign of love in all this cloudy day? Remember, dearest, that if 'we be without chastisement, whereof all are partakers, then are we bastards and not sons.' Will you give up the name of child? Will you barter eternal hopes for present comfort; a heaven of blessedness for a home of sunshine? No, you shudder at the thought, and are ready to exclaim with Cowper—

'Give what thou canst, without thee we are poor,
And with the rich, take what thou wilt away.'

"Think, sister, a heart of love warmer than ever glowed in yours, has ordered every step in your pathway, planted in it every thorn, strewed in it every rose, and all that it may end in glory. He who endured for you every conceivable agony, has determined to spare you all of pain and anguish that he can, compatible with your eternal blessedness, and no more. He knows that when his heaviest billows roll over you, all is but a ripple to the ocean of wrath that overwhelmed his soul when he took your place as a condemned sinner in Gethsemane, and on Calvary.

"Of you he has said, '*I will that they whom thou hast given me, be with me where I am.*' To fulfill that will, love, you must suffer much, often, or never be among the number of those 'who have come up out of great tribulation, and have washed their robes and made them white in the blood of the Lamb.' In tones of unaltered love he says to you, 'In a little wrath I hid my face from thee for a moment, but with everlasting kindness have I gathered thee.' Trust, dearest, implicitly in the burning, quenchless love of an unchanging Saviour. Lean your aching head on his bosom, repose your sad spirit in his arms, and, '*As one whom his mother comforteth, so will he comfort thee.*'

"'The Lord God omnipotent reigneth.' 'Tis the joy of heaven, the comfort of the church, our only hope. Soon this brief existence will close, and then of what moment the things that now so much concern us? As we unravel in eternity the seemingly tangled thread of Providence, the perfect order and beauty of the work of God will astonish our souls.

"You speak, love, of *spiritual* darkness; and here I touch the tenderest point, one, on which my views have much changed. Yet the remembrance of my past inconsistencies, my foul backslidings, make me ever shrink from urging on my beloved friends those attainments in holiness, that abiding in Christ, which shall secure to us continued peace and joy. Those same bitter recollections have sometimes clouded my own horizon, but they have not returned me to that love and fear of the world by which I know I was long governed. The world is crucified to me, and I to it, as never before. And though I would weep as one mourneth for her first born, over sins the evil consequences of which can never be recalled; I can but exclaim as I look to Calvary, '*I will greatly rejoice in the Lord, and my spirit shall be joyful in my*

God, for he hath clothed me with the garments of salvation, and covered me with the robes of righteousness.'

"I have at length decided to tear myself from an adored mother's fond embrace, sweet sisters' gentle cares, kind relatives and friends, the church of my love, the scenes of my girlhood, each loved, familiar spot, each sweet, hallowed association, and dear pursuit; to go far hence a stranger in a strange land, to labor, suffer, and die in the attempt to bring home to God some of the benighted daughters of Greece. And blessed be God for the honor, the privilege so undeserved. Yet the trial has been agonizing. The knife has touched the very heart strings, and my spirit has almost sunk beneath it. Yes, dearest, I have resolved to engage in this work, not because so very pious or so very fit for it, but because very peculiarly bound to suffer and sacrifice for a Saviour whom I have very greatly dishonored in the past. If I can thus more fully express my deep repentance, and my ardent love, my personal object is gained. But I think I do feel for those precious souls, and long to be laboring to bring them to Christ. The seat of the mission is in Corfu, the capital of the Ionian Islands, established just six years ago. I go to teach in a flourishing school intimately connected with the mission, containing English, Greeks, and Jewesses, under the care of Mrs. George Dickson, a Scotch widow lady of eminent piety and rare accomplishments. Pray for me.

"Fondly yours,

"EMMY."

The following note to her sister J., was written about this time:

"Whatever interpretation you may put on my decision, you will, I trust, never doubt the quenchless, the intense affection of my heart for my own dear family. For them I would endure any sufferings; death itself would be welcome, if it could bless them. But I am not, dearest J., either my own or theirs, but His who hath purchased me with his own precious blood; who hath rescued me from everlasting destruction, and laid me under infinite obligations to himself, and his dear cause. Let us look, love, beyond this vale of tears, which is not our home. May we but reasonably anticipate a meeting there, and it matters but little where, or how long we live below. Ah, sister, that is the sting of parting, that so many I love are unprepared for a home in heaven. God give you, dearest, an interest in the blood of Christ, which alone can cleanse from sin; and regenerate your heart by that blessed Spirit, unless born of whom we cannot see the kingdom of God. Seek more earnestly an inheritance among them that are sanctified. Strive to enter in at the strait gate, for it is a mighty struggle when the power of sin is broken within us."

CHAPTER X.

Letter to the church—They request the privilege of supporting her as a missionary—Her views of the Christian's privilege—Communication to the Board—Gives up her school to Miss S. P. C.—Testimony to her character as teacher—Letter to her Sabbath school class—Arrival of Rev. Mr. Love and family.

HAVING been led, as she thought, by the spirit and providence of God to decide upon accepting the appointment of the Board, Miss Waldo addressed a communication to the church of which she was a member, to see if they would grant their approval. In this letter she reviews the history of her past religious experience, and the rich privileges she had enjoyed for growth in knowledge and grace since she had been with them. "The truth," says she, "in all its beauty, harmony, and perfection, has been gradually unfolded to my view, till the gospel seems one glorious whole, reflecting in ten thousand varied lights, the dazzling brightness of Jehovah's character. The path of duty and holiness has been made more and more plain, and I feel myself bound by peculiar obligations to give myself wholly to Christ." She then recounts the providences by which she had been led to devote herself to the work of a missionary, and adds, "I rejoice in suffering and sacrifice for the dear Master I have too often dishonored ; and if he will but use me in promoting his glory, I can only wonder at his condescension. Such as I am, I am resolved to live henceforth for God, and glory to serve him any where and in any manner."

The church promptly responded to her communication, pledging themselves to follow her with their prayers, and accompanying their communication with the following resolution. "Resolved that a committee of three be appointed to communicate with the Board of Foreign Missions, and to request in our name the privilege of assuming the entire support of our sister, Sarah Emily Waldo, their missionary to Greece; we pledging ourselves to raise and to transmit to her the requisite funds."

This kind communication from the church formed the last link in the chain of providences by which she was to decide upon the path of duty. She immediately addressed a private note to Mr. Peck, signifying her readiness to communicate with the Board, providing it was still his impression that she ought to go. While waiting a reply from him she wrote as follows:

TO MISS S. P. CARTER.

"My dear Sarah:—I feel a remarkable tranquillity of soul in the contemplation of this great work. The kind sympathy and co-operation of the church in my behalf has endeared them still more to me, unworthy as I am of their regards. May they be led to feel for the darkened nations of Europe, and, when this wasted form shall have returned to the dust, may many a ransomed soul in Greece rise up to call them blessed.

"How is it, dearest, with you? Have you made a complete surrender of all to Christ, to be wholly, and forever his? Does God now dwell in you and walk in you, being a Father to you and making you feel that you are indeed a daughter? Is all laid at the foot of the cross, and are you, love, sitting at the feet of Jesus? Then blessed be rich grace, if not, the Lord make you speedily to know his great salvation?

"I believe it is the Christian's privilege to be raised above the world and filled with the love of God, to be *completely* consecrated to Christ, and thus enjoy already the bliss of heaven in his soul. With but one object, the glory of God, ever before him, unmoved alike by the smiles or frowns of others, he should devote every energy to the salvation, the sanctification of all whom he can influence. This, dear Sarah, is living. Something of its blessedness I have tasted, though not in its fullness. But I have allowed unbelief to lead me again into comparative darkness. Yet here I cannot stay; nor am I willing that you, the object of my strong affection, should remain here.

"Will the Saviour do no more for his people than allow them glimpses of joy, doubting hopes, and a few conquests over indwelling sin? Has he wrought out for us a no more perfect salvation than this? Is this all the believer can expect? How little do we glorify Christ, when we can only stammer out with hesitating tongue our slender hope of acceptance through his blood. Of what avail are all abstract demonstrations of the excellency there is in Christ, so long as we go mourning all our days in his service? Is this the victory that overcomes the world? Does not the language of our complaints and fears rather resemble the tones of the captive than the shouts of the victor? Is this being more than conquerors through Him that hath loved us? Is this rejoicing with joy unspeakable and full of glory? Is this the earnest of the Spirit, the antepast of heaven?

"No, Sarah, our hearts assure us that Jesus will be to us sanctification as well as redemption; 'that as sin hath reigned unto death, even so *shall* grace reign through righteousness unto eternal life.' Will you not then, sister, seek with me that living by faith upon the Son of God, which shall keep us from the dominion of sin, and fill us with the joyful assurance of salvation? Have we not been too well satisfied with the confession of our short-comings, and theoretical views of the grace of God, esteeming ourselves in a most gracious state when we felt ourselves most sinful, without that living, practical holiness of heart, which is as assuredly promised by the Spirit, as the conversion of the soul? We have talked a great deal about religion, but how much have we felt. Rather than fear we should express too much by our words, we ought to feel more than we can express. All our attempts to believe this state of mind impossible are but delusions of Satan, and evidences of the power which sin still has over us. May God speedily grant us both, grace to believe and to obey."

Immediately after hearing from Mr. Peck, she wrote the following communication.

TO THE BAPTIST BOARD OF FOREIGN MISSIONS.

" *Charlestown, Jan.* 28, 1843.

"RESPECTED FATHERS AND BRETHREN:—It is with the deepest emotion that I present myself before you as ready to accept the proposal made me by your secretaries, to engage in the Greek Mission. The consciousness of great unworthiness and unfitness, the remembrance of the many sins and inconsistencies by which I have so often dishonored the dear cause of Jesus, the magnitude of the work before me, and the preciousness of the interests involved in it, all conspire to make me shrink from the assumption of a responsibility which would dignify even an angel. Yet, remembering whose is the work, and hoping that the great weakness and baseness of the instrument will only the more surely turn the eyes of any who may be blessed by it, to the glorious right hand that is pleased to use it, I rejoice to lay this broken sacrifice on the hallowed altar of missions.

"More than seven years have passed since the first ray of heavenly truth pierced the thick darkness in which my mind and conscience were involved. Gay, reckless, and without one thought of danger, I lived for more than fifteen years without God; and when the startling truth that I was indeed a lost sinner first broke on my astonished soul, ignorant of the nature of my own feelings, I was left, without one earthly guide, to grope my way to the cross of Jesus. For a long time, like the blind man, I could only 'see men as trees walking.' But weakness was graciously made strong, and darkness light. After much mental suffering, I came out alone from my family, relations, and early friends, and united in June, 1836, with the First Baptist Church in Charlestown, in which I have ever since found a most pleasant home. Seven years spent in the school of Christ ought indeed to have rendered me fit for his service; but I have too often turned a deaf ear to his blessed instructions, and perversely gone away backward from him; at times even wandered far from his side, and brought reproach on his cause. Yet he has graciously brought back the straying sheep, and led me into green pastures, and beside the still waters. In view of his great forbearance and goodness, I desire to spend the remnant of my brief life for Him, who, having forgiven much, should be most ardently loved.

"The subject of missions presented itself to my mind on my profession of religion in all the freshness of novelty, and fascinated my attention by its absorbing interests. The embarkation of twenty-two missionaries of different denominations shortly after, awakened my youthful enthusiasm, and in the ardor of excited feeling, I was ready to resolve to devote my life to the heathen. These feelings, however, were not the result of a deep sense of the lost condition of the heathen, or of my obligations to them, nor such as I should call true missionary feeling. Yet the cause of missions has always been of thrilling interest to me, and information respecting them eagerly sought after. During much of the time, however, I have not so realized the necessities of the heathen as to pray much and fervently for them, or make sacrifices, and practice self-denial that they might have the gospel; and for three or four years, the idea of personally engaging in this great and glorious work never crossed my mind. My field of labor seemed to be at home, and my plans of usefulness were mostly limited to the circle in which I moved.

"Nor should I ever have proposed myself for this exalted service, uncalled. I should never have dared to imagine that God could stoop to employ me, who am most unworthy to perform the humblest labor in the least important field. The first proposal therefore to engage in missionary service was startling, and could not be indulged; especially as it was made at a time when a review of my past wanderings, had nearly driven me to despair of ever having been a Christian. And when light and joy again shone from Calvary upon my soul, and I had resolved to consecrate myself anew and wholly to God, the renewal of the subject was almost equally painful, and months passed, ere I dared to cherish the hope that it was indeed the will of God that I should go hence. I longed to go, yet feared it was presumption to believe that one who had been so disobedient and worldly could be forgiven, and be permitted to become a missionary. My earnest prayer was that God would guide; that his providence, which rules every event, and his Spirit, which controls every heart, would settle the question and cause me to hear his voice saying, '*This is the way, walk in it.*' I wished to put my hand in his and be led like a little child in the way he would have me go. Formidable obstacles seemed to disappear, expected opposition was restrained, and a burning desire kindled in my heart to spend my little all in this dear service. Sacrifice and suffering, privation and toil could present nothing to daunt me; and if so I could lead one wandering sinner to Jesus, I could bear the toil, endure the pain. My only fear was that I should go unsent by God, and thus injure instead of bless. But if I have erred in concluding, after many varied feelings, that, wonderful as was the condescension of God, he still had a work for me to do in Greece, my prayer is that he will overrule the mistake to his glory and the saving of souls.

"Having attended the embarkation of Messrs. Love and Pasco six years ago, the mission in Greece was always one of great interest. This had been constantly deepening, till the proposal was made to me to unite with the mission, and I need not say that the subject has ever since, engrossed my heart.

"To the salvation then of some of the daughters of dear Greece, I do, most joyfully and heartily, now, and as long as God shall give me strength, devote my whole being, soul and body, heart and mind, all that the wreck of sin has left me to offer.

"I shall rejoice to be under the direction and control of this Board, to whose measures I have ever cordially assented, and in whom I feel unlimited confidence. The church of which I am a member, have most kindly and generously resolved to assume my support, but I trust I shall be none the less a *child of this Board.* May your prayers bring down blessings on the labors of

"Your young and unworthy servant in Christ,

"S. Emily Waldo."

From this time she considered herself as belonging to the Greek mission; and though it was uncertain when she might enter upon her foreign labors, she endeavored, so far as she could, to prepare the way, by severing one after another the various ties which bound her to her loved home. Her first care was to procure a suitable person to whom she could give up her school. This beloved object, which for more than four years had engrossed so large a share of her thoughts, could not be resigned to chance. "I have felt a burden of anxiety," said she, "as to the course I should pursue in reference to my school; yet I have not been distressed about it, but have endeavored to cast this burden also on the Lord, whose guidance I have fervently implored." It was therefore to her an occasion for sincere gratitude when her friend Miss C. consented to assume the charge of it.

Writing to her soon after, she says, "I have had numerous applicants for my school, but that you should have it in your heart to come, was what I wished to consider as an intimation of God's will concerning myself."

That charge, which with so much solicitude she had assumed in December, 1838, was therefore resigned in Feb. 1843; but the influence of that school on many a mind will no doubt be felt forever. From the moment that she assumed the responsibilities of a teacher, she made it the prime object of her study, indeed the main business of her life, to become all that a teacher should be. She commenced the work with enthusiasm, nor did her zeal abate to the last. To one who seemed less happy in her employment as teacher, she wrote: "I think I have two qualifications for a teacher which you do not possess. First, I was a great rogue myself, and therefore am not so much astonished to find rogues in school; and secondly, I was the eldest of a large family who, loving and loved as they were, gave me ample proof that children are not akin to angels, so that I had a good apprenticeship before I set up. Your dear sisters, always so obedient, so gentle, but ill prepared you to govern obstreperous girls of a more sanguine temperament. You expect too much, and suffer more in the disappointment."

To one who was about to open a private school, she remarks: "Scholars must be convinced that you love them and really seek their good,—that you are not vexed, but grieved with their faults. Praise whenever you can. Reprove when you must; but be long-suffering. Cherish an affectionate manner; feel a sympathy in all their concerns. Cull for them every little flower that can be found in the steep, and to them often cheerless, path of science. Say what you will, scholars do, and must build up a school. Though a teacher have the genius of a Newton, or the eloquence of a Cicero, though he enjoy the puffs of all the papers, it is all in vain, if his pupils have not a good word to say for him. If your pupils are interested in you they will keep your school full."

On another occasion she remarks, "I have sometimes thought that teaching presented more temptations to heart-wanderings than a more mechanical employment. There is so much that is ennobling and exalting about it, so much to gratify the finer feelings, to satisfy the nobler aspirings of the soul, that I have thought there might be more danger of our resting satisfied without the presence of God, than in a calling less adapted to fill the capacities of the soul. But one thing I do believe, there cannot be a happier person than a teacher who is fitted for his work, if he has a diligent and affectionate school, and enjoys the light of God's countenance."

From the numerous testimonials which might be given of her success as a teacher, the following has been selected as a sample. It is from the pen of one who had been a member of her school two years.

"The two years which I spent under the instruction of Miss Waldo, were worth more to me than all the rest of my school-days. Not that I was learned so much more of what is usually taught at schools; but I was taught to *think*, to *reason*, and to *inquire*. But while our beloved teacher was peculiarly fitted to guide and direct the minds of her pupils, their hearts were won to love her, seemingly without an effort on her part. I never knew a teacher so greatly, or so generally beloved.

Her government was the perfection of the art. She governed without seeming to do it, almost without our knowing it, surely without our ever thinking it a restraint, or endeavoring to evade her authority. So much was she beloved that her slightest word was law; and she was respected, nay almost reverenced, as much as she was loved. She could mingle with her pupils at play-hours, sympathize with them in their amusements and enjoyments, and join in familiar conversation, without endangering her dignity.

"But her religious influence upon those under her charge was greater than any other. She never lost sight of the one grand object of her life, to serve God. I think her efforts to interest the young in the Saviour were uncommonly successful. The prayer meetings which at one time she held with her pupils were, I know, greatly blessed. She was much in the habit of writing notes to them upon religious topics. One of these, which I still have in my possession, and which I now value exceedingly, was the means of calling my attention to the subject of religion more earnestly than ever before; and, I know, that many others might bear the same testimony. Her prayers at the opening of the school were uncommonly spiritual, earnest, and fervent; so much so as to concentrate the attention of the most worldly of her pupils.

"But words are feeble to convey an idea of one so lovely, so pure, I might almost say so holy. It has always seemed to me that she was the embodiment of pure and undefiled religion, and yet I knew her, ere her character was fully developed, and before she had attained those heights which she afterwards reached. Those who were members of her school just before she left to prepare for a missionary life, and those who knew her in other lands, could doubtless say much more."

"E. A. C."

Her Sabbath school class was not entirely given up till just before she sailed for Greece, but as various duties called her from home, she was frequently obliged to relinquish it to the care of another, and in selecting a substitute, was always mainly anxious to secure the services of the most devotedly pious. The following letter was written while on a visit to her sister.

Salem, March 4, 1843.

"MY BELOVED CLASS :—Another Sabbath must pass away before I shall meet you again, and so I have resolved to write you a few lines, and thus hold some little intercourse with those so dear to me. Such little separations as the present remind me constantly of the great one just before us, which in all human probability will be to us as long as our lives. Such a reflection naturally suggests the inquiry, Shall we *ever* meet again? Shall I ever again hold pleasant converse with my dear girls, with whom I have passed so many happy hours? And as these inquiries lead me to the only source of light, the blessed word of God, my soul is filled with joy in

—— 'The hope, the blessed hope
Which Jesus' grace has given,
The hope when days and years have passed,
We then shall meet in heaven.'

"I wish I could say we *all* shall meet. But some of you, dear girls, are still unreconciled to God; some of you have still refused to accept the great, the offered salvation. Dear Sarah, Emily, and Maria, how my heart yearns over you, and longs to see you penitent and humble at the foot of the cross. Will you not come to Jesus? Will you not renounce the vanities of an ungodly world, and give yourselves to God? Will you remain unreconciled to God, and perish? O, I beseech you, as with my dying lips, turn, turn and live, for why will you die?

"And is it certain that all the rest of us are heirs of heaven? Can we read our 'title clear to mansions in the skies,' or is not our hope falsely founded? Is ours the faith that works by love, purifies the heart, and overcomes the world? Are we growing in grace, dying to earthly things, increasingly diligent in our Master's service? Is Jesus more and more precious, sin more and more odious, and the salvation of souls increasingly valuable in our esteem? Let us examine our hearts and hopes. Let us see if we are indeed the Lord's, and consecrate ourselves anew and wholly to him. For some of you I feel peculiarly anxious, because your volatile dispositions make you more prone to that lightness and trifling, so dishonoring to God, so ruinous to the soul. The Lord keep you from laying up for yourselves the bitter repentance which my wanderings from God have caused me. If the love and joy which a year ago glowed in your bosoms have abated, remember, dear girls, Jesus has not forsaken you, but you have wandered from him. May he keep you all by his sovereign grace."

On the arrival of Mr. Love and family from Greece, she sought an early acquaintance with them, and for awhile confidently expected to be associated with them in missionary labors. It was also determined that she should spend the summer with them at Saratoga, in the prosecution of the Greek language.

Writing to Mrs. Love under date of May 20, she says: "The brief days I was permitted to spend with you were most happy, and have been often lived over both in my waking and my sleeping hours. Soon I trust to renew the pleasure, and anticipate much happiness in passing the summer with you, though I regret to leave my dear mother. May the Lord make it a blessed season to our souls, and prepare us thereby for future usefulness. And can it be that I have really seen and conversed with those dear friends, for a blessing on whose labors in dear Greece, I have so long loved to pray? And shall I be permitted to labor with them, to spend my life in the same glorious cause, with them to suffer and with them to die? Indeed, my dear friends, I am most unworthy to be a missionary. How poor a preparation for this great work has most of my previous life been! How far short do I come of what you desire in a fellow laborer? Your patience and affection will often be tried, and your expectations perhaps disappointed. Habits of self-indulgence, impulsiveness of feeling, and strength of passion, though resisted and deprecated, may yet sometimes grieve you. In a word you will find me a frail, erring girl, willing indeed to labor and suffer, but often calling for your forbearance and forgiveness."

CHAPTER XI.

Visit to Saratoga—Ill health of Mr. Love—Necessity of deep piety in a missionary—Repeated detentions—Inquiry into the cause of their disappointments—Letter to Miss S. T. B.—Their designation—Extracts from parting notes.

Owing to various unforeseen circumstances, it was not until the last of June that Miss W. became quietly seated with the family of Mr. Love, in Saratoga. Though anxious to commence the study of Greek, and fearful that the summer would glide away without accomplishing much, yet she cheerfully left all with God. "These little delays and trials," says she, "are a part of the kind discipline of our heavenly Parent, and are intended to perfect our Christian character, no less than those sterner afflictions which shake our natures to their very foundation. O the illimitable love of God! Does it not surpass our highest thoughts, and is it not inexplicable on all the principles of earthly affection? How can the Holy One love us? How is it possible he can feel for us that tenderness, that interest, which his word, his providences, and our own experience so clearly exhibit? Well might Paul say, it '*passeth knowledge*.'"

Of Saratoga she remarks, "It is a very pretty town, only that it bears the marks of dissipation and ungodliness, and shows itself as Satan's seat. This withers up its beauties, and makes it in our eyes most unlovely. I do not feel, however, much of the *out-door* influence, though I would far rather be in some quiet nook, where rumor of folly, and fashion, and sin, might reach me no more.

"But my studies," she adds, "engross most of my time. I love the language, and enjoy much in its prosecution. Mr. L. is passionately fond of *Bible study*, and to me this is sweeter than my necessary food. His knowledge of Greek has already opened to my mind many a difficult passage; and I anticipate much pleasure from our Bible class for the study of the Gospels. How will my increased privileges augment my responsibilities, and with how much meaning might God say to me, '*What more could I have done for thee, that I have not done?*'

"To live for God is indeed a struggle, a mighty and unceasing conflict, in view of which my yielding soul is often ready to quail, and in supineness to feel that the armor is too heavy to wear so constantly. I have had more than one sharp contest within; and O I feel very weak and helpless, unable to accomplish any thing unless God help me most mightily. The deep sinfulness of my heart, its readiness to trust in an arm of flesh, to forsake the blessed fountain of living waters, and drink at earth's broken cisterns,—its accessibleness to temptations, its languor and its earthliness often fill me with dismay. A victory is hardly gained over some desperate foe to inward holiness, ere the attack is renewed with tremendous power on the very field of imagined conquest. O Saviour, pray for me, that my faith fail not. I have suffered greater variableness of feeling than is compatible with deep piety, and have felt much the breaking up of all my former religious routine. We have had much sickness in the family, which has tended to absorb feeling, occupy time, and distract thought. But may God give me grace in all things to glorify his name."

It was soon apparent that the health of Mr. Love was much more impaired than was at first apprehended; and fears began to be entertained that he might not be able to resume his missionary labors in Greece. This was a sad thought to Miss W. Her affectionate heart had already begun to cling to this beloved family as the home of her future exile. Yet with those chastened feelings which are the proper offspring of strong faith, she meekly bowed her will to that of her Heavenly Father, and cheerfully left the whole to his disposal. In a letter to Mr. Love dated August 26, after expressing a fear that the time of their departure might arrive before his health was restored, she adds,

"But the same mighty Saviour whose word of old said to disease, 'Thus far but no farther,' still knows the wants of his own cause, and can recall your departed vigor just as soon, and just as fully as is best."

And when afterward their most painful apprehensions were realized, addressing the same, she writes:

"For a moment my heart rebelled against this grievous disappointment, especially in view of the critical situation of our beloved mission. But it was *only* 'for an instant.' And though the tears would flow, I could kiss the rod. Yes, the lov[illegible] and wisdom of our most gracious Redeemer invite [illegible]r warmest confidence, and cannot for a moment be questioned. In him I cheerfully confide, though he [illegible]ad [illegible] in the dark, through deep waters.

" But above my own distress I feel for you. For you to relinquish this dear mission and settle in America is like the giving up of the ghost; it is severing the very heart strings. This child of your affection, begotten in pain of soul, nursed with tears, and cherished with prayers, entwined around every fibre of your heart, dear as life itself; how can you bequeath it to strangers? God help you, beloved friends. May He who hath broken, heal. In such an hour earthly consolation is a mockery,—to reason with, to try to soothe the breaking heart is folly. The tearful eye can see no ray of light but from the throne of God. O that from thence, sweet assurances of love may comfort you, and the soft hand of a loving Saviour wipe away your fast falling tears. The word of God alone sounds sweet to hearts filled with anguish. Let us betake ourselves to its exhaustless treasuries, and hear it saying, 'My son, despise not the chastenings of the Lord, nor faint when thou art rebuked of him; for whom the Lord loveth he chasteneth, and scourgeth every son whom he receiveth.' Let us then

'——— Praise him for all that is past,
And trust Him for all that's to come.' "

* * * * *

" How all important that those who engage in the cause of missions, be persons after God's own heart, deeply pious, wholly devoted. The Lord will not work with us, if we have talents only, natural fitness, or even every earthly qualification; if our hearts cannot be the residence of his Spirit, pure and holy as that heavenly Messenger, in vain are all our expectations of success and blessing. He will turn our wisdom into folly, our policy into disappointment, our efforts into nothingness. Confusion and shame will cover us, and our garments will be stained with the blood of souls. Such reflections have humbled me before God, and I have felt anxious to spend the few weeks that yet remain in earnestly seeking greater conformity to God, and deadness to the world; greater spirituality of mind, and more energy in struggling against sin. The warning character of the Christian life has been specially impressed on my mind, and the necessity of unceasing conflict with sin. I have great reason to reproach myself for self-indulgence, spiritual inertness, and a disposition to yield to every passing temptation. I regret especially that I have so often allowed my attachment to yourselves, and enjoyment of intercourse with you, to separate my soul from God instead of drawing me, as it ought, nearer to him. And I have felt justly chastened in being deprived of your loved society, since I had, in the enjoyment of the gift, neglected the Giver. O the forbearance, the long-suffering of our gracious Redeemer. If his love were like ours, how should we long ago have been consumed in his wrath!

"I want you to feel my precious mother to be a special trust committed to you, and, when the trying day of final parting must come, to afford her all possible support and sympathy, especially after I have left. I have given her to Christ. Indeed I entreated Him, who committed his mother in the flesh to a beloved disciple, to take my own sweet mother into his peculiar care."

Having been two or three times disappointed in the hope of sailing for Greece, they were now anxiously awaiting the arrival of the Catharine, which was daily expected, and would be detained only about ten days. But another disappointment awaited them in the very sudden death of Mrs. Arnold's father. This trying dispensation of Providence not only put a check upon their immediate embarkation, but for a while rendered it doubtful whether Mr. and Mrs. Arnold would be able to go at all. Under these circumstances Miss W. thus writes:

"How inscrutable are God's ways! Never was I so shocked as when I heard from the newspaper the first announcement of Mr. Allin's sudden death. I could not but lift my soul in prayer for poor Sarah. O may God help her in this hour of mortal anguish. She is ever in my mind, as well as her afflicted mother. I feel deeply for them all, and can appreciate their feelings most fully. To leave their bereaved and desolate mother at such a time as this, must be most distressing, and a thought hardly to be entertained. Should they feel constrained to renounce altogether the idea of laboring for poor Greece, I should think them perfectly justified by the dealings of Providence.

"Yet how can I relinquish the expectation of our long anticipated embarkation without tears? Still the Lord's time is the best; and if he says, 'Stay,' indeed if he never says, 'Go,' I will be still; for 'he doeth all things well.' If we view the present and past trials which God has brought upon the Greek mission, as only designed to try our faith, and test our love to it, and Jesus, we can bear up, and on, undismayed. But if God is *displeased* with us, if he mean to signify disapproval by these afflictions, then are we troubled. In God I can place unlimited confidence, but if he forsake us in anger, where shall we turn? It is a most painful thought that I may be the offending cause. I have always felt so unworthy of this glorious work in view of my early wanderings. But it is my most sincere and earnest prayer, that his chastenings may fall on my head alone, and that he will allow his other dear servants to go and labor. May he not chastise the mission for my sake. My desire to go was never so intense, nothing can quench it,—no trial, no service can alter it; but if the Lord go not with me, I cannot depart, though a host should uphold me.

"The Lord has been kindly preparing me for trial, granting me most gracious manifestations of himself, and enabling me to feel that in him I have a treasure that outweighs the world beside. But I was not supposing it was for such a trial. Yet I think I can say with the poet,—

'When I can yield my all to God,
  In trial's fearful hour,
Bow all resigned beneath his rod,
  And bless its sparing power;
A joy springs up amid distress,
A fountain in the wilderness.'

"Let us be constant in prayer, that God will show us his way and lead us in a plain path. Jesus' love is no less now in this hour of darkness than when the sun of prosperous hope shone unclouded on our path. Let us love him, let us cling to him in darkness and the deeps.

"I feel that there is danger of our taking undue comfort from the sovereignty and mystery of God's dealings, instead of seeing in his chastisements the just punishment of our wanderings. Who can tell but that God would have allowed us all to depart, and already have begun to bless our labors in Greece, if we had been, during the last six months, emptied of self, filled with the love of Christ, crucified to the world, and alive unto God, and the welfare of perishing souls? How ought such a thought to abase us in the dust, and fill us with penitence and shame. We have no right to comfort ourselves with the promises, nor take shelter under the providence of God, while we are estranged from him. Suppose Jonah had said, when the winds roared, and the waves tossed them to and fro, 'God is a Sovereign and afflicts his people only in mercy. This is to try my faith.' Would he not thus have added sin to sin? The Lord keep us from such iniquity.

"Such feelings as these have greatly afflicted me, and brought me, I trust, into the publican's place. God has graciously restored my wandering soul, and made me feel that I am not worthy to go,—that I deserve to be denied the privilege I had lightly esteemed. O that he may henceforth keep me by his side, fasten the eye of my faith unwaveringly upon him, and enable me to consecrate my entire being to his service. How can we ever content ourselves to live at a distance from Christ, after we have once had a view of his loveliness, his fullness, his infinite superiority to all beside? May we henceforth be absorbed in him."

TO MISS S. T. BOSWORTH.

"*Charlestown, Dec.* 8, 1843.

"My beloved Sarah:—You may almost be tempted to call in question my right to use the above address, after my long silence; and did not my heart from its very depths assert its unaltered affection for you, perhaps I should hesitate myself. But, Sarah, these have been weeks and months of sore and repeated trials; trials which I had not anticipated, and by which I have been almost overwhelmed. Yet no! The great Right Hand has graciously upheld me, and a Saviour's unchanging love been ever my sufficient refuge.

" When I bade you farewell, though my heart strings quivered with anguish at the thought of seeing you no more, yet I was then rejoicing in the hope that in a few weeks, with the beloved missionary band whom I had learned to love so well,—the dear Loves, the affectionate Arnolds, and the interesting Mr. and Mrs. Cross,—with these to leave this favored land, unitedly to labor for the rescue of perishing souls. But ere one week elapsed, that fond hope was blighted, at least partially so, by the sad decision of Mr. Love's physicians, who pronounced his return madness in the extreme. My personal interest in the family, and sympathy for them, bowed down as they were by this grievous disappointment, could not but make me weep tears of sadness with them. But when added to this, the new aspect in which Mr. Love's withdrawal placed this young and feeble mission, perplexed and disquieted the Board, and it became a question whether they could send us out in these altered circumstances, then for the first time I realized the strong hold which this dear mission had on my heart; how it had become inwrought with my very being; and the thought of renouncing it was agony. Except my father's death, it was the severest trial I ever endured. Yet conscious of my unworthiness, and confident in the wisdom and love of God's providence, I could only say, 'Not my will, but thine be done.' In the end the Board decided to detain Mr. and Mrs. Cross a year longer, and to send out this fall, Mr. and Mrs. Arnold, and myself. Unexpectedly they found a vessel willing to carry us directly to Corfu, to sail about the last of October. We made all haste to close our preparations, and were just ready to go, when the vessel was found to be too old and disagreeable for lady passengers. We were accordingly advised to wait for the Catharine, to sail about the first of December. And now, as all prepared we were waiting her arrival, the mighty hand of God is again laid upon us, and death, in a sudden and dreadful manner, is commissioned to tear from dear Mrs. Arnold her beloved father. It would be cruelty to leave her afflicted mother now, and therefore the Catharine sails this week, and we remain. God's ways have been in darkness and the deeps; his judgments are unsearchable, and his ways past finding out. Surely we may praise him that there is a rod in the covenant. Whom he loves he chastens, never willingly, but to produce afterwards the peaceable fruits of righteousness. Dear Sarah, God is '*a very present help in trouble*,' and never do we know how true this is, till experience of sorrow has tested it. He is a Refuge, a precious, blessed Comforter. Welcome the afflictions that have restored my wandering soul, and made me feel the sweetness of his love. Let him do with me as seemeth him good. I have no higher joy than to fulfill his will.

"You will not wonder then, my dear Sarah, that these weeks, crowded as they have been with events of absorbing interests to me, have left me no time to write you. And now, my beloved sister, let me ask concerning your own dear self. How is your health? What effect has the changing weather of the past autumn produced on your enfeebled system? But more especially, how fares your soul? Is it wholly given to Christ, and does he reign supreme without a rival there? Or do you still fear to look duty boldly in the face, and from the heart pray, '*Show me thy way, O Lord?*' By all the motives by which you would stimulate your unconverted friends to give up all for Christ, urge yourself forward, dear sister, to an entire consecration. There is not an excuse you can bring for not being a whole-hearted Christian, which they may not bring to sustain them in their impenitency. Either there is no God, no immortal principle within us, or else, as consistent beings, we are called upon to sacrifice every thing for God, and the welfare of the soul. There is no middle ground between these two extremes, though we, comparing ourselves among ourselves, have tried to establish a half-way position.

"It is my earnest prayer that I may be wholly the Lord's, devoting to him my entire being, and depending on him each moment to work in me, to will and to do of his good pleasure. I have thought much of the mental struggle which you said you sometimes experienced between duty and inclination. I would not, Sarah, if I could, satisfy your mind by my own reasonings on that subject; but one thing we both know. It cannot be *right* to feel so. And you may, beloved Sarah, through Jesus gain the victory, and rejoice in the belief and practice of the truth. The Lord give power to the faint. When we do not feel the preciousness of Jesus in our own hearts, we cannot feel deeply for those who know him not. It is only when in all his transcendent loveliness we lavish on him our most intense affection, and receive in return the sweet assurance of his love, that we are ready in sincerity to exclaim,

'O that every heart but knew him,
And could taste his mercy too.'

"And now, beloved Sarah, I commend you to God; praying for your sanctification, and entire consecration to his service. When we have suffered awhile may he receive us to glory.

"With unabated affection,

"Your own

"EMMY."

Though sorely afflicted, Mr. and Mrs. Arnold soon felt that the calls of duty were louder than those of affection, and their bereaved mother cheerfully surrendered them to the cause of Christ. They had lost the opportunity of sailing in the Catharine, but only awaited the arrival of the next vessel for that port. This proved to be the Potapsco, for the embarkation in which they at once commenced preparations.

The services of their designation were held in the First Baptist Church, Providence, on Friday evening, December 29th. On the day following, Miss W. returned to Charlestown, and addressed farewell notes to several of her friends, from which the following are brief extracts.

To one she says, "I am now writing my last letters from this my native land. In all probability I shall see the sun set but once more behind my childhood's horizon; and then I must tear myself from loving hearts and loved scenes, from the sacred privileges of the sanctuary, and the dear, dear refinements of cultivated society, and become a stranger in a strange land. Yet I am happy in God, and in the work before me, for '*He that is mighty is with me, the Lord of hosts is my refuge.*' "

To another she writes, "After repeated trials and detentions, kind chastenings from a Father's hand, God at length seems about to send us far hence. The services of our designation were held at Providence last evening. They were of a most interesting and deeply solemn character. Then, my beloved sister, as never before, I felt my utter weakness, my perfect helplessness. Then, with a depth of meaning which such circumstances alone could produce, I could say,

> 'Other refuge have I none,
> Hangs my helpless soul on thee.'

Such responsibilities as devolve on a missionary, such labors as are assigned to him, such trusts as are committed to him, make him seek refuge in an Almighty Friend, and constrain him to lean wholly on the arm of Jehovah; his is the irresistible might of weakness trusting in omnipotence. I feel in the immediate prospect of embarkation, solemn and sober, but cheerful and composed. I am not left alone, nor am I comfortless. To be sure my heart strings quiver, and are stretched to their utmost capability of tension, but Christ fills, and will fill every void."

To another she thus expresses the emotions of her full heart: "Well, my sister, my beloved friend, tried and true, the hour of parting has come at last. In the haste and excitement of preparation for our present sudden departure, I have delayed writing till I fear it is too la'e to inform you that we sail on Monday at 11 A. M. I fear I shall never look on your loved face again; never feel the imprint of another kiss from the lips that have ever uttered words of love to me. Never more hear that voice whose tones have been music to my ear. My beloved, my mother in things spiritual, Emmy bids you her last farewell, with throbbing heart, with quivering lips. Would I could once more pray with you for God's blessing on you. God bless you, best beloved. God Almighty bless you from his own infinite fullness; bless you for your early, constant, faithful love; bless you for your kind and forbearing admonitions; bless you for your thousand labors of love; bless you for your supplicating prayers.

"Ah, I need not tell you, dearest, that I love you, but shall I, can I, do I love my Saviour less? O no, no! Jesus, my own gracious, loving, faithful Redeemer. Jesus, none but Jesus. For him would I go to earth's farthest bounds; for him labor, suffer, die. Thanks to him for the blessed privilege, of making some sacrifices for him, of suffering for the cause which I have so often made to suffer. He is my Rock and support. In him do I now rejoice. Your arms can no longer shield me. But the everlasting arms are my refuge. Christ is all my salvation, and all my desire. My only hope is to live by faith upon him. Once more, dear sister, farewell. Pray for dear mother, pray for me, for my holiness, my usefulness, that I may win souls to Christ. Yes, pray ever for Your own

"EMMY."

Among many testimonials of affection received about the time of her leaving America, was a present from her

Sabbath school class, accompanied by the following note.

" To our dearly loved teacher, Miss S. E. Waldo, in behalf of her Sabbath school class.

" The time having now nearly arrived when you have decided to leave your native shore for the fair land of another people, it has been our desire to pay one parting tribute of respect to her whom we have loved so fondly and so long.

" For years you have labored with affectionate zeal to promote our highest interest, and we believe it has been your constant prayer that our names might be written in the book of life eternal. We rejoice that in some measure you have been permitted to witness the happy results of your exertions; but the bright link which has so closely connected us is soon to be severed. You have felt that duty called you to lend the aid of your laborious efforts for the lightening up of the darkened spirits in a distant land, and may the sentiments to which we give utterance, be the feeling of our hearts when we say, ' It is right.'

" And now, dear teacher, we would beg your acceptance of this slight memorial of grateful affection, and remembered kindnesses. And should your eye wander with pleasure over its pages, your thoughts will turn to us, and we will feel that your prayers will still ascend, though from the altar of the stranger, for

" Your loved

" SABBATH SCHOOL CLASS."

CHAPTER XII.

Embarkation in the brig Patapsco—Account of her voyage—Kindness of the captain and fellow passengers—Divine service on board—Description of seasickness—Phosphorescence of the sea, nautili, &c.—Passing the Straits of Gibraltar—African coast—Shore of Spain—Letter to Miss S. P. C.—To her mother.

On the first of Jan., 1844, Mr. and Mrs. Arnold and Miss Waldo sailed from Boston in the brig Patapsco, Capt. Bearse, for Corfu. Miss W. intended to keep a regular journal during her voyage for the gratification of her mother, but owing to continued sea-sickness she was able to write very little. Her first attempt is dated

"*Brig Patapsco, Jan.* 22, 1844.

"My darling Mother, and dear ones at Home:—To you shall be devoted the first lines which my hand has been able to trace since the hour of our parting. Yes, twenty-one long days have passed, and I am just convalescent enough to write. Really, I little anticipated such a siege. And yet I have not been, at any one time, so very sick as I had imagined. The first four or five days, I was less indisposed than I have since been, nor have I at any time experienced such excessive nausea, or extreme depression, as I had supposed constituted sea-sickness. My suffering has been rather from extreme lassitude, weakness of the bowels, loss of appetite, and great irregularity of the system. Some of the company have been sicker at times than myself, but I have been the last to get up, and my appetite still continues behind the rest.

"The long continuance of sea-sickness has doubtless been in a measure attributable to the very rough weather we have had. Until the 20th, we had a gale of more or less violence, with rain every twenty-four hours. But the good hand of our God, our faithful, gracious God, has been upon us, and we have reason to sing of mercy. He has hushed the gale, and given prosperous winds in answer to our prayers, and has preserved us from death and many dangers.

"Our captain, though not a religious man, is one of the pleasantest beings I ever met with. We have never heard one profane word on board the vessel, nor have we ever seen, or heard, the least unkindness or severity. He has paid us every possible attention, given us most freely of every delicacy he had provided for his own private comfort, and in every way endeared himself to us all. I beg you, mother, brother, and all my dear friends, to find out and show every possible attention to Capt. Richard Bearse of Hyannis. God bless him and his dear, kind wife. How much safer and better it is to leave the Lord to direct our way than to attempt it ourselves. I regretted that the captain was going to take his lady, but she has been a great comfort to us, and had she been my sister, could not have been kinder. Indeed, all on board have been extremely kind.

"Yesterday was the first Sabbath that we have been able to have divine service on board; and sweet it was indeed, to praise and pray on the mighty deep. Never is God so near, never do we more feel our dependence on him, and never is it so sweet to call, and feel him to be, Father, Saviour, Friend, as when tossed upon the treacherous seas, in a frail bark, alone upon the world of waters. As our little band united in singing,

'Where two or three with sweet accord,' &c.,

the words had a meaning unfelt before. Mr. A. preached from 2 Cor. 6 : 2, with feeling and appropriateness.

"I visit my dear home every night and hold sweet converse with each of you. Your loved image, precious mother, is ever before me, and it is my heart's dearest, sweetest, and most constant joy to pray for you."

"*Mediterranean, Feb.* 5.

"You may wonder, my beloved ones at home, to find this the date of my second record in my Journal, if such it may be called. But that sunny day of the 22d ult. has been succeeded by calms and head winds, which brought back our old companion, sea-sickness, and I have hardly been able to write until to-day. When I say *sick*, you must not think that I mean we are unable to be up at all, but rather that we live as follows: After rather restless nights, we wake with a feeling of nausea which will not allow us to dress, that is, put on a loose frock, without several pauses to relieve the disagreeable sensation. At nine, we languidly recline around our breakfast-table, after which you might see us bolstered up with pillows, half sitting, half reclining, attempting to forget in reading, the uncomfortable sensations which our breakfast has produced, and generally parting with it in the course of an hour or two. If the day be fair, we go on deck; and then you might see us in some nook or corner, reclining on each other, occasionally rising to look at some wonder of the deep, or in vain endeavoring to walk the rolling deck. We dine at 4 or 5 P. M., and when we have recovered from that, watch the sunset, or sing awhile on deck, till some sea dashing over us, or the damp spray penetrating through our garments, admonishes us to retire. Many an hour do we spend in talking of our homes; and in the tedious, sleepless hours of night, memory, with excited power, recalls the forms of all I have ever known or loved. I have lived over and over the scenes of the past, some with contrite sadness, some with sweet pleasure, till I have almost forgotten that I was on the mighty deep. And when slumber again enwraps me, your forms still fill my dreams, and seem to watch like kind angels around my pillow.

"Having read that the phosphorescence of the sea was caused by a glutinous kind of fish, like the sun-fish, we watched one day to see them, and witnessed a great number of various forms and colors, but all having one bright spot or centre. Occasionally they would adhere to each other, and form a long serpentine train of light, reminding me of electrical diagrams. We have had the pleasure too, of seeing some of those beautiful creatures, the nautili, or Portuguese men-of-war. They are perfectly transparent; but as the sun-light strikes their tiny sail, it is now a delicate pink, and then of azure blue or silvery white. They are borne along on the crest of the toppling waves, expanding or contracting their sail as the wind varies. And again we have been delighted to see the merry porpoises, leaping from billow to billow as if in sport, or a gull flapping its wings in the distance.

We have also descried several vessels in the distance, but have approached none near enough to hail them.

"But I must pass over what has taken place in these long weeks, and tell you something of the interesting and exciting scenes of to-day. We had tacked and re-tacked, till we almost despaired of reaching the straits, when this morning, the joyful news of 'a fair wind and land ho,' made us hasten from our berths and ascend to enjoy the prospect. On Saturday morn, indeed, the wind was fair, and the captain and some others could see land, but it was too dim and distant for my vision; and a squall soon striking us, followed by head winds, drove us out to sea again. Yesterday, in some of our tacks, the black coast of Africa was dimly seen, and we gazed with interest on *Terra Firma.* But it was reserved to to-day to awaken in us that intense excitement, which the sight of pasture lands and green fields, and the abodes of man, produces after a sea-voyage.

"As we had been driven to the south, the coast of Africa was first visible, craggy and dark, and seemingly uninhabitable by man; comprising huge masses of rock, covered with a mere mould or low furse, with here and there a green patch. At length, in a sheltered cove, were revealed to us through the glass, some high towers and a few buildings, but nothing with distinctness. It was the town of El Arish. Cape Spartel for awhile bounded our vision; we came within a quarter of a mile of the land, and amused ourselves in trying to find some signs of life. Having passed the point, the distant shore of Europe loomed up on the north, but before we could see it with any distinctness, we passed the quiet bay of Tangiers, on the opposite shore, far in whose sheltered southern side lay the city which names the bay, and whose white buildings looked like bits of chalk.

"At length the sunny shore of Spain, rock-bound, indeed, but white with limestone crags, attracted our admiring gaze. I never saw any thing so grand, so beautiful. Sheltered among the hills on the sea-shore, lay the pretty town of Tarifa, whose high light-house tower first attracted our attention. We could just see a long wall through which cannon peered, and beyond were the white houses built of plaster, which make these towns conspicuous, though distant. On the verdant slopes still farther east, were the green vineyards, with here and there a red-roofed cottage.

"We could not pass very near Gibraltar, and satisfied ourselves with admiring its steep sides and sharp summits, with only a glimpse of the town below. It is separated from the main land by a low isthmus, and sometimes has the appearance of an island. The zig-zag paths which lead to its lofty summit, Point Europa, the Calpa of the ancients, seemed like scratches on a stone.

"We felt ourselves somewhat recompensed, however, for the loss of a near view of this famed Rock, by the sight of Centa, the opposite cliff on the African shore, which in height exceeds Gibraltar. This, though on the coast of Morocco, belongs to the Spaniards, who have strongly fortified it; and behind it, stretching far to the right, lay the magnificent city of Centa, at least it seemed splendid in the distance. We looked and looked, till our eyes were weary, and our heads ached. We bade farewell to the broad Atlantic, which washes our own New England, and which had many a night rocked us to sleep, and, borne by a rapid current and strong breeze, we entered the old Mediterranean. A gorgeous sunset closed this most interesting day; and we could not be induced to come below, until a good sea most unexpectedly washed over us, and sent us below with dripping garments.

"But I must close, hoping that you may find something to interest you in Emmy's descriptions, which will not, however, bear a critic's eye. How sweet to feel that there are hearts that love, and some who pray for me, in dear old Charlestown. Yes, and One who loves me with more than a mother's fondness, who cares for me with more than a sister's tenderness, and protects me with more than a brother's care, is ever, ever with me. He, I trust, 'is mine and I am his; what can I want beside?' May he be your all-sufficient portion, dear, precious loved ones."

"*Feb.* 14.

"We are now within forty-eight hours sail of Corfu, and I must hasten to close my letters home. Since my last date we have had one or two occurrences of sea-sickness, but are again well and rejoicing in our rapid approach to our destined port; though we cannot repress a feeling of sadness at the thought of leaving our pleasant companions, and in parting with the good brig Patapsco, thus severing the last tie that binds us to dear New England. But we have had blessing upon blessing, and commit ourselves trustingly to the good hand of our God and Redeemer, assured that all things shall work together for our best good, if we but love, obey, and trust him.

"The fine breeze which wafted us through the straits continued until Thursday, and we advanced with unusual rapidity on our course, making two hundred and thirty-three miles in one day. It, however, died away, and was succeeded by head winds and gales which drove us to the northwest extremity of Sicily. The coast of Sicily looked beautiful, and we could easily understand how it was once the granary of Rome. On the 11th we had the great pleasure of being hailed by the brig Uncas, from Boston. We were near enough to see a number on deck, though we could not distinguish their faces. Long did we gaze on the noble bark as she ploughed through the waves, our own star-spangled banner floating to the breeze. We have seen a great many vessels since we entered the Mediterranean, but generally at a distance. Europeans can be distinguished almost as far as they can be seen, on account of their canvass being of a much darker color than ours.

"I feel, beloved ones, that this is but a poor apology for a journal, but you will not attribute it to an unwillingness to write, especially if you should ever be the unhappy subjects of sea-sickness, from which I have never been wholly free, and which produces a lassitude which makes the least exertion a mountain. I have had, too, a great deal of headache, especially when I read or write more than a few minutes at a time. Many a letter to you do I compose in my berth, many a long talk do I have with you, and many a fervent prayer do I raise for God's blessing on each one. However widely my footsteps may roam, my heart will cling with unchanging love to my own dear home,—to the mother whose bosom has so often been my pillow,—the dear brother who was my pride and love,—the sisters whose devoted attentions welcomed my return, and endeared my home more than all splendor and pomp—the dear uncles, aunts and cousins, who always met me with a smile—the loved friends—and the dear church whom the love of a common Saviour has bound to me. Sweet home! the blessing of the Highest rest down upon thee; kind angels watch over thee; rich grace abound to thee."

TO MISS S. P. CARTER.

"*Mediterranean, Feb.* 9, 1844.

"MY DEAR SARAH:—When my heart yearns for home, it thinks too of the loving spirit with whom soft communings were so sweet, and whose sheltering arms were ever ready to protect me from a cold world. I love to link your name in prayer with those dearer than my own life, and to recall, when I think of my loved home, the scenes in which we have mingled. I love to dwell upon those seasons when together we have talked of the past, the present, and the future—of the concerns of time and the hopes of eternity—of ourselves, our Zion, and a lost world—of sin and sorrow, of penitence and pardon, of faith, and hope, and joy—of our long-suffering Father, our adorable Redeemer, our gracious Sanctifier. And O, I love to think of those hours, more sacred still, when together we sought our covenant God, and poured forth our desires into the ears of our ever-prevalent Intercessor.

"Yet do not think, dear Sarah, that your Emmy is sad, because she recalls these by-gone hours. God has been more gracious to me than my fears, and never more so than on the trying day of our parting. That morning was one of doubt and trembling. I feared I could not endure the trial before me. The Lord's face was clouded and I mourned. But I entreated him that yet once he would be with me. He heard me in that I feared. The sweetest peace filled my soul, and I wondered at my own feelings, as these blessed words of Jesus came to my mind, '*Peace I leave with you, my peace I give unto you, not as the world giveth, give I unto you.*' And he enabled my precious mother, too, to inscribe in my album, 'In his hands I am *happy* to leave thee.' O sweet is that declaration; a pledge, I humbly hope and pray, that Jesus may be to her more than many daughters. Yet sometimes my heart fails me when I think of her as sad and sick on my account. Tell me, Sarah, tell me faithfully how she bore it all after I was gone. Sometimes I have sweet hopes, that our own dear ones at home may be led by our separation to seek an interest in Jesus, to fly for refuge to the hope set before them in the gospel. God grant it for his dear Son's sake.

"In another respect, too, has my gracious God far exceeded my hopes. He has not only preserved me from depression but given me unusual cheerfulness. All that a brother's devoted attention, or a sister's confiding love, could do to refill the void, I have in dear Mr. and Mrs. Arnold. All that kindness could effect towards relieving necessary evils and securing all possible comfort, our friends on board have done. Were they but as anxious to please God and serve him, as they have been from the first to make us happy, we should have nothing to ask for. Our feeble efforts for the precious souls on board as yet manifest no good effect. But God may raise in power the seed sown in weakness. We have a fine crew, moral, but not religious.

"Yes, I am cheerful and happy, and feel more anxious to engage in my work than ever before. But O, how unworthy to enjoy this privilege, how incompetent to fulfill the duties of my station without large communications of divine grace. Tell your dear father, mother, and sisters, that Emily thinks often of her second home, and of the prayer which soothed her last farewell to it. Say to the dear mothers in our Israel that the memory of that precious prayer-meeting has been a joy to my heart; for I hope its supplications were registered in heaven. Ask them to pray for sailors; for many are the snares laid for their feet, and few of them are in the fold. Ask my young sisters to labor on for Christ and for a dying world, remembering to pray always for the feeble band in the mighty field. Often and anxiously have I thought of our Zion, and of the cloud that seemed gathering over her. I have found no refuge but in casting all on Jesus."

TO HER MOTHER.

"*Feb.* 10, 1844.

"As there is some probability of our stopping at Malta for water, we have concluded to have letters in readiness. Perhaps you imagine that we have already reached our destined port. We did not, however, pass the straits till the fifth inst. Previous to this time, we had almost constant storms, so that we lost five days in laying to, under close-reefed sails, rocking and pitching about most unpleasantly, the decks washed every few moments by heavy seas which occasionally poured down the companion-way into our cabin and state rooms.

"But since the sunny fifth we have had most delightful weather and favorable winds, so that on one day we sailed 233 miles in twenty-four hours. However an unbelieving world may smile, we cannot but remember that this same fifth was the monthly concert for Foreign Missions, when many a heart was pleading for us, and we felt in these favoring gales the breath of prayer. It is not a vain thing to call upon God; and we delight to remember that we are in his hands, whose throne is bound by the golden link of prayer, to the dear ones we have left behind.

"We saw the waving handkerchiefs long after we left the wharf, and waved ours in return; and our saddest thoughts were for those we left behind. Your image, darling mother, was ever before me, and my prayer was for you, that God would strengthen and comfort you. Do not grieve and mourn, my own beloved parent, but rejoice that He, who is better than many children, still remains to you. To know that you are well and happy, both temporally and spiritually, will be my greatest solace and comfort; and my chief anxiety is the fear that I may make you sick or unhappy. Your sweet words in my album are an unspeakable comfort to me; and I hope that He who enabled you to say, 'In his hands I am happy to leave you,' will be your stay and staff, through long, long years to come.

"I could discern Charley's tall figure for a long time. Dear, dear brother, how often in my slumbers do I dream that he is by my side. But we have reason to sing of mercy, for great has been the loving kindness of God, especially towards me. Had my own kind Charley, or dear Susey been on board, I could not have enjoyed more devoted brotherly attention or sisterly tenderness, than I have received from dear Mr. and Mrs. Arnold. And every one has been kind and affectionate. Not one cloud of disagreement has ever cast its shadow over our little company."

"*Corfu, Feb.* 20.

"By the exceeding goodness of God we are allowed, loved ones, to date from this city of our destination. We did not stop at Malta, as our passage up the Mediterranean was so short as to render it unnecessary. We entered the harbor on the morning of the 17th; the water smooth as glass, unrippled by a single zephyr, and the sun shining down upon us with almost summer intensity. The city, crowned by the picturesque and towering citadel, lay before us. All that was disagreeable being too distant to mar the pleasure with which we watched every object. Soon after we cast anchor the health officer came along side, to whom I delivered a note to Mrs. Dickson. Having followed orders, and obtained permission to go on shore, we were welcomed to Corfu by Mr. Taylor, to whom we had letters of introduction from Mr. Love, and who very politely came forward and accompanied us to our house. Here we were most cordially embraced by our astonished friend, who, until she received my note, had no knowledge of our arrival. She was well, and happy indeed to see us, and our hearts melted in gratitude at the rich, unmerited goodness which had at last permitted us to meet. We have met with the greatest kindness and politeness, and warm welcomes have at least seemed to betoken interest in us; to God be all the praise. We had callers on the very day of our arrival, and every day since, so that we can hardly realize that we are among strangers.

"We have been taught one of God's designs in detaining us so long in America, from the fact that a somewhat fatal epidemic has raged in Corfu which laid low Mr. Love's friend, Dr. Uriglio, in whom we should have found a kind and valuable friend. But God, who knows all our needs, has, we trust, taken him to himself. Had we sailed at the time first proposed, we should have been exposed to it; but now it is past. Dear mother, is it not good to wait patiently for the Lord, to seek his guidance, and never set up our will in opposition to his? O, is he not always right, always kind, 'most merciful when most severe?' We feel a sweet pleasure in committing ourselves into his hands, in feeling that he is our Protector, our Sun, our Shield, our constant and able Friend, our all in all. Never in our dear, dear homes, did God seem so near, so kind, so unspeakably precious, as here where we are shut up to God, where we feel as if he alone knew us, as if he were our pledged Guardian, our nearest, dearest Friend. Indeed, I cannot express the peculiar emotions awakened by our new situation; but they are such as fill us with sweet peace, and real happiness.

"I might occupy a sheet in telling you how very dear Mr. and Mrs. Arnold have become to me.

> 'Our souls in love together knit
>   Cemented into one;
> One heart, one soul, one mind, one voice,
>   'Tis heaven on earth begun.'

Mr. A. is all that a Christian, a friend, a brother, could be to me; ready to do any and every thing for our happiness, cheering us by his prayers, and the precious consolations and promises of God, and leading the way before us in whatever is lovely and of good report.

"And dear Mrs. A. is such a loving, open-hearted, winning creature, that one's heart must be incased in steel, not to love her dearly. Most favored indeed am I to have such friends, the most precious of all earthly blessings, and I desire to humble myself in view of the goodness of God to one so unworthy. Dear Mrs. Dickson, too, we all love her dearly, and look up to her as a mother. Such a kind, pleasant, and pious lady is seldom to be met with. It is wonderful to see a woman of her age so active and energetic, especially when her constitution has been long racked by disease and enfeebled by sorrow and toil. She dearly loves to teach, and will, I believe, never cease from her favorite employment while life remains."

CHAPTER XIII.

To the First Baptist Church in Charlestown—First letters from home—Baptism at Corfu—Description of the country—Religious privileges—Her school—To Miss S. P. C. Baptist brethren in Corfu—Difficulty of rightly estimating the religious character of inquirers.

Soon after her arrival she addressed the following letter

TO THE FIRST BAPTIST CHURCH IN CHARLESTOWN.

" *Corfu, March* 16, 1814.

"Beloved Brethren and Sisters:—Though no longer permitted to see your faces in the flesh, I still rejoice to tell you, as in days gone by, of God's good hand upon me, and his gracious dealings with his unworthy child. The Lord graciously heard your prayers for me on the trying day of our departure, and filled me with unexpected peace and composure, even when sundering the dearest earthly ties; so that, though heart and flesh failed, the Lord was the strength of my soul. We experienced a long succession of unpleasant weather during the former part of our voyage, but on the very day of the February monthly concert, as if the breath of prayer had sent them, we had fair winds, and fine weather; and so rapid was our passage up the Mediterranean, that we were but eleven days from Gibraltar to Corfu, a distance of some 1800 miles.

" In consequence of continued sea-sickness, we were able to have divine services on board only twice during the voyage; but those were precious seasons. Never, in his temples at home, did God seem so solemnly near, as on the lonely deep; never did we so deeply feel our constant dependence on him as when tossed on its billows. It was sweet to praise him, surrounded as we were by his wonders, and daily receiving his manifold mercies; and it was delightful to pray to Him from whom no distance could remove, no changes alienate us. Our almost constant sea-sickness prevented us from doing much for the good of the ship's company; but we distributed tracts, and implored the gracious influence of the Holy Spirit to accompany every influence calculated to awaken and renew them. Though we had not the pleasure of seeing any of them converted, yet God graciously disposed every heart to kindness; nor was there any profanity or intemperance on board.

* * * * *

" A few days after our arrival, an interesting lad called on Mr. Arnold as an inquirer, begging the privilege of a Bible class for himself and some other lads, who accordingly meet every Saturday evening for the study of God's word. Some of them, we trust, are not far from the kingdom of heaven. You probably know that there is a large military force kept here by the English, some 2000 soldiers, mostly hardened sinners, far from God. Some of these called, and desired that there might be a public religious service for them on the Sabbath. We therefore, ' in our own hired house,' like Paul of old, ' preach the kingdom of God, and teach those things which concern the Lord Jesus Christ.' Thus you see that though a long time must elapse before we can tell the Greek in his own tongue the things of salvation, we still have enough to do.

"With respect to the Greeks, I would say that the bitter persecution of those baptized a year since, and also before, has intimidated many an anxious inquirer. An interesting Greek, who once seemed truly converted, comes occasionally to read the Scriptures with us. His mind is evidently enlightened to see the truth of evangelical religion, but he does not avow it. You may be ready to censure; but remember, dear brethren, he was fearless, until the pistol and the dagger were aimed at him; and how many of you would dare say that you could face such obstacles?

"We long, we pant for the outpouring of the Spirit on this valley of dry bones, that they may rise and live. Never did I so feel my helplessness, my nothingness, my entire dependence upon God. Stripped of all the helps, the favorable circumstances, the abundant means of grace enjoyed at home, with obstacles of no ordinary kind hemming up every path, knowing that every convert made by our instrumentality, must wade through seas of opposition and suffering if he would follow Christ, and with nothing to offer the carnal hearts around us, as an equivalent for the sacrifices they must make, except that heavenly blessedness, which the earthly mind cannot appreciate, what hope have we but in God? Yet this simple reliance on him is sweet. Yes, God is here; and O how near does he seem to be. Will you not then unite with us in praying for the Holy Spirit? His influence neither Jew nor Greek can withstand."

Of the reception of her first letters from America, she thus writes:

"*March* 21.

"The precious letters from home came on the 19th, and for a while I was well nigh beside myself. We felt quite sad on Monday, the proper day for the arrival of the mail, to see no vessel telegraphed. But just after tea, on entering my chamber, I glanced at the citadel's top, and lo, a signal. I cried out in ecstasy to my friends, and running to examine the explanatory card, we found to our joy it was the signal for the English steamer. A friend passing the evening with us, kindly volunteered to endeavor to obtain our letters that night, but they were not ready. Early next morning, Mr. A. hastened to the post-office, and received the precious package. I eagerly opened it, pressed the precious papers to my lips, and hastening to my chamber, with streaming eyes commenced their perusal. Darling mother, and dearest J., S., L., and P. O how did I look at each loved signature. It was as a reviving cordial to a fainting frame. And how delightful to read of all God's goodness to my dear ones, of his gracious answers to my supplications in your behalf. Oh, he was better than my fears, as he always is. Let me trust him and never be afraid. Nothing was so sweet to me, dearest mother, and sister J., as that you find your happiness in God, and having turned away from the broken cisterns of earthly pleasures, quench the thirst of your immortal natures in the glorious Fountain of perfect bliss. Thank you all for writing so frequently, and minutely, and thus keeping me apprised of the run of things in dear old Charlestown."

After replying to the various items of intelligence contained in her letters, she says of herself:

"My health was never better; I have an excellent appetite, and sleep so soundly, that I only regret the loss of my sweet dreams of you all. The weather is mild and the air balmy as summer. We have occasionally cool breezes, and the people here talk about the severe cold, and piercing air; it seems almost a farce. We have a great deal of rain, and occasionally heavy thunder and lightning."

A short time after their arrival, Mr. Arnold had the happiness of baptizing a young English lady who had been for some time cherishing a hope in Christ. Of this baptism Emily wrote as follows:

"Our little company set out for the water at halfpast seven, P. M. It was cloudy and rained a little, the sea breaking on the shore with some violence, when we knelt beside these waters and invoked God's presence and blessing. Mr. A. having sounded the bottom, led down our dear sister into the watery grave, and there baptized her into the holy Trinity. Her composure was remarkable, and her satisfaction no less so. At her request, on our return, we sang, 'Hinder me not,' and 'Fearless of the world's despising.' Our hearts were filled with rejoicing, and our tongues with praise."

TO HER MOTHER.

"*April* 19.

"We often wish that our dear mothers could look in upon us and see how well and happy we are, that they might not feel anxious and troubled about us. We have every possible comfort, and all enjoy most perfect health. The weather is now delightful. The snow has melted off from the neighboring mountains, and the chilly winds no longer blow. Balmy and fragrant breezes give the air a uniformity of temperature which greatly contrasts with the ever changing weather to which I have been accustomed. We have a beautiful situation in one of the most healthy, airy, and pleasant parts of the city, commanding a view of the harbor, citadel, palace, and esplanade; indeed, all these are almost within a stone's throw. We have delightful walks, too, in various directions, and a mile from the city brings you into as beautiful a country as could be desired, exceedingly picturesque and fertile. But, beloved mother, though this place were Eden itself, it could not estrange us from our dear homes. Our hearts revert with fond tenderness to the homes of our childhood, and gushing tears alone can relieve our throbbing hearts at the remembrance of them. We speak of the beauties of this spot, and of our domestic happiness, because we know it will gladden your hearts to be informed of all that ministers to our comfort and cheers our absence.

"We have not had the trouble about servants which we anticipated. Our man, for men do all the cooking here, is a pleasant, obliging young Greek, who reads the Scriptures with us daily, and, what is a great thing for one of his nation, kneels in prayer. He also spends an hour every Sabbath afternoon in reading and studying the New Testament with Mr. A.; and not satisfied with this, he last Sabbath begged to have another hour in the morning. O that the Lord may open his eyes and renew his heart.

"We have, too, some pleasant religious privileges. Every Sabbath at 2 P. M., we have divine service in the house, attended principally by the English military. Then every Sabbath, and Friday evening, we have a prayer meeting with the pious soldiers, and some of these are very, very precious seasons. We have also a prayer meeting among ourselves on Wednesday evening, when we talk over the prospects of the mission, our joys and sorrows, fears and hopes, and pray for a blessing on the work of our hands. Of course we can yet talk but little in Greek. Still we try to read the Scriptures, and explain a little to those who come in. There is one old man who comes almost every day, and who gives some evidence of being really a Christian. Both he and another interesting inquirer, seem much astonished that I am neither the sister, nor cousin, nor in any way a relative of Mrs. Arnold, and yet am here without a husband. They can hardly believe that I do not belong to some religious order, vowed to celibacy; for they can hardly understand how closely a common faith in a common Saviour binds us together.

"My school continues interesting and prosperous, though many foes to religion have sought its injury. You would be pleased, I know, to see my little flock gather around me, as I go into school; one taking my bonnet, and another my shawl; one bringing a sweet nose-gay, another promising to do her best. O children's hearts are always warm; and cold and stony must be that heart that draws back repulsively from them. Very many of them show a deep interest in the study of the Bible, and sometimes listen to our instructions with tearful eyes."

TO MISS S. P. CARTER.

"*Corfu, April* 30, 1844.

"MY FONDLY LOVED SARAH :—It does almost seem sometimes as if I must enjoy at least an hour's intercourse with you ; must once more pour out into your confiding bosom, my oft burdened feelings. I sigh for the sympathy of that heart of love, which ever beat in such strange, sweet union with mine. Not that I have not dear friends in brother and sister A., and my dear Mrs. D. O no, they are all I could ask, affectionate, kind, sympathizing, devoted; I do not wish them to be more so. But you know, dearest, ours is no common love ; and I cannot tell you how delighted I am to find that others can see and appreciate its peculiar tenderness and sympathy.

"How much more beautiful this morning landscape would be, if you could enjoy it with me, dearest. This is indeed a most beautiful country. The equableness and blandness of the temperature form a striking contrast to the climate of New England, and the richness of the verdure, the novelty and variety so attractive to the foreigner, present themselves to us in all their freshness now. It is the season of roses ; the monthly, an exotic you know with us, is here very abundant and hardy, forming the hedge on many a road-side. They are very beautiful, but by no means so fragrant as our common rose, which is here much valued on account of its sweetness. My scholars daily bring me sweet little nosegays o f roses, geraniums, and the like; and my chamber is often scented with the orange blossom, the carnation, the rose, or the geranium.

" The view from my chamber window is very beautiful, and as I often gaze on it, I will try to describe it to you, that you may imagine yourself leaning out of my window, beholding it with me. Directly under, and in front of my window, lies the esplanade, where the military parades daily take place, and fine bands fill the air with martial and amateur music. This for a while we liked well to hear, but are already tired of it, as our school, our studies, and our devotions, are daily disturbed by it. This large open space, a miniature Boston Common, is bordered by horse chestnuts, acacias, and lilacs, and between these rows of trees, on either side of the Mall, are flowers of various kinds. Towering behind these, rises the principal fortification, the lofty Citadel. This has so much picturesque beauty about it, that I never become weary of admiring it. Terrace rises above terrace. The natural rock, hewn and altered by art, yet with its rich green moss, clinging vines, and clustering shrubs, is still possessed of nature's wild beauty. It rises, I should think, 200 feet above the level of the sea, which flows at its base. Its sides and base are one nest of intricate fortifications, and crowded barracks ; and an incredible number are contained within its walls. The little bay of Corfu lays in glassy stillness on the left, save when the Sirocco blows violently, and then the breakers dash on the craggy shores of Greece most musically. The Governor's palace fills the nearer left fore-ground, with a small green in front of it enclosing a fountain. And far away to the right is the noble Mediterranean, bounded nearer in, by the beautiful country around us.

15

It is a lovely scene by moonlight, and could you enjoy it with me, I would not wish a lovelier landscape.

"When will you come and visit my school, love? I assure you my scholars have warm hearts, and quick perceptions, and are far more interested students of the Bible, than I was accustomed to have at home. Their tearful interest and silent attention are most affecting; or when the subject is of a different character, their inquisitiveness is not less so. Do plead, dear sister, for the quickening spirit to make the gospel the power of God unto their salvation."

"*May* 4.

"To-day has been so memorable and interesting a season, that I cannot retire to rest without enjoying a little converse with you, love. It has been observed by all the members of the mission as a day of fasting and prayer for the blessing of God on our labors, and it has been a solemn good day to us. I felt the need of it. My school, and the study of the language, make large demands upon my time, and I had allowed them to come in the way of communion with God. Though he was still as a fruitful garden, yet I was leaving my soul too much to a wilderness. True I had enjoyed some sweet seasons, especially at our last communion, and in Sabbath school. Yet I felt a longing desire after some gracious manifestations. I longed and prayed to be humbled and restored. God has heard my prayer, and has brought me low, till I have abhorred myself, and wondered at the riches of his grace. It is indeed marvelous how God has borne with me. Well might he have said to me as to wayward Israel, '*For of old time I have broken thy yoke, and burst thy bands; and thou saidst I will not transgress.*' O how often have I said this, and yet wandered again. Were it not for the blessed invitation, '*Yet return unto me*,' I should not dare to come again. But O how ready is Jesus to receive; and how does that blessed Fountain in Judah ever avail to cleanse away sin. And then our covenant meeting this evening was so sweet, how I wish you could have been here. Tomorrow is the precious sacramental season. You can hardly conceive what sweet pleasure this feast brings to us here."

"*May* 9.

"There are seasons, dear sister, when my soul yearns for you with unutterable longings; it is so to-night. How appropriate and soothing these lines:

'Sweet is the thought, the promise sweet,
That friends, long sundered friends shall meet,
That kindred souls on earth disjoined,
Shall meet, from earthly dross refined.'

Shall we, darling, meet again, shall we, in the courts of the blessed renew our communion? Hope trembles at the greatness of the bliss, its contrast with the rich desert of heavy sins. But if redeeming love can stoop so low as to reach me, and raise me to the blessed home of our dear Lord, if I shall first depart, how will my waiting spirit leap to welcome you to glory, and be the first to guide your ransomed spirit to the throne. O what hopes has Jesus purchased for us. And the cost, the mighty cost! Dear, precious Saviour! Is there any cross for his sake too heavy; any sacrifice too painful to make for him? O no. For him I can give up my beloved mother, for him resign you, love.

"We had a most delightful season last Lord's day. It

was a blessed day every moment of it; a spot of brightness in my pilgrimage.

> 'Jesus came down my soul to greet,
> And glory crown'd the mercy-seat.'

I enjoyed something of that precious boon, a broken heart, and never did I sit at the blessed supper with such delight. I don't know that I ever told you, but it was one of the severest trials to me, in anticipating missionary life, to think of sacramental seasons—of the change from that sweet fellowship with hundreds of dear believers to two or three; and I used to think if there ever would be an hour of loneliness and desolateness, it would be then. But it has just been the reverse, and not with me only, my dear companions have felt the same. O the strength and sweetness of the tie that binds our little band together. Shall I introduce you to the Baptist church in Corfu? Dear Mrs. Dickson, our mother in Israel, Mr. Arnold, who is exceedingly interesting at such seasons, and his dear wife; these you know. Then there is our dear young sister, recently baptized. O I wish I could just bring her to see you. She does build so wholly on Christ and the gospel, and must always have a '*Thus saith the Lord*,' before she advances a step in religious matters. Then our dear brother C., who is such a simple, godly, straight-forward Christian; so familiar with the Bible, so simple in his faith that I love him more and more every day. Amidst all the seductions of a military life, and they are appalling, he has had grace to live for God, and many a careless scoffer listens with respect to his faithful exhortations. Next comes his gentle, timid wife, rescued from papacy; and last our other soldier brother, R., an interesting young man, brought up amid the same delusions, but converted and baptized in Halifax, by Rev. Mr. Crowley.

"I do not know, dearest, as I can make you understand the difficulties attending a right estimate of character here. There may be a great change in a Greek, and yet he may never have been born again. So much is he under the influence of early prejudices, that an active mind, when once aroused to shake off the fetters which have held it captive, comes into a new world. Throwing aside the authority of man, and the doctrines of a church which forbids all within her pale to decide for themselves, the whole soul is excited to the highest degree. A hundred varying passions are awakened, such as pity for the still enslaved multitude, exultation at self-deliverance, and an intense curiosity to know more of that wondrous gospel, which was so long a sealed book. Yet, you see, all this may be without any real brokenness of heart, or sincere faith, and such we find to be the actual case. Indeed, but for the bitter persecutions of the converts at Patrass, there might have been a large number ready to profess Christ, the defect in whose piety it would have been hard to detect, but for the furnace of trial. With all the ardor and activity of the Greek mind, they examined the gospel with enthusiasm, and were delighted with the simplicity of our sentiments. To no character could Christ's description, '*They received the word with gladness,*' apply more forcibly; and with equal truth might the rest be added, '*When tribulation or persecution arise because of the word, by and by they are offended.*'

"There are two interesting young men here, who in a high degree answered to the above description, and gave many interesting evidences of being followers of Christ. But one of them was in the house when the ferocious mob sought the life of Mr. Buel, and their shouts of vengeance have rung in his ears ever since. The other was fired upon in his own house as a heretic, and the flash of that pistol seems ever before his eyes. The other interesting inquirers here and in the vicinity, are under their influence, and kept paralyzed by fear. It is to me most affecting to see their appreciation of the excellence of the pure gospel, hushed by their intense fears. Do you wish to know for what to supplicate in behalf of this people? O pray that God may neutralize this terrible dread of suffering for Christ, and substitute that perfect love that casteth out all fear. This one thing seems to raise an almost insurmountable barrier to the acceptance and confession of the truth."

CHAPTER XIV.

Her filial affection—To her younger sisters—To Miss S. T. B.—Description of three converted soldiers.

By letters received from home on the 18th of May, she learned that her mother was somewhat unwell. The following touching paragraph illustrates the strength of her filial affection.

" *May* 21.

"Your dear letters received on the 18th, made the tears flow fast and long. Do not write again, my precious mother, when it hurts you so, for unspeakably dear as your letters are to me, I would rather be denied them than obtain them at so great a cost. O, mother, how I longed to fly to your bed-side, and try to soothe your pain, or minister to your relief; and how the impotency of the wish filled me for a season with bitter anguish, which could only be relieved by going to that gracious Saviour, to whom alone I can commit you with confidence. I knew that for his dear sake I had come far away here, and I believed he would accept the trust I gave to him, my heart's treasures, the inmates of my home. Many a time, dear mother, ere I left you, when my heart was wrung with anguish at the thought of what you might suffer, I have wrestled with God for you, and have felt ready to bear any thing, or to suffer any thing, if God would only support you and be your stay.

I remember one time in Salem, when for two or three days my feelings had been most distressing on your account, when all the burden of my soul was for you, that the Saviour would not leave you comfortless but would come to you—I recollect how soothingly that touching scene came to my mind, when on Calvary the dying Saviour thought of his mother in the flesh. I felt an assurance that he would be to you more than many daughters, and I think he has heard my cry. O that he may spare you from further suffering, and may make your hours glide sweet away, cheered by his life-giving presence. There is a blessedness in being taken off from every earthly trust, and in being able from the heart to say with David, '*All my springs are in Thee.*' It is a happiness which the world cannot understand, but which the soul that has felt it, values above the highest earthly good. May this be your sweet experience, dearest mother; and, while one spring of carthly comfort after another is dried up, may the full flowing waters of life be poured into your soul, and its deepest thirst be quenched.

"The sad news from our dear church almost broke my heart. I could hardly credit it. This is indeed a severe chastening, the heaviest of all troubles. Perhaps we have boasted too much of our union, and stood in our own strength. This is enough to humble us. I need not guard you, dearest mother, against judging of our religion, or our church as a body by this, for, bedimmed as the light now is, it will break forth with purer brightness; much as may be the dross apparent in this furnace, the pure lustrous silver will be found remaining brighter from the contrast. Yet O, how sad such an event.

"That my beloved and revered friend, Dr. Bolles, had been released from his sufferings and taken home to his

Master's presence, was not sad news to me; for I could but rejoice that he who had so long groaned in this tabernacle, being burdened, was now clothed upon with immortality, reposing where the weary are at rest. May I be found as ready to render up my last account, when the Lord of the harvest summons, as was this faithful servant.

"The season is now beautiful beyond description. The dark, yet feathery foliage of the olive is relieved by the fresh delicate green of the budding vines; the roses, geraniums, and orange blossoms, load the air with fragrance; beautiful and romantic views open to us on every side in our afternoon walks, and we only want you with us to consummate our delight."

Miss W. was in the habit of writing to each of the family in turn. The following extracts are from letters

TO HER YOUNGER SISTERS.

"*June* 13.

"When we first came to Corfu every thing seemed strange, and we thought it would never seem like home to us. As the landing-place is at some distance from here, we saw considerable of the city as we walked up to the house. The streets were very narrow and no sidewalk, except a sort of arcade formed by building porticoes in front of the houses. Here were little shops, not bigger than a small bed-room, all open, and containing every variety of goods. The streets resounded with cries, (for here almost every thing is sold in the street,) the din of which is heard from morning till night. We passed some men in loose black robes, with long beards, and hair down their backs; these were Greek priests. Others were seen with a tighter black robe and a turned up hat; these were Italian priests. Others wore red caps adorned with long blue tassels, with a white skirt and embroidered jacket, or a blue skirt gathered round the knee; these were the native Greeks. The Maltese, too, look singularly with their odd black mantillas over their head. Indeed, there is here every variety of costume, and most motley are the assemblages which are often grouped together about sunset on the esplanade. A great many of the people here are very dark complexioned; the laboring classes are quite the color of Indians; but some of the men are fine looking, intelligent, and active. Singing is much more common here than at home. As soon as the sun has gone down, the streets are full of singers, not all of whom indeed are blessed with very sweet voices. Ragged little urchins, seemingly as ignorant as the animals around them, sing in the most perfect measure and union, snatches of Italian songs, &c. But, poor creatures, they know nothing else, but are a miserable, neglected, and depraved company. The people in the country, instead of living in neat wooden cottages as at home, occupy little plastered houses of one story, and often only one room; generally having a ground floor. Though often in such a room, with only the bare earth under your feet, you will find a black walnut bureau, or a bed with ruffled pillow cases. Indeed, much more importance is attached to finery than to comfort. Alas, these poor people know little or nothing of God, or Christ, or salvation; and so that they make the cross sufficiently often, or kiss the picture of some saint enough, or burn a wax candle or two, that is all of religion they suppose needed. And the worst thing is that most of them do not wish to know any thing better, and get angry when any attempt is made to enlighten and improve them." * * * *

"Your miniature, my dear P., now lays on the desk before me, and often do I kiss it while the tears fill my eyes, that I cannot see the dear original. Yes, my darling, Emmy's heart yearns after her little sis, and I can only find comfort in praying that God will prepare us to meet in heaven. This, you know, love, can never be, unless our hearts are changed by the Holy Spirit, and our sins forgiven for Christ's sake.

"I am glad that you like your studies, and hope you will never neglect your lessons for amusements. What new studies have you commenced beside French? I hope you will have great patience so that you will be able to write me a note in French, sometime. My teacher in Greek does not know a word of English, and the only way he can explain a difficulty, not understood in Greek, is through the French, though he generally gives all the lessons in Greek. I can understand educated people tolerably well in conversation, but the poor people make such a jumble of the language that I can hardly understand them at all. I hear the Italian more than the Greek, and as I studied that at home, it comes easier to speak Italian than Greek. So sometimes I talk Greek, sometimes Italian, sometimes French, but generally English. If I gave much attention to Italian, I could soon speak it with ease.

"There are a great many ragged, miserable children here in the street, who do not seem to have any one to take care of them. Every Saturday, many of these, together with the poor old men and women, go round and beg; and everybody gives them something, or else they would starve, for there are no poor-houses here, and they find it hard to get work. The principal thing on which they depend is the olive, which they use for food, and make into oil. There are tens of thousands of these trees in the islands. The trunks are perforated with innumerable holes, some very large, so that it seems impossible for the sap to find a place to run up into the tree. They have, too, a great many fruits; medlars, plums, cherries, apricots, mulberries in abundance, almonds, pears, figs, currants, grapes, strawberries, &c.

"My scholars love to read the Bible with us, every day, and some of them have learned a good deal about the Scriptures. I think they could tell me more than you can. Will you not read the Bible more, dear sister, and tell what you read? For if you do not read the precious word of God, how can you be saved? I want you to read it, not because you *ought*, but because you love it. I want you to repent and come to Jesus, taking his yoke upon you which is easy, and his burden which is light. And now may God bless my dear little sister, and give her grace to love and serve him, so that we may meet in heaven through Jesus.

"Your loving sister

"EMMY."

TO MISS S. T. BOSWORTH.

"*Corfu, June* 13, 1844.

"MY MUCH LOVED SARAH:—Your letter was a blessed feast to me. I read it over and over again, when dimming tears did not obscure my sight. Very dear, my sweet sister, have you been to me since those 'days lang syne,' when we exchanged our little notes and held brief conversations on the great subject of salvation. Each interview for the last two years has greatly strengthened that tender tie. May God seal its consummation in heaven. Yes, precious indeed has been a throne of grace, a refuge unspeakably sweet in this distant land. There the anguished heart has been soothed and consoled; there anxious forebodings, exchanged for trusting faith; there the soul, unbound by space, has borne in earnest supplication before God the absent loved, with whom in this holy exercise it was again united; there the flagging spirit has been strengthened to wield the armor of the gospel with fresh vigor, and there mountain obstacles have vanished into naught. Many intensely interesting subjects are daily pressing on my mind here, and fill my heart at the mercy-seat with petitions. But at the evening hour, I love to bring before the throne my loved ones far away, and sometimes I have sweet enjoyment in praying for them. There may we often meet.

"I cannot tell you, Sarah, what my feelings were at the moment of leaving my native land. I awoke that morning, troubled and doubting; my soul shrunk from the terrible trial, the bitter parting before me. I felt a fear that I should faint in the trying hour, and my soul was distressed for my darling mother. I wrestled with God for light, for strength, for faith. Like Sampson, I prayed that for *this once*, the Lord would uphold. I begged, I implored, I could not be denied; and I felt a sort of assurance that the blessed text for the day, '*As thy days so shall thy strength be*,' would be verified. Some of my dear family left early in the morning, and my soul was wrung with anguish. But when the hour came that I must bid farewell to that precious home, where was all I held dearest on earth, when I visited room after room, each dear to memory by a thousand hallowed associations, though I felt my cheek blanch, and my heart beat fainter, yet in that moment, that text came with most soothing, sustaining power, '*Peace I leave with you.*' Yes, it was peace such as I scarcely ever felt before; a calm, quiet, composed trust in God, that took away the sting of even *that parting.*

"The vessel was thronged with dear pupils, and the wharf lined with loved friends and schoolmates. A few brief words, a hurried kiss, one last embrace, and then having sought God's blessing, the last link was severed of earthly, visible communing. The hymn sung was that commencing,

'O'er the gloomy hills of darkness,'

and the prayer was offered by our pastor, Mr. Green. Every feeling was absorbed in one intense desire, that God would support dear mother, and I have reason to bless him for his gracious answers in her behalf.

"We had a stormy passage, but were never in any imminent danger, and passed the straits of Gibraltar, on the fifth of February. That was a most exciting day to us. The sight of land again and habitable abodes, the new and picturesque scenes on every side, the gorgeous Mediterranean sunset, never witnessed before, all conspired to impress it deeply on our minds. Thence we had a very quick, delightful passage to Corfu, where we landed on the 17th. The city presents a very picturesque appearance to one entering the harbor; but, like most Eastern cities, its beauties grew less as we entered within its confines.

"There was a desolateness about the deserted house, which, you know, had been occupied by Mr. Love, and a strangeness which was saddening to the feelings. But I never enjoyed the presence of God, or the sweetness of dependence on him, more than during those first days. We felt alone, yet not alone, for God seemed nearer than even in our happy land. Our dear friend, Mrs. D., had suffered much for some months before our arrival, having first fallen from a carriage, and afterwards been run over by a horse; both of which accidents were followed by fever and repeated attacks of illness. She was, however, busy in her labors of love; and the first day of March I entered upon my duties as her associate. The dear flock under our care is composed of Greeks, Jews, Italians, Maltese, Scotch, English, and Irish. These are Protestants, Catholics, members of the Greek church, of the Jewish synagogue, &c. The English are the children of the soldiers stationed here by England, to protect the Ionian Isles; the rest are natives of Corfu. Most of the latter understand English or Italian; which last is the language of the Jewesses, and indeed to a great extent of Corfu; for this island was so long under the Venetians, that the Greek language is quite supplanted in the city. All who can read, read the Bible daily; and I, who cannot yet speak much in any other tongue, spend a most delightful hour daily in my English Bible class. Six of the number are Corfuotes who understand English. Very often much tenderness is manifested; and our prayer is for the life-giving influences of the Holy Spirit, that it may not prove like morning dew. The Jewesses too are a very interesting company, and I feel a strong attachment to many of them. They at present study only the Old Testament; our object being to lead them to see that Jesus of Nazareth is He 'of whom Moses in the law and the prophets did write.'

"You know that this is a garrisoned city. There are some two thousand or more English soldiers here, mostly ungodly, immoral scoffers, under the command of officers who may be more secret in the indulgence of vice, but who are equally lovers of pleasure, and children of wrath. Yet here, as in Sodom, God has 'a little remnant according to the election of grace.' Of this very small number, two are Baptist brethren, and these have united with us in a semi-weekly prayer meeting. These meetings, which have been unspeakably precious, God has been pleased to bless to the conversion of two very interesting young men, and the restoration of another who had wandered from the fold. These three are now requesting baptism, and most delightful has it been this evening, to listen to their account of the dealings of God with their souls.

"In view of these precious mercies, you will not expect me to write of regrets, and wishes to return. No, yearning as my desires often are for home, and a sight of those I love, I wish to remain, while the Lord permits, in this part of his vineyard; and I bless him for the privilege. I greatly feel my need of qualifications, especially of humble, close walking with God. Corfu is very different from a missionary station among the uncivilized and rude. All the ensnarements of fashionable Christianity, the seductions of polished society, and the artificiality of European manners, are met with here, and it requires great grace to resist them. Pray for me, dearest, in view of them.

"You speak of feeling dissatisfied, because your present circumstances will not allow you to do all you could wish for missions. Indeed, love, while you can pray, you can do very much. It would afford me more joy to hear of one who was praying fervently and believingly for our dear mission, than to learn of a donation of hundreds of dollars. It is the Holy Spirit we want, and that 'gift of God cannot be purchased with money.' With his influence, the smallest means can accomplish mighty results—two may chase a thousand; but unblest by his presence, the most formidable array of men and means will be as useless as a straw. All that men and money can do has been done for Greece; at least very much has been done thus; but all that God can do has *not* been tried. This is emphatically the one thing. If you will offer for us the effectual fervent prayer, it will be a richer donation than thousands of silver. Besides, dear sister, this is the gift God asks at your hand. To murmur that it is no other, is to rebel against him.

"I feel for you, dearest, in these dark hours. I know you suffer keenly the loss of what once secured you much earthly enjoyment and influence. But do not doubt the love of that kind Physician who mixed the bitter potion. If his dear hand present the cup, drink it to the dregs, assured that his own soft hand shall yet wipe away every tear."

The following is her description of the three converts referred to in the preceding letter. "These soldiers have warmly interested me. The difference and yet oneness of their feelings are alike pleasing. A. is simple, frank, and whole-hearted. Lack of religious privileges has prevented him from obtaining as clear views of the way of justification through an atoning Saviour as we could wish. But this deficiency in the outset, has made us experience more delight in witnessing his growth in grace, and in the knowledge of divine things. There is a quiet, abiding happiness manifest in his every feature, which tells of peace within.——" B. is tender, child-like, devoted; his countenance ever expressing the sadness of deep penitence mingled with sober joy in God. He is also more clear in his views of sin and reliance on Jesus.——C. has a distinctness of perception, a strength of purpose, and a high fervor of soul which lead us to hope that he is a chosen vessel, destined for peculiar service in the cause of Christ. There is a thoughtful resoluteness in his face which shows that he has counted well the cost.

" Differing as they do in these characteristics, there is a striking uniformity in their entire renunciation of their former bad habits, their thorough abandonment of their dissolute companions, their great delight in reading the word of God, and in prayer, and their strong attachment to us and to each other.

" These prayer meetings are refreshing as the oasis in the desert to the parched, weary traveler. Amid the spiritual deadness around us, whose paralyzing influence we dread to feel, these blessed hours have had a most vivifying, strengthening power. Brother C. feelingly remarked last week that he thought God had sent us to the Rifle Brigade. We hope, indeed, that was one of his purposes who is wonderful in working. These converts will, we trust, be baptized within a month. Two of these had pious mothers. It is affecting to see the tears roll down their sun-burnt cheeks, as they express their regret for their long inattention to the pious counsels of their dear parents, who went down to the grave unblest by a sight of their children's conversion.

"One of them at the time his seriousness commenced, was engaged to act in the theatre here. For the English officers employ the soldiers to act plays for them, and indeed sometimes appear themselves on the stage. But this young soldier, though already prepared, resolved to give up his part, and no persuasion or ridicule could induce him to alter his purpose. He has since said, that alarmed in view of his danger as an impenitent sinner, he was resolved to give up all these unhallowed pleasures, though, supposing he should always feel a craving for these sinful amusements, which he was fully determined to renounce, he expected never to find any more happiness. But to his astonishment, when thus willing to give up all for Christ, he found that not only was the love of these pleasures taken away, but in its stead his soul was filled with a pure and holy joy, compared with which all the happiness he had ever found in the world was nothing. It is indeed delightful to hear him talk and see the change."

CHAPTER XV.

Baptism of three soldiers—Mrs. Dickson visits Scotland—Visit from Mrs. Buel—Dependence on the Holy Spirit—Their missionary labors—Visit to the country—Description of their country residence—Meetings with the villagers—Interest of the scholars in missions and temperance—Of society in general—Letter to Mrs. Crocker.

The first day of July, 1844, was another bright spot in the experience of our dear missionary friends at Corfu; for on this day the three soldiers, who had for some time given pleasing evidence of a change of heart, received the solemn rite of baptism at the hands of Rev. Mr. Arnold. Of this interesting season Miss W. thus writes: "Our three soldier brethren having unitedly addressed a letter to Mr. Arnold, requesting baptism at his hands, our little church held a meeting for the relation of their Christian experience. We had enjoyed many opportunities of conversing with them, and their daily lives bearing delightful testimony to the sincerity of their Christian experience, we felt abundantly satisfied that they had been born of the Spirit. Accordingly on the 1st of July, at 5, A. M., we rode out, about two miles, to the place which had been selected for the ordinance, where we were met by our other two brethren and the three candidates who had walked out together. It was a beautiful spot on the sea-shore, where a little romantic cut in the hills opened a path to the water's edge. The green banks rose on either side, crowned with the olive, and decked with wild flowers; while beyond lay the glassy waters unrippled by a zephyr, reflecting, as from a perfect mirror, the golden rays of the rising sun. Not a sound was to be heard save the singing of birds, warbling their matin lay. The candidates having been prepared, we gathered on the sea-shore, and the songs of Zion, probably for the first time, rose from that little lonely dell. Those rocky cliffs then echoed to the voice of prayer, as, bowing before God, we invoked the presence of the adorable Trinity, in whose name this ordinance was to be performed. As we rose, two or three Greek caiques crossed the bay, and one of them, being attracted perhaps by our singing as our voices again rose in praise, struck their oars and witnessed the, to them, unwonted scene. Our beloved brother Arnold administered the ordinance with the solemnity and propriety which mark all his religious services, and we were all ready to say,

'Lord, what on earth can sweeter be
Than thus to come and follow thee?'

"Re-assembling in Mr. Arnold's study, we had a most delightful prayer meeting; and never were there happier beings than these young soldiers as they poured forth their broken, tearful thanksgivings for God's rich grace to them-ward."

But though their hearts were delighted and refreshed with these sweet streams by the way, they felt that their work was particularly among the Greeks. Of these there were some inquirers who appeared interested, and who at times seemed to manifest the spirit of Christ, but of none of them had they confident hopes that they had been born again. Speaking in reference to one of these, whom their little church had declined receiving, Miss W. remarks :

"It seems vastly important, that in restoring pure religion to a corrupt church, the first models should be cast in the finest mould, should bear a marked resemblance to the blessed Original, and present a striking contrast to that which here bears the name of Christianity. The attention of the people must be arrested by witnessing the living power of vital religion in the life,—a holy walk,—a sensitive conscience,—a close and manifest adherence to the principles of the gospel in all the minutiae of daily duty,—these, in the hands of God, seem to me the most effectual weapons with which to batter down the strong holds of superstition. The power of argument, or force of reasoning, may induce some to come and hear the new thing, but will never affect the heart. The first examples then of real Christianity which we offer them, should meet this exigency; and for this reason, it seems to me, we should look well at the character of the stones at the foundation; if these be defective what can we expect from the building? I would not indeed be *over-cautious*, nor expect perfection from those just emerged from darkness, but I would be slow to act."

On the 6th of July Mrs. Dickson left Corfu, with the intention of spending a few months in Scotland. This threw the care of the school principally upon Miss Waldo; though Mrs. Buel came from Athens and spent six weeks with them, so that she had the assistance of Mrs.

Buel in the forenoon, and of Mrs. Arnold in the afternoon.

"We feel deeply," says she, "the absence of our dear and valued friend, Mrs. Dickson, the savory influence of whose godly and faithful instructions was felt by all the members of the school. The children parted with their loved instructress with many tears, and earnest wishes for a prosperous voyage, and a speedy return. I almost shrink from the responsibility of taking upon myself the care of a school which she has so long and so well conducted, sustaining so varied relations, and involving so many important interests. Young, and inexperienced in the peculiarities of this peculiar place, knowing that one misstep might entail sad consequences, I realize more than ever my own weakness and deficiencies, and the need of constant guidance and strength from above to keep me in the right path."

"Were there but one class of pupils in the school, one interest to consider, one end to accomplish, there would be less cause for anxiety. True there is but one great object before us, the everlasting salvation of our charge, and their instruction in what is useful, so far as this is in our power. But a plan which may seem best calculated to accomplish this for the English, may be injurious to the Greeks, or be to the neglect of the Jewesses. How these three divers interests, requiring three different classes of means, and the use of three entirely different languages, can be secured, is often a subject of anxious thought, and not the easiest of problems to solve. I am now enjoying the invaluable services of my dear sisters, Mrs. Arnold and Mrs. Buel, to both of whom I am most deeply indebted."

"It would seem that with so much help I should have but little to do; but one needs to fill the place, in order to form any idea of the amount of labor to be done. Our school now numbers 60, not a dozen of whom regularly bring work of their own to school, so that work must be cut out and fitted for the rest daily; their writing books must be ruled, as well as have copies set; and then they have been so little accustomed to order, that the constant regulation of the school requires no small amount of time. One must be addressed in English, another in Italian, and a third in Greek; and a look here, or a word there, are almost constantly required to restrain their volatile dispositions. Yet they appear interested in their studies, desirous to improve, and not wholly unmindful of their everlasting welfare. Most of those who have been any time in the school, can answer almost any question on Scripture history, or evangelical doctrine, with correctness, and sometimes with peculiar appropriateness. They love to examine subjects by proof texts, and are never more pleased than when referred to chapter and verse. They like too to have their feelings excited, and perhaps are too prone to a sort of self-complacency, when a close appeal to their consciences produces tears. One or two of them, however, have, I think, often had very serious feelings; but in these cases we have had to bear the disappointment of seeing them detained at home by their parents, on some trivial excuse, till other subjects have diverted their attention from their soul's welfare. This was the case with a little girl who understands English very well and could therefore be more profited by Bible instruction. But her profligate mother could not endure the reproof which her child's seriousness administered, and soon put an end to it. Another interesting little Catholic, whose pensive face often spoke of inward feeling, and whose falling tears often wet her Bible as she listened to the truth, has been kept at home for some weeks. Sometimes they inform us that they have told their parents or sisters that they ought to have new hearts, and have met with only ridicule and rebuff. O pray for the descent of the Holy Spirit on these dear youth; without his quickening influence all will be in vain. Never did I so realize that it is eminently his work to convince of sin, as since I came here. Man can do every thing else, but here his power fails; and never does one feel so impotent as when attempting to make a sinner *feel* the truths to which his understanding assents."

Speaking of their missionary work in general, under date of July 22, she writes: "To one a stranger to this field, it might indeed seem a day of very small things; but to one on the spot, who can realize the numerous and weighty obstacles in the way of the spread of truth, things would wear a different aspect. The great means employed by us is the reading the gospel with them, and making such explanations as our exceedingly imperfect knowledge of the language will allow. Mr. Arnold has had thirteen different Greeks to read with him, sometimes seven at a time, and these interviews have often elicited most pleasing remarks and feelings. Mrs. Arnold has a class of Greek girls, some thirteen or fourteen in number, of whom seven or eight are sometimes present together. They have more than once been affected to tears by her appeals, translated to them by our servant, who herself seems not far from the kingdom of heaven.

17

I have had some very pleasant readings with one or two poor women who do not know a letter.

"You would have been interested had you been in my room last Sabbath. I had been reading to them, and trying in my stammering Greek to explain a little, when I was called away for a moment, and they began to talk with each other about the ignorance in which they were kept. As I returned they exclaimed very earnestly, 'Why don't they read what we can understand in the church? We don't know what the priest reads.' Ah, said I, how can you do God's will if you don't understand it? Then by some familiar illustrations, I endeavored to realize to them the necessity of knowing God's word if we would do his will. They felt the force of my remarks, and shaking their heads significantly, sighed, and said, 'How can we understand?' I then told them how it was in our country—how the people were instructed in the gospel every Lord's day, and at other times. They listened with deep interest, casting approving glances, and uttering exclamations of delight. I then told them we had come here, because we had heard in our own country that they had none to teach them, and we wanted their souls to be saved. We had not come for money or pleasure, but in hopes to save some of them. At this they expressed still greater delight and astonishment; but when I told them I had a dear mother in America, who wept much when I came away, but who said she was willing I should come, if I could only be the means of saving some one, the tears came into their eyes, they raised their hands in wonder, and prayed that it might be so."

On the 5th of August Mrs. Buel returned home to Peireans, and Miss W. having suffered much from exhaustion and headache, occasioned in part by the extreme heat, but mainly resulting from her increased responsibilities, concluded to take a vacation of a few weeks. Just at this time, Mr. Arnold and his family received an invitation to spend a few weeks at the house of a friend of his, near the village Gasturi. This house, which was called Palatino's place, from the name of its owner, was, according to the custom of the country, furnished, but not occupied; and as it was offered them rent-free, they very gratefully accepted the invitation.

In a letter to her mother, dated August 13, 1844, she thus describes their temporary home:

"The house we occupy stands on quite an elevation, commanding a fine view of the city, and the circumjacent country. The green vineyards and the quiet lake lie between us and the distant fortifications which cover the principal heights in the city. Behind us towers the lofty summit of Santa Deka, whose base, and the intervening valley, are shaded with the soft foliage of the olive; while to its very top, interspersed among the rocks, may be seen the terraced vineyards, defying the burning sun and the parched earth, to deprive them of their rich, soft verdure. When I tell you that we have not had a single shower from the 5th of June till the 11th instant, and then not much rain fell, you might suppose that not a green thing could be left; but, on the contrary, the whole country around wears the softest, richest, freshest green. Instead of fields of grain or vegetables, of clover or meadow, as far almost as the eye can reach, can be seen only the grape and the currant; and these requiring heat rather than moisture, flourish through all this long drought.

"These fruits are now ripening, and are indeed superior to any thing in the United States. The clusters of the currants especially, are unlike any thing I ever saw; being as long sometimes as the arm between the wrist and elbow, and crowded on the stems as compactly as possible, so that nothing can be seen of the stalk to which they are attached. They are of a light purple, and of honeyed sweetness. Of the grapes, the Mascatella, a very spicy fruit, is just ripening; and here we find the Sweet Water, the Malaga, and other varieties. The portico, in the rear of this house, some six or more feet wide, and extending the length of the building, is entirely overshaded with beautiful vines, whose pendant clusters, of varied size and hue, might tempt the most epicurean taste.

"We have secured one blessing here which was quite beyond our reach in the city,—that of quiet; and you should live in Corfu a month, to appreciate the greatness of this blessing to us. The busy streets of Boston may echo to the din of rattling wagons and noisy artisans all the day, but with night comes the stillness suited to repose. But in Corfu the stillest hours in the twenty-four are between noon and 2, P. M., and the evening ushers in a series of noises which bid defiance to sleep and rest. The streets are so narrow, that even elevated as our flat is, we seem all 'out of doors'—as we used to say; and all the conversation of the streets, echoed back from the high plastered walls around us, may be heard quite distinctly. When these street-walkers and musicians sleep, is more than I know; but at any hour of the night their loud songs and hideous noises may be heard, as to and fro they pace the streets and lanes. And then much of the religion of the Greeks consists in ringing bells. You may conceive of the distraction of having six or eight bells, within a stone's throw, ringing as our fire bells do, ten or a dozen times a day. But now, to our delight, we have got quite out of the hearing of bells, except at evening, that distant chime which is always grateful to the ear. The locust's hum, and the cricket's song are our only music here.

" But you will think I have forgotten that I am a missionary, if I have so much to say about all these worldly matters. No, dearest mother, I hope not; only I am the same being that I ever was, sensitive to the same annoyances, and alive to the same delights, as in other days. But we are trying to be missionaries even here, and indeed we are more pleased with the opportunities that this place affords of doing good to the Greeks, than with the city. The family that live on this place and have the care of it, consisting of a man, his wife, two bright, but wholly uneducated boys, and an infant girl, have been in at our family devotions in Greek, every morning and evening since we came. And besides this, the villagers, from the distance of two or three miles, have come to hear the Scriptures read. On Sabbath last, we had twenty adults and a number of youth who sat an hour or more listening to us, while we read to them the gospel. One only of the whole company could read. How delighted you would have been, dear mother, to have seen that interesting group, seated on the grass in front of our house,—mothers with infants on their arms, and interesting young maidens in their national costume, all listening so attentively to the word of eternal life.

They are much delighted with our sacred music as we sing Greek hymns to *our* tunes.

"We find these villagers, particularly the females, unable to read or write, and yet naturally bright, and willing to learn. One man offered to build us a house, and get us plenty of scholars, if we would come and teach the children in his village. Yet no doubt if we should remain long among them, and labor with any success for their spiritual welfare, we should experience much opposition from these very country people, now so kind and courteous. They have the same sinful hearts which all men possess, and do not naturally love or desire a religion which will cut them off from all hope of being saved, while they live in sin and ungodliness. It is easier for them to fast, and go through all the burdensome requirements and ceremonies of their church, than to give up those cherished sins of heart and life, which the holy word of God denounces and proscribes without compromise. This innate love of sin, of which every human being is conscious, and which, if honest with himself, he must confess, is the real foundation, the main spring of all the opposition which the truth experiences, either in Christian, or heathen lands. While man remains what he now is, so long, dear mother, must the faithful teacher of the truth of God meet with opposition. What the apostle said almost two thousand years ago, is still true, '*The carnal mind is enmity against God,*' not merely is it at enmity, but it is enmity itself, the very essence of hostility.

"And now, dear mother, how gladly would I exchange this slow pen for the use of speech; how I should love to whisper in your ear the dear name of mother, and feel again your warm kiss on my brow. Yes, dearest mother your dwelling is my earthly pole star. But is it not sweet to think of that city not built with hands, whose inhabitants go no more out, where the pang of separation is never felt, nor the dread of losing what we love ever harasses us? There, dearest, we shall meet, I hope. There may God allow me to welcome you home, and O may none of our dear little circle be missing there; so that when

> 'One by one we pass away,
> As star by star grows dim,
> May each, translated into day,
> Be lost and found in him.'"

By the same mail she writes of her school as follows:

"School closed quite interestingly, and I am longing to return to my dear charge, hoping to re-commence my labors in the strength of the Lord. The last Bible lesson we had together, was an occasion to be remembered, when a number seemed to feel the importance of setting their faces Zion-ward; though, alas, they soon forget the impressions which God's truth makes upon them.

"They have, for some months past, taken up a little collection among themselves on the first Monday in the month. As our school closed on the Saturday preceding the monthly concert, they asked if they might bring their contributions on Saturday. On Saturday morning they reminded me that I had promised to tell them about missions, and would not be satisfied until I had assured them that I would do so.

"Nor have they forgotten what was said to them some time ago in reference to temperance. We have rather refrained from saying much on this subject, or of urging them forward in this matter, knowing the strong prejudice which almost universally exists here against total abstinence, and aware that many were ready to say, the children were forced into an engagement the nature of which they did not understand. In view of all this it has been very pleasing to witness their repeated manifestations of unabated interest, and especially to hear them inquire 'When may we take the pledge? Have we not been tried long enough? We never wish to taste any more wine.' Some of them, under very strong temptations, have manifested a firmness of purpose in reference to this matter, which we could hardly have anticipated."

Of the society in general at Corfu, she remarks, "This is a very wicked place, and great indeed must be the supplies of grace which shall enable one here to walk with God—to lead that hidden life with Christ, which the world knows not of. It is not the gross licentiousness, the open immorality here, which are a snare to the Christian's feet, but it is the subtle, insidious influence of a worldly Christianity. It is not the superstition of the Greeks, but the earthliness of a temporising Protestantism whose deadening influence dries up vital piety, true godliness, and heavenly mindedness. To defy this influence, seems like attempting to breathe a pure air amid the fetid vapors of a putrid marsh.

"Ours are not the sufferings and exposures, the toils and privations of the missionary to barbarous tribes; we are not compelled to dwell in a rude hut, a log cabin, or a frail mat tenement; we are not deprived of wonted nutriment, and forced to an unwholesome diet; we do not suffer from the severities of an Indian winter, nor are we scorched by the burning sun of Siam and Burmah; we are not cut off from the refinements of civilized life and cultivated society. No, ours are the trials of hope deferred that maketh the heart sick, of weary waiting for some sign of returning life among the dead, of longing for some opening door through which to enter with the gospel of salvation to thousands who are perishing. These trials are not so tangible as the former, they may not so easily arouse the sensibilities, and awaken the sympathies of others, but they wear far more upon the spirit, they call even more for the prayers of God's people."

The same day on which Mr. and Mrs. Arnold and Miss W. sailed from Boston for Corfu, Rev. William G. Crocker and wife sailed from the same port for the Bassa mission on the western coast of Africa. The news of the death of Mr. C. having reached Greece about this time, Miss W. addressed the following note

TO MRS. M. B. CROCKER.

"My Beloved and Bereaved Sister:—Little did I imagine when I parted with you on the wharf last new year's day, that our first intelligence from you would be of so afflicting a nature. My heart did indeed sometimes misgive me, when I looked on your face flushed with health, in the fear that Africa's burning fever might lay you low, but that you would so soon be left alone in a land of strangers did not enter my mind. Mysterious indeed, my dear Mrs. C., are God's dealings with his children. '*His paths are in great waters, and his footsteps are not known.*' But how sweet to the child of God to be able to cast himself undoubtingly on that unchanging love which orders alike the sunshine and the shade; which mingles in the most healthful proportions the bitter and the sweet. When such a hand administers the cup of sorrow, who would not drink it to the dregs? I rejoice to learn that his consolations have abounded towards you, and that you have been enabled to stay yourself on him. May he continue to be your light and strength, and preserve you to labor long for him in dark Africa.

"When this melancholy news arrived, my mind instantly reverted to the little closet in Newburyport, where we bowed together in prayer, seeking direction and help from above; and I felt assured that the prayer you then offered was heard, and would now be answered in blessings and comfort, by the '*God of all consolation.*'

"In such sorrow as this human sympathy seems almost an intrusion, and the stricken spirit loves in silence to commune alone with God—with that dear Redeemer who '*Suffered being tempted, that he might be a merciful and faithful High Priest' for us.* To him therefore I fervently commend you; and unable myself to offer any balm to soothe your anguish, I would implore for you the sweet solacings of the blessed Comforter.

"That he may ever be with you, prays

"Your attached and sympathizing sister,

"EMILY WALDO."

CHAPTER XVI.

Affectionate remembrance of home—Account of some of her friends at Corfu—Mrs. Arnold's illness—Her religious feelings—Return of Mrs. Dickson.

From the time Miss W. first decided upon connecting herself with the Greek mission, she never seemed to give place to a single regret, at the sacrifices she had necessarily made. True her sources of happiness far exceeded those which many of our missionaries enjoy. She ever spoke in the strongest terms of the kindness and devoted attentions of her fellow missionaries. She was happy too in her work, and ready to notice and enjoy every rill of pleasure which a kind Providence had placed in her way. Yet with a heart keenly alive to the endearments of home, and which never could forget the sweet attractions of early and sanctified friendship, it was impossible that she should not, at times, feel the greatness of the sacrifice she had made, though her love to Christ forbade any wish to recall it. Her letters abound in expressions of strong attachment to her friends, excelled only by her stronger devotion to Christ, and the work to which he had called her. It would therefore be injustice to that loving heart of hers, did we not occasionally give place to the deep gushings of its warm affections as expressed in the following extracts.

TO MISS S. P. CARTER.

"*Sept.* 12, 1844.

"I wonder, Sarah, if you ever feel those strange, deep yearnings after me, which I feel at times for you. I can't describe them; they must be felt to be understood. At such times my heart seems drawn almost to painfulness towards you; the links of love that bind me to you, tighten and tighten around my heart till the compression is almost more than I can bear. My spirit yearns for that unburthening and commingling of heart, which was the honey-drop of our intercourse. Say, do you thus think of me, dear Sarah, especially at that noiseless hour we chose to consecrate to mutual prayer?

Whether safe moored in love's retreat,
  Or severed wide by mount and sea,
This hour in spirit we would meet,
  And urge to heaven our mutual plea.
Oh tell me if this hallowed hour
  Still finds thee constant at our shrine,
Still witnesses thy fervent prayer
  Ascending warm and true with mine.
Faithful through every change of woe,
  My heart shall fly to meet thee there;
'T would soothe this very heart to know
  That thine responded every prayer.

Yet do I need an assurance? Do I not know that it does thus respond? Forgive the doubt. But will you never again place your arm around me, never more imprint your fond kiss on my cheek, never more whisper words of affection in my ear? How can I resign all hope of this? O faith! rise above earth; anticipate that blessed reunion of the redeemed in heaven. Think how sweet to meet, all purified from sin, all delivered from temptations, all free from fear of parting more, possessed with angelic power to love intensely, sincerely. O may this hope never prove presumptuous, unfounded. But ah, 'these gloomy doubts that rise! Yet, Jesus is my only trust, my sole portion; and his precious blood, O will it not wash away my crimson stains? A few more days of toil, a few more nights of sorrow, and the pilgrim race is run, the goal is gained, we meet in heaven."

TO HER MOTHER.

"*Corfu, Sept.* 19, 1844.

"My Most Beloved Mother:—Surely there never was a child blessed with such a dear, devoted mother as your unworthy Emily has. How do these three closely written sheets that lie before me, tell of a mother's undying remembrance of her absent, though ever present child. O that for one hour, my blessed, my all but idolized mother, I could once more press you to this heart, that throbs with such quick pulsations as your dear image fills my mind. O why did I not oftener enjoy that precious privilege of emptying my heart into yours when I was by your side? Why did I so often allow that secretiveness, which is a part of my very being, to shut up thoughts and emotions that often ached to be set free? I feel sometimes, when my heart yearns so for you again, that I cannot be denied, that just one hour, just once more, I must see you. O I had such a sweet dream a little while since, when I went home and saw you all and was just as I used to be. It quite comforted and refreshed me; though it could not give such comfort as the hope that I shall meet an angel-mother in the blessed family of the first born in heaven.

"But your dear letters! Most acceptable, most precious was every word; all the minutiae of changes and improvements; yes, every sentence was of deep moment to me, and had I time I would dwell on each. The wedding in particular, must have been very interesting, I could almost fancy myself there. Dear, dear Charles! O may he ever be true to those sweet and holy vows, and long, long enjoy the bliss of a happy home. But for my beloved brother and his sweet wife, I must wish something even more than this; and nightly do I plead for them that they may have a treasure in heaven, a home of cloudless joy above.

"Those papers too—you can hardly imagine my emotion as the familiar words, *Evening Journal*, met my eye, and the well known type, form, and arrangement, recalled to me the days when the question, 'Has the paper come?' was uttered by one dear sister after another, until the wonted rap announced its arrival. And still more tender are the memories of that tea-table where it was read, at whose head sat my darling mother, and around, loved sisters, brother, cousins, and friends. The room, each article of furniture, the table, all, O how vividly do they now rise before me. I can almost join in the pleasant chat, and taste with you the tea and cakes. How pleasant to think that those papers had been in your hands, your eyes had rested on the same words, you had uttered similar expressions of sorrow at the awful events narrated therein, and raised the same prayers to heaven for its gracious interposition.

* * * * *

"We have found one pleasant Greek family here-with

whom I believe I have never made you acquainted. It consists of a gentleman and lady, two interesting daughters, and a little son. The girls, merry, laughing creatures, remind me so much of my own dear sisters, that as they twine their arms around me, and call me Emily, I can almost imagine it is a sister near, till the attempt to reply to their ceaseless questions in this strange tongue dispels the charm. The lady is such a dear motherly woman, so domestic, so cheerful, and making one so much at home, that she often brings my dear mother to mind, especially as she is of your height and figure.

"The father is a most interesting, well-read, and intelligent gentleman, though a thorough Greek in his faith, or rather practice. We have very many interesting conversations on the truth, and he often makes concessions in reference to our belief, and his own church, at which we wonder. He has, however, two strong holds in which to take refuge from all the attacks we would make upon his errors from the word of God. First, the church's irreversible authority to decree what she please, either in matters of faith or practice. Here he rests secure, and this point he will never yield; from her authority he dares not appeal. A second, which is his uniform argument against the pure and spiritual faith, is the belief that the temperament of the Greek nation requires a material religion, one of visible objects of worship, something tangible by the senses. He says that in northern temperaments, among people more cool and immaterial, a pure faith may flourish without all these external symbols, but not among Greeks. While he possesses such feelings, we cannot hope that he will accept the unadulterated gospel; yet we cannot but feel deeply interested in such a man, as also in his very kind family.

"Among our English friends is an interesting family of ladies, Mrs. ——, her mother, and an only daughter, a sweet girl of twelve, sensitive, graceful, witty and loving, the pet of all who know her. Mrs. P's history is one of deep interest. Her father was an English consul at Algiers, and resident for many years in different parts of the Mediterranean. She herself was born at Gibraltar, under the American flag, and, with her only brother, was the idol of her parents. When a mere girl, her father was lost at sea, and soon after, his property, through some technicalities of law, was taken from his family who were left in comparatively straitened circumstances. At this time, she became acquainted with a young, fascinating Greek, of family, but not of great fortune, and still very young, married him. But alas, the bright sunshine of domestic joy was soon darkly clouded. The young bride found that her husband was a profligate, and all entreaty and persuasion failing to reform him, she bade him farewell, and returned broken-hearted to her early friends; preferring labor for her support rather than life with such opprobrium. A sweet babe became a relief to her sad heart, and in that child her life has been bound up. About two years or more since, she was led to find a friend in Jesus, faithful and true, and her lacerated heart has found a healing balm in the faith of the gospel, the promises and the grace of God. This blessed change she attributes in part, under God, to the instrumentality of dear Mrs. Buel to whom she is devotedly attached. She came here a year ago to teach, but is now expecting to leave for Malta in October, much to our regret, for we have found in her, more than in any one else, a kindred spirit. Though not American, yet she is so gentle, affectionate, pleasant though sad, that we cannot but love her, especially when is added that strongest of all bonds, common love to a common Saviour. When the evening shades have gathered around us, and we are weary with the cares of the day, it is very pleasant to slip on our bonnets, and run over to Mrs. ——'s, where we ever have a warm welcome, and spend a pleasant hour; or to hear their footsteps on the stairs, and share with them our home joys.

"We have also very kind friends in Rev. Mr. and Mrs. Lowndes, missionaries of the London Missionary Society. They are older than we are, but are especially kind in sickness and sorrow. They are now absent on a journey, and we miss our pleasant visits at their hospitable dwelling.

"You see then, dear mother, that we are not shut out from Christian society, or Christian friendship; but in this far away isle, a few hearts are becoming linked to ours by the chains of love. But never, O never imagine that they loosen in the least degree those golden cords, that, stretching across the broad Atlantic, bind me to my home, my early friends. Far otherwise; they but freshen, and quicken remembrance of that by-gone, that sweet intercourse, till busy memory makes the past present, and we are again among the scenes of our native land.

"You speak of change, dearest mother, and truly it is written on all below. Were it not, what would unlink these earth-bound hearts, and raise them to the skies? Our father wishes to bring his children home, and dearly as he would have them love each other, and grateful as he would have them be for his kind provisions by the way, it must be a grief, humanly speaking, if his offspring turn no wistful gaze to their Father's house, and feel no earnest longing to see that Father's face, in pure, unalloyed bliss. God grant, beloved mother, that all our little company may meet in heaven,—that none of us may be so beguiled, either with the shining dust, or the gay flowers that deck the road, as to refuse to look upward to the dazzling glories of the upper sanctuary, our heavenly home. When shall this anxious heart find rest in a well-grounded hope of such a reunion? Dear brother and sisters, O do not fail to seek admission to the mansions of rest, ere the door be closed. And now, dearest mother, I commend you anew to that gracious God who has thus far heard my prayers for you. May he ever bless you, prays

"Your own fond

"EMMY."

TO HER MOTHER.

"*Oct.* 21.

"As usual this month finds me at a late hour commencing a letter to my beloved and distant parent. Indeed I am unusually pressed; for the dear friends of whom I wrote you in my last, Mrs. P. and family, are just leaving Corfu, and their lonely situation, aggravated by the unkindness of some here who should have been friends, has deepened our affection and sympathy for them, so that we could not deny ourselves the happiness of devoting every leisure moment to such expressions of kindness as affection prompted, and which were most soothing to their tried feelings. I know my own sweet mother would love them so much, and would devote herself so much to them, that I feel 'tis her own guardian spirit that prompts me to ask, What can I do for these sad hearts? They embarked on Saturday, the 19th, but being driven back by a storm, are now with us, waiting for a change of weather. When I came home from school to-day, Emily came running down stairs to meet me, just as my own dear sisters used to do, when foot-worn and weary, I returned from school to my own loved home. And dear Mrs. T., the grandmother, said as I came into my room, 'I have been looking with so much pleasure at your mother's miniature, it is such a sweet face, I know I should love her.' And that, you know, dearest mother, made me love her so much more. You will not blame me then, mother, I know, that I have less time to write you, especially as I shall write again by the middle mail.

"Matters with us pursue the even tenor of their way. Among the Greeks there is nothing of special note. Some are very kind, but have no desire to receive any religious instruction; and others who have been enlightened are yet afraid to avow their desire for a purer faith. Yet we trust there is a little leaven in this vast mass, which by God's effectual working shall leaven the whole lump. The feeble efforts which we put forth seem to be as nothing; but God, we rejoice to remember, delights to use the weak things of the world, to confound the things which are mighty, that none may glory in his presence.

"Hoping for his aid and blessing, I have recently attempted to open the school devotions occasionally in Italian; by far the greater part of my pupils speaking this as their mother tongue. I use in prayer, chiefly selections from Scripture, which I prepare beforehand, but which, offered in the spirit of prayer, will, I trust, be presented by the great Intercessor, and be answered in his name. I am becoming more and more interested in my pupils, particularly in the Greeks and Jewesses; the little English girls in turn have been delighted to hear the letters which my Boston, and Sabbath school scholars have sent me. These are promised them as a great reward on Friday afternoon, if they are very still.

"Mrs. Arnold still assists me in the school, though I have persuaded her, the last week, to give up going in the afternoon, for she could not bear the confinement; and she has also found it peculiarly injurious to pass over our stairs, nearly 100 in number, as she must do four or six times a day. The Sirocco winds affect her very unfavorably, and she is growing pale, so that I felt unwilling to have her attempt so much. They are the same kind brother and sister to me, and I have reason to be grateful that I am in one of the happiest families on earth."

A few weeks later she remarks, "My dear Mrs. Arnold has been obliged to give up the school altogether, though very reluctantly, and not so soon as her exhausted energies required. She suffers very much from the Sirocco winds, which to her are like an atmosphere of death, both enervating and depressing. They sometimes prevail here for days together. To me they are balmy as the summer breezes, infusing fresh life through my whole system. But they have a most withering effect upon dear Sarah. We hope however that this is only the process of acclimation, and that a second year in Corfu will be less injurious to her decidedly northern constitution. God bless the dear, dear one, and spare her long to be the joy of loving hearts."

After Mrs. Arnold left the school, Miss Waldo was for a while alone, but finally secured the assistance of one who relieved her from much of the manual labor of the school. "I have not," says she, "been heavily overburdened, yet you will, I am sure, appreciate the joy with which I am anticipating the return of dear Mrs. Dickson. Dear woman! how happy shall I be, again to enjoy her society and counsel. Nor I alone. The face of every child in our little flock beams with joy at the thought of meeting her again, and a warm welcome awaits her from many a heart in Corfu.

"I feel the need of keeping ever in remembrance the great object of all instruction, the salvation of the precious soul: and I have daily reason to see the importance of improving, as they pass, the golden opportunities I enjoy of making Christ known to these dear children. Already a considerable number have passed from under my care, and I can no more point them to the cross. 'Now is,' emphatically, 'the day of salvation;' and it adds a fearful weight to my responsibilities to know that, with many of them, it is the only season in their lives in which they will have any one to warn them to 'flee from the wrath to come.' God forbid that any of them should receive greater light only to experience a heavier condemnation.

"Yet how vain are all our efforts, unless the Spirit move upon their hearts. Never did I more fully realize my utter dependence on Sovereign grace, than when teaching my little flock the way of salvation. O that it may lead me to more earnest and believing prayer in their behalf. I feel the need of prayer for my own soul's sanctification. I breathe a tainted air, filled with worldliness, which is death to the soul,—and I often feel its pernicious influence. I am exposed to temptations, and called to encounter spiritual foes, the power of which is far greater here than at home; and no common degree of grace is requisite to keep alive and glowing in the soul the flame of heavenly love.

"We have indeed many helps which I had not expected, and for which I would be thankful to God. Besides our own little meetings, we are blessed with the acquaintance, and privileged with hearing the preaching, of a most godly minister of the Episcopal church. Rev. E. Hall, to whom I allude, is a preacher so thoroughly evangelical, so sound in doctrine, so truly practical, so simple, so elevated, so humble, so fervent, so rich in all the good things of the gospel, that we feel it a great privilege to listen on Wednesday evenings to his soul-nourishing discourses. Nor is he more practical and evangelical in the pulpit, than heavenly in his conversation, and exemplary in his life. We esteem it a great blessing to know such a dear servant of God, and trust the acquaintance will indeed minister to our spiritual good."

"*Nov.* 14.

"God is graciously quickening me, and giving me an unwonted longing for seasons of converse with him. He is enabling me to shake off the deathly lethargy which seemed to rest like a pall upon my soul, and is making even such a guilty worm taste the river of his pleasures. The dear Saviour is present now. Would that I could talk with you of his love, and of the blessed home he is preparing for us. Is it not unbelief that would make me despond of abiding in Christ? I have sometimes almost despaired, but I trust God is now drawing me nearer to himself, and renewing his covenant with my soul. O is he not a gracious God? Was there ever forbearance like his towards me? You cannot tell the riches of his grace to me, for you know not what deep, dark stains he has blotted out. May I ever live near his cross and feel the melting, burning influence that comes from it. Blessed Jesus, bind me to thyself.

"Amid all the cares of the past week the blessed Saviour has been peculiarly gracious to me, and kept my treacherous heart from wandering from him, and thus losing the sweet relish of his love. When I read this morning the precious text for the day, '*Thy Maker is thy husband*,' I felt that God did indeed sustain each tender relation to me, and that I need not, should not, feel alone."

Mrs. D. having been detained in Scotland far beyond her own expectations, or those of her missionary associates, did not arrive in Corfu until the close of the year. During her whole absence Miss W. was obliged to sustain an unwonted amount of care and responsibility, which was every day becoming more trying from the increased debility of Mrs. A. "I cannot," says she, "think of myself, while I see Mrs. A. so feeble and depressed. She has had no settled disease, but has been gradually losing strength during the fall and winter. The physician has recommended a visit to Athens, hoping that a change of air and scenery may prove restorative. For this we earnestly hope and pray, but with many fears. I cannot look forward at all, but rather live by the day, doing the work each hour brings, in the strength of the Lord and with a view to his glory."

CHAPTER XVII.

Return and illness of Mrs. Dickson—Encouragements in their work—Letter to her former Sabbath School Class—Change in the arrangement of the school—Trials of missionary life—Thoughts on addressing Christ in prayer.

THE commencement of the year 1845 found Miss Waldo rejoicing over the return of her fellow-laborer, Mrs. Dickson, who reached Corfu, Dec. 31st, after an absence of nearly six months. Mrs. Arnold's health had by this time become so delicate that it was seriously feared she would be unable to endure the climate. To try the effect of a change of air, Mr. A. repaired with her to Athens, leaving the mission in the charge of Mrs. D. and Miss W. They had been absent but five days, when Mrs. D. was taken suddenly and seriously ill, so that a double weight of responsibility necessarily rested on Miss W., who, with all the affection of a daughter, watched by night and day beside the bed of her suffering friend. It was to her a season of severe trial, causing her sensitively to feel that her only hope was in God. To him she most fervently prayed that if possible the life of her dear friend might be spared. God was pleased to grant the desire of her heart, and her gratitude for this great mercy is thus expressed in a letter

TO MRS. BUEL.

"*Corfu, Feb.* 10, 1845.

"MY VERY DEAR FRIEND:—Will you not 'magnify the Lord with me and let us exalt his name together?' We were brought low and he helped us. The sorrows of death seemed to be taking hold on our beloved Mrs. D.; 'we found trouble and sorrow.' But 'gracious is our God and merciful.' He hath 'chastened her sore, but he hath not given her over unto death.' My heart is so full of thankfulness that I feel as if I could do nothing but bless the Lord."

After giving some particulars of the illness of her friend, she adds:—"This morning she said to me, 'To tell the truth, Miss W., my recovery is a disappointment to me. All my thoughts and feelings were towards heaven, and I hardly want to come back to this dark sinful world. But perhaps it was selfish. God's time is the best.' As I looked on the happy saint, I was almost tempted to reproach myself for wishing to keep her from her crown,—for desiring to detain her from her adored Redeemer. Such a heavenly, solemn place has that chamber of suffering been, that I, too, shrink from going out into the world again. Should the Lord spare us to meet, I should love to tell you what a rich experience has been afforded me of the gracious condescension and faithfulness of our covenant-keeping God. I would not exchange the experience of these few days for all the pleasure earth can give. I have been permitted to see with my eyes how the grace of God can sustain and cheer the soul under intense suffering and in the direct face of death, and a reality and preciousness has been given to religion such as I had never before felt."

"*Feb.* 19, 1845.

"This has been an eventful month of my life. Indeed February will be a month in the year of no common interest to me. In Feb. 1841, the proposal to become a missionary was first made to me by Dr. Bolles; in Feb. 1842, five of my dear Sabbath school class were converted, and three baptized; in Feb. 1843, I closed my be loved school in Boston; in Feb. 1844, I arrived in Corfu; and events of deepest interest have been crowded into Feb. 1845, which make it one of the most interesting periods of my life. What shall mark its next return God only knows.

"The anniversary of our arrival was a very solemn day to me. It brought with it a painful sense of unfaithfulness and guilt. O the long-suffering of God that has spared such a cumberer of the ground. I have felt constrained to come as a guilty sinner to the blood that cleanseth and devote myself anew to Him, who hath called me to be holy. Indeed, I find no little watchfulness and prayer needed, to maintain a walk with God such as it is my privilege to enjoy."

"*March* 27.

"There is a great deal of gayety in Corfu just now, attending the Prince's departure, but it is all uninteresting to me; not that I have become a misanthrope, or feel embittered against the world; marred as it is by sin, it is still God's world, and full of his goodness. All that is his work is bright and beautiful as his own glorious nature, and all this is a source of joy. But the gayety and folly of the gairish world is not of him, and forms therefore no part of my happiness. But for him this lovely island, with all its verdure and beauty, would be a lonely spot to me. But in the assurance of his favor and the hope of his blessing, I can be happy, though separated from all the loved objects of my early days. Is it not a blessed thought that God is everywhere, that his children cannot wander where he cannot follow and bless them?"

"*April* 1.

"Mrs. D. has recovered much more rapidly than was at first anticipated, but is still feeble, and strongly inclined to a recurrence of the same disease. Yesterday was the first time she entered the school-room. Truly the Lord's promise is sure:—'*As thy days, so shall thy strength be.*' Had any one asked me a few months since, if I could keep school two months longer alone, I should have felt disheartened at the thought; for on the return of Mrs. D. from Scotland I thought I had gone on alone just as long as I could. Yet how soon was she laid on a bed of suffering? and through how much has the Lord since carried me? making me happy in it too, preserving my health and cheering my heart.

"God has also vouchsafed to us rich spiritual mercies, in the hopeful conversion of two or three interesting individuals, and the gracious quickening of some silent disciples who had not dared to be decided Christians. The former converts seem to hold on their way, and an increasing number attend our meetings, and seem to love them. We trust the Spirit is moving on some hearts. The last two Sabbaths our chapel has been well filled.

"Would that I could speak of some things equally encouraging among the Greeks. From Mr. Arnold's letter to the Board, which goes by this mail, you will learn some interesting particulars respecting Greek preaching, both missionary and native, of which I have not now time to speak. On one point I have changed my mind since I came here, that is, the possibility of a revival of vital religion in the Greek church, aside from any extraneous influence. I think it quite as possible that from the Greek church itself a renovating influence might arise, as was proved in Luther's time to be true of the Catholic church. This does not make me regard our mission here of less importance, but somewhat alters its relative situation. O that God would raise up from among them a second Luther to work even a more thorough reformation than that of the sixteenth century."

The following extract from a letter to her former Sabbath school class shows that it was not in the Greek church alone that she felt the need of a renovating influence from on high. The letter is dated April 26, 1845.

"My greatest comfort in thinking of you arises from the hope that most of you have turned your feet into the way of life, have received that Saviour of whom it was once my delight to speak to you, and are daily seeking from him those supplies of grace which you so imperatively need, and which he is so willing to bestow. But this is not a comfort unmingled with fears. For some of you I hope with much trembling. Though in those of you who by a public profession had put on the Lord Jesus Christ, I did think I saw evidence that you had become new creatures in Christ—that you felt something of the power of his love—yet I often saw much evidence that you were still in some measure carnal. The love of the world, of its fashions and its pleasure, was not always under foot. The warm sisterly affection which should always characterize believers in a common Saviour, was not always manifested. Love for the prayer meeting, for close religious conversation, for the more self-denying duties of a child of God, was often languid and cold. The desire to make known Christ to those who know him not, and pity for the dying heathen, were often in feeble exercise. The meek and quiet spirit which is in God's sight of great price, was often wanting among you. I know, my dear girls, that you are not the only professing Christians who come short in these things, nor do I mean to hold up myself as a pattern, but I mean to say that these things shut out the full assurance of hope that you are indeed the Lord's chosen ones.

"How is it now with you? Are you adding grace to grace, gaining one victory after another over sin, increasingly devoted to Christ, and walking in love, as Christ also loved us and gave himself for us? Do you love the souls of men more, and are you laboring and praying more earnestly for their salvation? Do you weep over the heathen and do what in you lies to give them the gospel? Do you watch and pray, ever looking to Jesus? Ask yourselves these questions, examine your hearts and see whether Christ be indeed in you. I cannot decide the question for you; it rests with each of you. Each must give account of herself to God.

* * * * *

"And now, my beloved class, farewell. The God of salvation seal you as his own, and unite you in his blissful presence. To him I commend you, for he alone can keep you. Abide in him; for out of him you are helpless, exposed to all the shafts of the devil, and a prey to your own natural corruptions. But a little while and we shall bid adieu to all earthly scenes. O, may we then have One to cross death's dark valley with us, and welcome us to the home of the redeemed."

About the first of May a change was made in the arrangement of the school of which Miss Waldo thus writes:—

"*June* 6, 1845.

"I have been very happy in my school the last month, in the successful carrying out of a new plan. We have separated the Greeks from the other girls, and I have taken them under my special care, for the purpose of increasing their interest, and at the same time improving myself in the language. Though it is only a few weeks since I commenced, the result has already been very favorable. I have under my care fifteen Corfuotes, ten of whom are full Greeks. We have in all twenty-four natives, beside the Jewesses who number twenty-eight. Indeed, we have only about ten English girls; so that our school is quite a foreign mission school,—just what I always wanted. They seem to feel attached to me, and I have begun to pray with them in Greek. O how I long to see some of them converted. They do begin to think on subjects which till lately seldom had a thought, and one or two seem much interested.

"I suppose we shall not have the Jewesses much longer. The Scotch society which has so long sustained us, or rather their English brethren of the secession, will take the school into their own hands. This is not from any dissatisfaction on their part, but only the carrying out of their original plan. When Mrs. Dickson visited Scotland, four years ago, she was requested, by some ladies belonging to the Glasgow Jews' Society, to attempt an opening among the Jews, with the promise of their support if she succeeded. In pursuance of this request, on her return to Corfu in 1841, through the influence of a Jewish friend, an opening was made and a few Jewesses secured. Last year their agent visited us to see the state of the school; and, finding we were pressed by more applications from Jewesses than we could meet, proposed the formation of a separate school for them. On Mrs. D's late visit to Scotland, the society showed her every mark of attention, and requested her to become their missionary to Corfu. But as this called for a separation from our Board to join one of another denomination, she declined. The auxiliary society in London have therefore resolved to send a teacher, and as she cannot live alone, they will send a missionary also. If they are as good as some of the dear Scotch seceders with whom we have met, it will be a valuable acquisition to our little circle.

"*June* 18.

"Our new plan of separating the Greeks, with the blessing of God, is working well. The suggestion, I trust, came from him, and on him is all our present hope of success. I have now, beside my English classes, eighteen who speak Greek. These children are, I humbly trust, the answer to prayer, and this has given to them an interest such as never clothed the school before. It is a pleasure even to exhaust one's self in such labor. But, O my dear sister, what a responsibility is laid upon me. I tremble at the thought, and want to feel the same disposition to look to God for direction in each little particular, which comforted me in the distressing illness of Mrs. D. Then I felt that my only hope was from God. I prayed him to teach me how to nurse her, when, and what medicine to give, what treatment to pursue, &c., and I did not feel uncounseled."

Under the same date, speaking of some remarks respecting a deceased friend, she adds,—"I very much dislike these eulogiums of the dead. I am no friend to biographies in general because they are so untrue. How differently in many cases would the departed spirit describe his past life were it permitted him. Only when an individual's life is connected with some important work, is there an excuse for a memoir; except indeed it be such a memoir as that of J. B. Taylor, fitted to arouse the Christian from the lethargy of sin, and lead him to high attainments in piety. Indeed I think many of the published memoirs are a curse to the church."

She often expressed fears that her friends should think more highly of her piety than they ought. Addressing one of them about this time she thus writes of herself:—

"You think of me probably as a missionary who has, for the sake of Christ, left all that heart held dear. But do you also consider that I am a resident of a gay and fashionable city, where the laws of etiquette, and the rules of polite society exercise iron sway?—a garrisoned town, where no one can live in seclusion, but where every word and act, almost every feeling, is the subject of general surveillance and comment, where one never can be alone except he lock himself up in his own chamber? Remember that it is not the gross practices of uncivilized heathenism which surround and tempt us, but the form of godliness without the power, fashionable religion, worldly piety, if such paradoxical expressions are allowable, these lay snares for us in which we shall surely be taken, unless the rich grace of God hold us up.

"Imagine yourself, dear sister, a newly arrived stranger in a strange land, placed there indeed, it may be, to teach salvation to lost sinners. But now you cannot speak their language. Weary days and months, nay years, will hardly find you a proficient in it. During this time you are the same creature of affections, susceptibilities, and social needs, as you ever were; nay, more so; for the severed fibres of your heart still bleed and are sorely sensitive. Kind words greet you in your own tongue, hospitalities are proffered you, and friendship is manifested. Are you a human being, and can you be insensible to all this? They speak of your heart's Lord, your adored Redeemer; they love him too, at least profess to; can you be indifferent? And yet this acquaintance, thus began, thus necessitated almost, how many entanglements does it bring with it! how many subtle influences, how many soul-seducing snares!

"I do go to God with all these difficulties. I should sink if I could not. But I am often afraid that I ask for direction with a pre-biassed mind,—an unsubdued will. These are things that few anticipate in engaging in missionary work; yet I am convinced they are more or less common to all missionaries who are in colonial provinces. They are things about which Christians think too little, and pray too little. But I tell you that you may know how to pray for me."

"The greatest draw-back to my pleasure of teaching is the imperfect manner in which I can express my thoughts in Greek. When I read a few days since in the Magazine that Miss Vinton could take the charge of a school the first year of her going out, I wondered if she made as stammering work with the Karen as I do with the Greek. It is a great restraint to feel one's heart full, and be unable to express it. This I feel especially in the Bible class. The life and interest ordinarily awakened by that exercise, are restrained by the constant effort to remember forms of tenses and cases, or the forgetfulness of some word which could express my meaning. One great difficulty arises from the extreme corruption of the language by the common people. The language that our poor children use as little resembles that I am learning from books, and from my accomplished teacher, as the dialect of the Gascon peasant resembles that of the Parisian. This evil is aggravated by the mixture of Italian, both in pronunciation and in the words themselves. I know of no remedy but to learn as fast as I can these corruptions, and, to a modified extent, to use them."

It was a great comfort to Miss Waldo, amid the discouragements of her missionary work, to have frequent opportunities, by means of her pen, to enlighten and encourage those who from her native land looked to her for instruction. Such letters are for the most part too personal to be given to the public. The following extract from a letter dated July 19, 1845, may serve as a specimen of the readiness with which she entered into the feelings and trials of those who thus sought her counsel.

"I cannot tell you, dearest, the deep feeling with which I read that part of your letter in which you spoke of your feelings towards the dear Redeemer. How they recalled the days of mental conflict when the light first broke in upon my own dark soul,—when the first thought of the divinity of my adorable Saviour flashed upon my mind,—when I awakened to the consciousness that I was trusting for salvation in Jesus, and yet had believed him an arm of flesh,—when I prayed that God would reveal himself to my soul as he really was, and show me indeed the truth of that declaration of Christ himself, 'That all men should honor the Son even as they honor the Father.' How your words recalled the trembling with which my lips first whispered that dear name in prayer,—when I first came to my great Advocate, committing my cause to Him who 'ever liveth to intercede.' Well do I remember how strong early bias made me doubt and fear, till, in the sweet assurance that each prayer was heard and answered, my long harassed and troubled spirit found rest.

"Why, dearest, why that indescribable desire to utter the love and gratitude which the heart feels for Jesus, if it were sin? I do believe that Jesus has led you in a way you knew not, has taught you to trust in him and to love him, and that it is the moving of the new-born soul that struggles within you, when you would, but dare not speak his name in prayer. You would not do worse by addressing him than Thomas did when he exclaimed, 'My Lord and my God.' You would be no more blameworthy than the myriad hosts of heaven, who cast their crowns at his feet saying, 'Worthy is the Lamb that was slain to receive power, and riches, and wisdom, and strength, and honor, and glory, and blessing.' You would not displease God more than the angels; for they obey Him, who when he brought his first begotten into the world, said, 'Let all the angels of God worship him.' Yes, dearest, my joy is that the day will come when you shall see the King in his beauty, and, without one feeling of misgiving, shall tune your harp to his praise, and lift your soul in adoring worship to that 'Lamb that sits in the midst of the throne.'"

CHAPTER XVIII.

Question whether the mission should be continued—Her feelings in respect to it—Discouragements—Evils of a military establishment—Increase of Mr. Arnold's congregation—Removal of their place of residence.

Miss W. was now beginning to feel at home in her work, happy in the society of her missionary friends, but especially happy in her school, and rejoicing in the privilege of making some sacrifices for Christ. Though she often spoke of strong yearnings of heart for home, yet she could add, "Is it wrong? Does it prove me unwilling to labor here for God? O, no, no. I thank God for giving me the little flock that now look to me for instruction. I thank him for allowing me to show that I loved him much, for I was much forgiven. For no other could I have made this sacrifice, but when he spared not himself from the cross, what can he ask that I would withhold? He left a brighter home to come to a desert world, whose beauties were but the shadows of heaven's loveliness. He left those that loved and adored, for those who hated and reviled. He left the right hand of the Father, for the cross of Calvary; and is any thing too dear to give to him? O that I could have laid a pure offering upon his altar. Alas, I could only bring one stained and marred by sin."

Her attachment to the school was, however, soon to receive an unexpected test. The expediency of continuing the mission began to be seriously agitated at home; and about the first of July, she was prematurely informed by a correspondent that the Board had decided to bring it to a close. The following extracts express her feelings on the reception of this intelligence.

"You cannot tell the conflicting emotions produced by the tidings that the Greek mission might be given up. The first flashing thought was, shall I be clasped to my mother's bosom again? But the next was my dear school, just beginning to realize my hopes and meet my expectations,—that little group of Greek girls just collected around me, just beginning to manifest affection, just commencing to exhibit some interest in God's word —these rose next to my view. The hopes I was beginning to cherish of them seemed too precious to be given up; the tears would come, and I prayed, Lord, spare this mission. Mother, my home is dear. Kind as are the hearts around me, my heart has no home here. The unclasped tendrils of its affections, separated from the objects to which they early clung, still reach after them and take no new hold here. But, darling mother, life's sun hastens to its setting. A few brief years and the chill touch of death will hush this heart's warm throbbings. These few years, I would spend for Him who having forgiven much, is much loved; and if I may but teach one poor child to lisp his praises, I will wait for heaven's reunion with the early loved. Yet God's will be done. If he has no more for me to do here, I would hasten hence. Nothing else binds me here. O, may I be found ready for his will.

* * * * * * *

"You cannot wonder that the question has often

arisen, Why did God ever allow me to come here? A question which I cannot fully answer, and yet I think it has been at least of some benefit to myself. One blessing derived from it has been a knowledge of my own heart, such as I never had, and never could have had at home. Another has been preparation for the realities of life. I have been taken out of the soft, bland air of a loving home, and thrown on my own resources for society, for comfort, and for happiness. I have learned that 'not to be ministered unto, but to minister,' was the great duty of my life. Beside other directly personal benefits I might mention, I have learned the value of the Bible as the only standard of faith. I have seen the danger of departing from it to follow the traditions of men, and the withering curse of a dead Christianity. We cannot think too much of this one great truth, that it is of saving importance what we believe in matters of religion. The Bible teaches us very plainly that sincerity in error cannot save a man. 'There is a way that seemeth right unto a man, but the end thereof is the way of death.' O, then, of what infinite moment is the question, 'What is truth?' How important that each should ask, What do I believe? The word of God cannot teach things diametrically opposite. Does it teach what I believe? is a question which no one should decide lightly."

The steamer of July 18 brought them official letters from the Board which somewhat modified the information previously received. This communication called for an expression of their own views and feelings on the subject, with opportunity to plead for the continuance of the mission.

" The responsibility," says she, " is now in a measure thrown into our own hands. The question is not altogether will the Board recall us ? but will we return. How this question will be answered I cannot now tell. In the mean time let us look to God in prayer that we may be prepared for all his will,—that our own will may be swallowed up in his. Such a state of mind will prepare us for any event, and will make us far happier than to attempt to pry into the future, and lift the vail which hides coming events from our ken. How sweet to feel that our times are in God's hands, and that, though a man's heart deviseth his way, the Lord directeth his steps. *He* appointeth the bounds of our habitations. That should satisfy us. I trust it does satisfy me. The future is impenetrable. I cannot see a step before me, or form an idea of what God will do with me. But cheerfully and undoubtingly can say,

'All my fondest hopes had planned,
To his wisdom I resign.'

" Universal regret, I had almost said, is expressed by the English residents here at the idea of Mr. and Mrs. Arnold's leaving Corfu. They are much beloved for their quiet, unassuming manners, and readiness to do whatever good they can for the people. Were this the feeling of the Greeks, how happy should we be, and how much pleasure would Mr. A. feel in laboring for this people. As it is, he hardly knows what to decide upon. Mr. and Mrs. A. have lately established a charity school, which has found liberal support both among Greeks and English, and already numbers some eighty or ninety. It is intended for very small children, who swarm our streets, wretched, ragged, and dirty creatures as you ever saw. Thus far they have met with unlooked for success, and this little beginning may lead to large results.

"We have all felt much sadness of heart at the manifest want of success attending efforts here. While the simple Karen hears the gospel and at once believes, while the prejudiced Chinese receives the truth as a little child, while the Indian hears the missionary's message with weeping eye and softened heart, while Armenians and Nestorians pray to be taught a purer faith, and for love to Christ and truth, take joyfully the spoiling of their goods, the Greek indignantly repels the very idea of receiving religious instruction, and haughtily asks the humble missionary, Dost thou teach us? Yet we know there is a power that bringeth down every high thought that exalteth itself; a power that can make the despised gospel, the wisdom of God to those who once saw no beauty in it. And we wait for the revealing of that arm. We tarry for the coming of that salvation."

Writing to her mother, under date of July 6, 1845, she says, "I think I feel resigned to whatever God appoints —to labor in any part of the world, where he pleases to call for my poor services. I would not lift my finger to say where. Yet, dear mother, I often feel sad at the dark cloud that hangs over our unblest field; a blight and not a blessing from the Lord seems to rest upon us,—there seems to me scarcely one token for good. No new cases of inquiry or concern among the Greeks; but on the contrary some who have encouraged us as interesting inquirers, give proof that there is no love for the truth at the foundation of their inquiries. After more than a year's labor, when Mr. Arnold has begun to speak the language with ease, only from two to six assemble on Sabbath evening to study the gospel. And then in the soldiers we have much to try us. Some overcome of temptation, others manifesting unchristian tempers, and no careless sinner aroused to inquire the way to be saved.

"Ah, mother, the Christian exile can count it a light thing to have parted with all life holds dear, when he sees his humble efforts blessed in the salvation of lost souls. But when amid the desolateness of a dark land he feels that God too has forsaken him, then is his heart weighed down with a bitterness the stranger knoweth not of; his days are days of heaviness, and his nights are nights of tears. This makes me sad, though skies are bright and soft breezes blow around me, though a thousand comforts are afforded me and kind hearts cheer, yet there lies a weight upon my heart, a heavy load that all fails to remove.

"And then comes the conviction of unworthiness and unfaithfulness, and a feeling that if some other had filled my place a blessing would have been given. And with a breaking heart, I can only pray, O my God, if thy blessing cannot be with me, take me hence. If indeed Corfu is to continue such a moral desert, unblest with the visits of God's grace, it will cost me no struggle to leave it. But may we not hope for brighter days? God grant they may be at hand."

"*Oct.* 30, 1845.

"O how good is God to the chief of sinners, how manifold his mercies to one who deserves only wrath! How he has ever blessed me all my life, while my ungrateful heart has only returned goodness with disobedience, loving kindness with ingratitude. I feel to-night unworthy to look up to him and call him Father; for where has been the honor and service due from the child? Yet he follows me with his mercies, and one of the sweetest of them is your unchanging love, fondest of mothers. And yet, mother, how weak is even that, compared with his! Yours is the love of a parent towards a daughter, of whose faults you know too little, and whom you imagine possessed of excellences which eyes less fond cannot discover. But his is the love of a holy, sin-hating God to a rebellious, sinful, worthless being,—a mere dependent on his bounty. Your love watched over my cradle, bore uncomplainingly sleepless nights and weary days in nursing my helpless infancy, had patience with the waywardness of childhood, and the faults of youth, and is still a gushing spring which flows out unrestrained by distance or absence. But his love gave his only begotten up to suffering, yes, to the *cross*, to save a soul whose every corruption from the first lay naked and open to his pure sight. Yes, He who was the brightness of the Father's glory must lie in prostrate agony in dark Gethsemane and cry, 'Let this cup pass from me,' and yet drink it. He, whose pure nature never knew the defilement of a sinful thought, must exclaim in his mysterious anguish, 'My God, my God, why hast thou forsaken me;' and all this that we might be saved. O love, love! let all else that is called love sink into nothing at the mention of this. If my heart is often sad, when I recall my ingratitude and selfishness towards you, dearest mother, what anguish should, yes, *does* rend this heart, as conscience brings up the long array of dark and aggravated sins against my God and Saviour, from childhood unto womanhood. But for the cross, I should not dare to hope, I would not ask for pardon; but in its shadow comes the sweet assurance of forgiveness."

* * * * * * *

"What a little world are these hearts of ours! How many rival sovereignties, what hot conflicts, what warring desires, what strangely mingled emotions! O to have them entirely subdued by the blessed Captain of Salvation, tuned to sweet harmony with his nature and service, and consecrated to him as sole Lord and King. Be this thy bliss, my heart, to feel a Saviour indwelling, enthroned, casting out every impure and high thing, sending light into each dark recess, and kindling there a flame of quenchless love that shall all vainer loves expel. O the bliss of loving Jesus, of being conscious of affection to him, and the misery of that doubt and uncertainty which to the inquiry addressed to the heart's inmost recesses, Do I love the Lord? hears nought but the dismal echo, Do I?

"It is sweet to love any thing, a mere flower, a bird, a sweet unconscious babe—to love another loving heart, —but O, to love perfect, concentrated love; this is the essence of heaven's bliss. Let us pray for love, cultivate it, cherish its every development, and seek to know the height and depth of that love which passeth knowledge."

TO HER COUSIN, MRS. E. A. BOWERS.

"*Corfu, Oct.* 4, 1845.

"MY DEAR COUSIN ELLEN:—I have just re-read your long and interesting letter of January and February, received April 5th, and though I cannot promise to write you an equivalent, I will at least prove to you that you are still Emmy's *dear* cousin, affectionately remembered, amid all the changes of passing years. Your letter was so like yourself, and in every sentiment and expression, so vividly recalled past happy days, that it revived early affection with unwonted force and made the warm tears flow. I feel grateful that amid your many pressing cares and important duties, surrounded by dear objects of your heart's fondest love, you still find a place for one who has so often forfeited her hold on your heart. I feel it the more because you add another to the little circle of my praying friends, and I trust often remember before the mercy seat your far-distant, tried, and oft disheartened Emmy. May yours ever be the prayer of faith that avails much.

"Time and space would fail me, Ellen, to allude to all the interesting topics of your letter. I can only briefly advert to a few. Thank you for all your good advice about husbanding health and strength. For your comfort I will tell you, that I do regard it as a religious duty to do so, and am far more careful and regular than I used to be. The climate, too, suits my constitution better than my native air, so that I have enjoyed the most perfect and uninterrupted health, ever since my arrival in Corfu. I attribute much to regular exercise. English ladies walk, as regularly as they wash or eat, and I have found the adoption of this habit of great service. And then we have such beautiful walks here. Roads almost as even and smooth as a marble floor, bordered with luxuriant hedges, which in all seasons except summer are enameled with beautiful wild flowers; and then such picturesque scenery! The old citadel rears its moss-covered head to the clouds; the antique massive fortifications which encircle the town, so wholly unlike every thing we have seen in America; and then the beautiful green vineyards, the soft waving olives, the bright fragant orange and lemon trees, covering the sunny slopes and hill sides of this most lovely island, in the light of a Mediterranean sunset, form an enchanting scene. And yet I will confess, dear Ellen, that that gorgeous grove, bedecked with nature's jewelry, which you so beautifully described, spoke to my New England heart more than all these southern beauties.

* * * * * *

"I followed you, dear Ellen, in your interesting journey, and enjoyed with you all its beautiful sights and pleasing events. I don't know any one who enjoys traveling so enthusiastically as yourself; and I am glad you have it in your power to gratify the taste. While you have been thus enjoying pleasant journeys from one part to another of our favored land, I have limited my travels to this little isle, and to a very small part of that. I have crossed, indeed, the broad Atlantic, and sailed through the stormy Mediterranean, but I know no more of Europe than before, except the little spot I inhabit.

"Corfu, the city, lies in a quiet harbor on the Eastern coast of the island, and is a small garrisoned place, not covering a larger area than the North End of Boston. Yet in this little place are crowded, in addition to a population of sixteen or seventeen thousand, two thousand British soldiers, more than a thousand of whom are quartered within the circumference of the citadel.

"We are surrounded on every side by all the apparatus of war. Almost every third person in the streets is a soldier. Every summit is crowned with massive fortifications, planted with heavy cannon. The ruins of old parapets, and bastions built by the Venitians, extend far into the country. Daily reviews and drills, with mimic fights, realize to you that this is not the kingdom of the Prince of Peace. All the train of evils that uniformly accompany a military establishment are found here. Licentiousness, drunkenness, and Sabbath-breaking, meet one at every corner. And the more insidious and subtle, but not less fatal influence of gayety, fashion, religious formality, and a dead profession, makes it a place full of danger to the Christian.

"As you may have anticipated, the English residents and military have furnished a cheering and encouraging part of our field of labor. Mr. Arnold has baptized five, and two others give hopeful evidence of conversion. About forty attend preaching on Sabbath eve, and fifteen or sixteen attend a weekly prayer meeting on Friday. Until the last four months, there were always more or less inquirers; but of late there seems no movement among the dry bones; and even from our little church of twelve members, we are about to exclude one, and suspend another. This has been a very sore and painful trial, and has weighed heavily upon our hearts. I never felt such oppressive sadness as I have felt for the last month in view of these and other troubles. May I not implore your most earnest and constant prayers in our behalf? Write me when you can, and believe me

"Your attached

"EMILY."

TO HER MOTHER.

"*Nov.* 20, 1845.

"The steamer has been again delayed, and patience has had an additional trial this afternoon, for through a mistake we cannot get our letters till tomorrow morning. Our Scotch friends are involved in the same mistake, but it is doubly trying to them, as this mail brings their first letters from home. O, these *first* letters! How the wanderer's heart longs for them, and with what intense feeling does he read every word. And yet perhaps his feelings are scarcely so intense, as when years have begun to slide away and the fear creeps upon the heart that time and absence are chilling love. How the heart then trembles at every fancied change, and thrills with pleasure when it reads the sweet assurance that our place in the hearts of the distant and the loved is still all our own. That happiness, all undeserved, has been mine as often as I have received your precious letters, fondest of mothers. O that I were worthy such love.

"It is said, I know, that no child fully realizes the intensity of parental solicitude, or the tenderness and depth of a mother's love till he or she comes to experience the same deep emotions. But I think such an ocean-wide separation as I have been called to, teaches as effectual a lesson. Yes, conscious as I am that I have sadly failed as a daughter in the love and service I should have rendered you, dearest mother, yet my heart turns as confidingly to you, and rests as assured of your forgiveness and affection, as if I had not been thus unfaithful. The thought has just passed my mind while writing this, Why should I not thus confide in the forgiving love of a Heavenly Parent, for though my sins against him infinitely outweigh all my waywardness to you, dearest mother, so does his love as infinitely exceed all you can feel, glowing as your heart is with maternal fondness. Yes, let our sinful soul strust in him. O, a mother! whose hand so tenderly smooths the pillow of sickness, whose eye so anxiously watches each symptom of disease, whose heart so quick to take the alarm, and dread the first stealthy, silent footsteps of decay or trouble of any kind? The gracious God illustrates his own love by it when he says to the sorrowing Israel, '*As* one whom his mother comforteth so will I comfort thee.'

* * * * * *

"Mr. Arnold's English congregation is quite enlarged; nearly seventy now attend on Sabbath eve. He alternates with Mr. C., the Jewish missionary, and maintains in all things the kindest fraternal relations with him, such as Christians ever should. A number of his congregation are serious minded persons, Methodists, Presbyterians, and Episcopalians, as well as Baptists, but who lay aside sectarian prejudices that they may shed a united light in this dark corner. But, alas! the simple doctrine of salvation by the cross, is a stumbling block to the Jew, and foolishness to the Greek of Corfu, as much as to those of Paul's time; and it is still true that the power of God alone can teach either, to receive him as their only Saviour.

"*Dec.* 5, 1845.

"We have just been removing our place of residence, for the sake of securing a lower rent. We shall lose the beautiful views of the harbor, citadel, and Albanian hills, with the pretty esplanade, but, as we get a better house for one hundred dollars less, and reach it by a dozen steps instead of sixty or seventy, we are reconciled to a less beautiful prospect, and less pleasant situation. The new house is on a very elevated spot, and, if possible, more healthy. It is little matter to me where I live; why should we care, when in a few years at the longest, the narrow house will hold all of us that belongs to earth. O it does seem strange to me that the great realities, God and heaven, judgment and eternity, have had so little influence over me. Surely I should have been another being than I have been, had I by faith realized these things. May I not, too late, have begun to feel that they are the only realities, all else is a dream.

"Our school is quite full now, over fifty in regular attendance, so that the larger part of my time out of school hours is necessarily spent in preparing for its duties. I have about twenty regularly attending Greeks, Italians, and Maltese, a very motley set I assure you; speaking such a gibberish of Grecized Italian, and Italianized Greek, as would defy an Athenian to understand. Only five or six of them can read the Greek gospels, two or three the Italian Bible, and the remainder are only learning to read and spell. Quite a number are very small. But I love the little things, and hope yet to see some of the fruit of my labors."

CHAPTER XIX.

Importance of holiness to the Missionary—Account of her Bible Class—Her interest in the Jews—Season of Mental Darkness—Letter to the First Baptist Church, Charlestown—To her Mother—To the Sabbath School Missionary Society, Watertown.

THE mind of Miss Waldo seems to have been at this time deeply impressed with the intimate connection between the holiness and the usefulness of Missionaries. Addressing one of her correspondents she says, "Do pray that none but holy missionaries may be sent abroad, such as are wholly Christ's, living in and for him. It is not gifts but grace, not knowledge but holiness, not a ready tongue but a sanctified heart, that this work needs. Pray that those who possess these may be sent into the harvest." To another friend she writes, "If you would confer the greatest happiness on your unworthy friend, pray that her sinful heart may be purified, her earthly nature spiritualized, and her whole being consecrated to the service of her long-suffering Saviour. Remember that I am beset with temptations on every side, with a heart that has not yet learned to look in steadfast faith to a willing and mighty Saviour. God brought me here to prove me, and he has found much, much dross. Tell all who pray for and love missions, to pray for the holiness of missionaries. If they are holy all is sure; if they are not, all else is utterly futile. A holy God cannot, and will not bless."

Of her school she remarks in a letter to the Board, dated Dec. 23, 1845,

"So unvarying is the routine of my daily duties, that the history of one day is the history of weeks, with only the variety of now more, now less attention on the part of the scholars; at times interest, soberness, and docility, and again heedlessness, indifference, and strife. O, what a momentous and soul-stirring event would be the conversion of some of these dear children to God! But alas, no day has been marked by such a blessed record.

"Perhaps, however, it may be of some interest to you to hear a little more particularly about the small Greek Bible class of from five to seven girls, from eight to fifteen years of age, who read every morning a chapter, or a part of one, from the New Testament, and listen to such questions and remarks as I may be able to make to them. Eleven in all have, during the past year, been at times members of the class, some attending very irregularly throughout the year, others having remained in the school only a few weeks or months. On the first of January they commenced the gospel of Matthew, and have read through the four gospels and the Acts, together with select chapters from other parts of the New Testament.

"At first it was almost impossible to obtain any answers from them, as they did not seem to think of associating any ideas with the words they read. But by degrees they have seemed to comprehend, and sometimes have given very appropriate and interesting answers. For a long time they could not be made to apply to themselves any condemnation from the word of God. Hell was for bad men, but they loved God, believed in Christ, and would go to heaven. But it seems as if this false confidence had been in some degree shaken. When asked now, if they love God, they hang their heads in silence. If asked if they can go to heaven as they are, though they will not often say, 'No,' yet their looks express that they feel unfit for that holy abode. Last summer, when an old scholar returned who had been absent for some months, during which time this great idea had seemed to be entering the minds of some, I remember how surprised she looked, as she heard some of them admitting, in answer to questions on the lesson, that indeed they were in danger of perdition.

"No abstract assertion of their unbelief and depravity could convince them, but the comparing of some plain requirement of God with their daily conduct has seemed most effectual. And as they are exceedingly given to bickering, and selfish in the extreme, no command has ever been to them so effectual a convincer of sin as that 'New commandment,' 'Love one another.' 'By this shall all men know that ye are my disciples, if ye love one another.' 'He that hateth his brother abideth in death.' Such declarations, they could not but see, cut off their hopes. Yet alas, this conviction has seemed to produce little abiding effect. A transient seriousness has been the only encouragement. They are most interested in the gospels, particularly the narration of Christ's sufferings and death, in which they seldom fail to manifest much interest.

"I have been discouraged, however, to find that all the knowledge of the word of God which they have acquired, as yet fails to convince them of the falsity of creature trust. O that that Spirit, who alone can make the carnal mind understand the things of God, would convince of sin so deeply, and effectually, that they would flee from every refuge of lies unto the only Hiding place for the lost sinner.

"This Bible class, and the reading of the Scriptures on Lord's day, with some poor women, has been about all my missionary work. Had that little been done in faith, and with a single eye to God's glory, would it not have realized some fruit? The other scholars in my department are not yet able to read the Scriptures, and I find it very difficult to give religious instruction to the little ones in Greek, as they are not accustomed to hear conversation on such subjects, and so do not seem to understand what it means. The school presents a small field of labor, yet, restricted as it is, there is much to do. O that it could be done aright. Patiently waiting for what further developments of God's will he shall be pleased to make us,

"I remain yours,

"S. E. Waldo."

By the same mail she wrote as follows

TO HER MOTHER.

"*Corfu, Dec.* 22, 1845.

"Dearest Mother:—Why have you let your fond heart dwell too soon on the idea of my return? Do not lay up for yourself disappointment and distress. Wait, dearest, God's time, and then you are safe. The same mail that brought your letter speaking so decidedly of return, brought me one from the Board, saying, it was the opinion of the Secretary that we should be continued. I did not know how to reconcile the two, and I trembled lest you might be laying up for yourself disappointment and regret. I do not think of return or continuance, but only of the present moment. I do not feel myself worthy to go home and be again among those who loved me far, far too well, nor yet worthy to stay on missionary ground. I can only say, The Lord do with me as he pleaseth.

"As to the over-land return, with my present feelings, I have little heart for such an undertaking. I shrink from the publicity and confusion of a journey across the continent, and will be quite willing to get a quiet berth in a fast-sailing vessel. With what heart could I look on strange cities, and foreign scenes, if I am returning an unblest missionary from an unblest field? Rather would I find some secret place, where, unknowing and unknown, I might weep over my sins and unfaithfulness before a holy God. Yet in this too, I desire to be passive in God's hands. The Board will no doubt direct or advise if they recall us, and I shall wait their decision.

"I have felt a peculiar interest in the Jewish nation, ever since I came to Corfu. The prophecies concerning them have acquired a far deeper interest, and my own views respecting the destiny and prospects of this nation have not a little changed. At home I scarcely ever saw a Jew, or heard any thing about them. The glowing prophecies with which Scripture is full, concerning Israel's future glory, I had been accustomed to hear applied to the church, and I had none of that peculiar feeling towards this people of God which has here been awakened. It is not that there is any thing particularly interesting in the Jews here; they are a cunning, deceitful, selfish race, and neither outwardly nor inwardly offer much to attract interest towards them. Yet the actual contact with the descendants of God's ancient and chosen people, the daily manifest fulfillment of prophecy in them, could not fail to awaken attention, and lead to the more careful study of what God has revealed concerning them. Here I have met, too, with some deeply interested in this once loved people of God, and could not but imbibe some of their spirit. Besides, I have learned more here of what is being done for the Jews. The Scotch missions among them are being richly blessed, and we are frequently hearing of most interesting conversions among them. Yes, Israel is indeed to be gathered in, and as she has drank to the dregs the cup of shame and oppression, so shall she receive at the last double for all her sins. As great shall be her glory when she who has been loved with an everlasting love shall again be the joy of the whole earth.

" The Jewish missionaries here, I mean our Scotch friends, find some encouragement, and we hope will yet be blessed in gathering into the true fold some of the lost sheep of the house of Israel. The recent death of Alexander, bishop of Jerusalem, a converted Jew, will be a sad disappointment to those who hoped that he would be one by whom Israel should arise."

TO MISS S. P. CARTER.

" *Corfu, Jan.* 13, 1846.

" My very dear Sarah :—Your deeply interesting letter of Nov. 29th was received a few days since, and I cannot describe to you the emotion with which its thrilling tidings were read, and re-read. When I came to that sentence, ' The result is, the debt is paid, and no mission will be disbanded,' I burst into tears, and could proceed no farther. The involuntary ejaculation burst from my lips, O my God, give me then the light of thy countenance, or I cannot stay. This one feeling for a time at least swallowed up every other, and though there came an after pang as the thoughts came home, Then I am still to be a lonely stranger in a strange land, unblest with a mother's fond caress, and the embrace of dear loved ones; yet this was the first, and has been the dominant feeling, O that God may bless, or continuance is no blessing.

"I have been feeling, dear Sarah, the thick darkness of a soul to whom God has said, 'Thine own wickedness shall reprove thee, and thy backslidings shall correct thee; know therefore and see that it is an evil and bitter thing to forsake the Lord thy God.'

'The awful message came,
The Lord of spirits said,
I know thou hast a living name,
But thou art dead.'

"How often, Sarah, have we prayed, 'Set our sins in order before us.' But O, it is a fearful thing to have that prayer answered—to see sins long gone by, stand before you with the vividness of present action, and in all their aggravatedness, inexcusableness, and loathsomeness, ever, ever present to you, whether alone or in society, busy or unoccupied,—when the crushed and despairing spirit feels the very pangs of death taking hold upon it, and yet cannot but say as one of old, 'If I say I will forget my complaints, I will leave off my heaviness and comfort myself, I am afraid of all my sorrows, I know that thou wilt not hold me innocent.' When the thought of a crucified Saviour casts only a blacker hue over guilt whose aggravation is, that it has been against his very cross and blood,—O this is fearful; yes, Sarah, the sins of a professing Christian are awful. Is there sorrow, is there anguish deep enough for such a heart to feel?

'My guilt appeared but small before,
Till I with terror saw
How perfect, holy, just and pure,
Is God's eternal law.'

"O what a light has flashed upon the law of God from a sight of his fearful holiness. I thought I had only to feel willing to give up the world wholly, to have peace and holiness come at my bidding, till a sovereign God made me feel, when the world had become a loathsome and distasteful object, that I might call and he refuse. O the misery of a dead heart that feels nothing, but is withered and dry. Yet still at the footstool of mercy would I plead,

'Jesus save my dying soul,
Make my wounded spirit whole;
Humbled in the dust I lie,
Saviour, leave me not to die.'"

A few weeks later she wrote to the same:

"Blessed be God, that long night is breaking, and humbled by it in the dust, my trembling soul adores redeeming love, and dares to say, 'My God will answer for me.' O Sarah, but for that blessed doctrine of *transfer*, of *substitution*, despair would have fastened upon my soul, 'He was made sin for us.' O what precious words. No other idea can possibly bring relief to the burdened conscience. No other consideration affords the least consolation."

TO THE FIRST BAPTIST CHURCH CHARLESTOWN.

" *Corfu, Jan.* 21, 1846.

" Beloved Brethren and Sisters :—When I bade you farewell, the saddening thought that I might see you no more on earth was relieved by the hope that frequent intercommunications would lessen the distance the broad Atlantic interposed between us, and make me feel that I was not quite an amputated member of your dear body. But the long and painful trial through which as a church you were called to pass, after I left you, and the equally protracted, and not less distressing position in which this dear mission has of late been placed, have conspired, with some additional reasons, to occupy us each too much with our own trials and sorrows, to allow us either time or heart to write.

" Your very kind letter of April 12th, came after your sea of troubles had been crossed and the Lord had restored to you peace and union, under a loved and faithful pastor ; and this tardy reply comes to you just as we, of the Greek mission, who had feared that our candlestick was to be indeed removed out of its place, have been assured that a gracious God has visited his people, and constrained them rather to resolve to strengthen the things that remain and are ready to die, than to disband and recall, and thus quench the smoking flax.

" Need I tell you that this has been to us indeed a dark and cloudy day. Our hearts have sunk within us, and sorrow and despondency were settling down upon our souls. Without were fightings, and within were fears. We were told that few believed there were any blessings for Greeks, and fewer still prayed that there might be. The withering influence of this shutting up of prayer in reference to this field, seemed to manifest itself in the decaying verdure of our little green hill of Zion here, which had been the refreshing of our souls in this thirsty land. As the voice of prayer and the plea of faith died away from the lips of Christians at home, brotherly love, and spiritual union languished among our brethren here, and the inquiry ceased to be heard, 'What shall I do to be saved?' So in proportion, doors of access and hope of good seemed to close upon us, and we have been almost ready to say with desponding Israel, 'There is no hope.' And when inward darkness and doubt have united with outward discouragements, like sinking Peter I have only been able to cry, 'Lord save, I perish.'

"You sympathize with the missionary who has only a rude shed for a home, who daily endures the discomforts of half barbarous life, who is worn out with weary journeys under a burning sun, or feels all the pain of disease with none of the alleviation of home. But if with all these, his labors are among a people thirsting for the word of Life, such hardships are not so heart-wearing, so soul-sinking, as efforts made for a people who repel every thing that touches their darling errors, even though such a missionary may have every comfort civilized life affords. That Zion's voice should go up in prayer for the simple Karen, begging for teachers of salvation, for the Chinese opening wide the doors of the gospel, for the Cherokee, blessing her for the light of truth, this is not wonderful, nay the contrary would be strange. But O, let her plead too, and with beseeching cries and tears, for the caste bound Hindoo, the dead-souled Burman, the Apathetic Siamese, and the proud superstitious Greek. The gentle touch of God's hand, if I may be allowed the expression, seems to move the hearts of the former; but Jehovah's outstretched arm alone can bow the latter. I have no hope for the Greeks, unless the church be baptised with a spirit of prayer in their behalf. But if that Pentecostal voice shall ascend for Greece, the mountain barriers that seem now to shut out the truth from the hearts of her sons will become a plain. Pray then for Arracan, for China, for the Indians; but beseech, implore, agonize for a blessing upon Greece. When I look at myself, I cannot wonder at our want of success. But when I think of perishing souls around me, I am constrained to cry, 'Do thou it for thy name's sake, Lord, though our iniquities testify against us.' * * *

"Affectionately yours,

"S. E. Waldo."

TO HER MOTHER.

"*March* 6, 1845.

"I suppose you remember the terrible winter of last year, when I wrote you respecting six weeks of terrific thunder, hail-storms, and incessant rain with howling winds, so that you almost thought this could hardly be called a sunny isle. But this winter has been the reverse of all that. Probably your brightest May days will represent our February and March weather. More than one day in February, we sat in school with open windows, and in our walks, admired the rich verdure and the sweet wild flowers; and if you could see the clear blue sky that arches now daily over us, and feel the soft balmy air, you would think that poets had not so falsely represented Spring as I used to think in New England. This is emphatically the farmer's time in Corfu; as the summer dries up every thing, and the heat of the sun forbids labor, five or six hours of the day. I suppose that cold east wind, the thought of which makes me shiver now, is whistling around you, and a good coal fire blazing in your chamber. How I should like to draw around it this evening, and link myself again with that dear sister band.

"How gracious has God been in sparing to me those who are dearer to me than life. Here in this strange land have I learned what it is to have a mother, and precious, precious indeed is that mother to me. Yet, if I give you God's place, if your love is more prized, your sympathy more sweet, your existence more necessary to me than his, then will He, whose excellence infinitely transcends all creature good, be grieved at my ingratitude and punish my folly. To him I yield the throne—Him first, dearest, chief. Him I must honor or perish; all else, though very dear, cannot affect my salvation. To Him who has borne with my innumerable and aggravated transgressions against his law and grace, has saved me at the cost of his only begotten Son, and whose mercy has even stooped to lift the dark cloud that has hung for months upon my soul, and say, 'Live, for I have found a ransom,' to him I owe all, I give all.

"You spoke with a mother's tenderness of the feelings of sadness I could not hide from you, and my very heart was touched by your fond earnestness. It was no fancied sinfulness that distressed me; but because I knew I had not lived conscientiously up to the light given me. But He, whose nature is full of mercy, who waits for the returning prodigal, has spoken pardon once more, and in Christ Jesus is, I trust, a reconciled God and Father. While I would not think less of my sins, I think of

Christ more, and rejoice in the precious declaration, 'If any man sin, we have an advocate with the Father, Jesus Christ the righteous.' O that precious advocacy!

"I was much interested in the account you gave of the change in dear ——. Is it not a great change, mother, to have cherished a hope of salvation, and expected a place in heaven, and then to find ourselves destitute of the requisites for entering that world? How important that we examine the foundation of our hopes. Let us ask in earnest; let us dig deep; for if we mistake in this matter, it will be an eternally fatal error. Good works, falsely so called, are indeed a poor foundation; for which of us has any good works to plead! Who will dare in the presence of spotless purity, before Him who knows our inmost being, to ask for a place in heaven on account of any good he has done? There is but one plea, but one name that will tremble on the lips of any of our guilty race in that day, when the judgment shall set and the books be opened. He that is brought within the dazzling effulgence of Jehovah's unstained holiness, unless covered with the robe of Jesus' righteousness, will feel that there is no hotter fire of torment than the presence of that consuming, ineffable holiness. How many an astonished sinner, who has thought God altogether such an one as himself, will feel that he is indeed of purer eyes than to look upon sin but with abhorrence. Yet if we have cast ourselves on his own promise, 'Though your sins be as scarlet, they shall be white as snow,' coming to that fountain which has been opened for sin and uncleanness, washing our robes and making them white in the blood of the Lamb, we need not shrink even from the presence of Him before whom the seraphim vail their faces.

'Forever here I rest my cause,
I make this only plea:
Christ hath obeyed thy righteous laws,
Christ hath expired for me.'

"It is wonderful that a guilty sinner can ever be made to come to God with confidence;—that that sense of guilt, which it might be supposed would fill him with trembling and alarm, can all be taken away, when he believes that 'God is in Christ reconciling the world unto himself, not imputing their trespasses unto them.' Truly this is the amazing love of God."

The Sabbath School Missionary Society in Watertown had frequently assisted the mission, both with money and books, and in return received from Miss W. several interesting letters. The following is an extract from one of them.

"*Corfu, June* 8, 1845.

"DEAR BROTHER R.:—Let me address through you the loved and generous Missionary Society who have perhaps thought me ungrateful for all the interest they have shown in my little flock, but to whom I feel deeply thankful for what they have enabled me to do for poor Greek children.

"Accept then, dear friends of the Sabbath School Missionary Society, my sincere thanks for the sum of forty dollars placed at my disposal. It has enabled me to clothe, in part, four poor country girls who have come in from the distance of nearly two miles to attend our mission school. The oldest of the four is a very plain Greek country girl, who has received the larger portion of what has been expended of your donation. She sews very neatly, and is thus able now to earn the clothing I have been accustomed to give her, which you will all think is much better. She reads, too, very well, writes neatly, and knows a little arithmetic and grammar. But you will say, Is this all she is taught? No, dear friends, this is not what I left my home for. Every day when she comes to school, she sits down with the Bible Class, around my little table, and we read together the precious gospel of Christ. I try in their language to explain it to them, and tell them that it teaches them they must be born again in order to be saved. I try to show them, that they have sinned against God, and must ask forgiveness of him alone, and not of man. I also try to convince them that 'not that which goeth into a man defileth him, but that which cometh out;' for they are taught that to eat meat on a fast day is an awful sin, while lying, anger, stealing, and Sabbath-breaking, are comparatively trifles.

"And do you ask, What does this Greek girl, whom you have clothed and enabled to come to the school, think of this? I may say she likes the Bible lesson, and has often said, when it was a little delayed, Shall we not read the gospel to-day? She is always very sober and attentive, and sometimes reproves the others when they are inattentive and playful. But I must add, she does not like the truth; she is like that Pharisee of whom Jesus told, who thanked God that he was not as other men, he fasted twice in the week. She keeps all the fasts with great strictness, and will not work on their sacred feast days for any thing you can give her. But I fear she trusts in all these good works, and keeps all the vain observances she is taught at home, believing that she will thus recommend herself to God.

"Dear friends, you know it is only God who can open her blind eyes, and show her that she is a poor sinner, dependent on Christ alone for salvation. Will you not pray for her that she may be taught of God? She has been comfortably clothed by your kindness, but O she has not yet the precious garment of Christ's righteousness to cover her naked soul.

"All the poor are very poor. If you should go into their houses, with only the ground for a floor, you would think you could never live in such a little, dark place. Their parents cannot buy them clothes, but they show their thankfulness by sending us little presents of goat's milk and eggs. There are some other poor little children in school, who have had some help from the fund you have supplied, but I am obliged to be careful how I give from it, or it would be spent in vain.

"And now there is another class I want to speak to you of. Do you know that there are about two thousand soldiers, English, Scotch, and Irish living here? They are sent here by the British government to protect these islands. They are not soldiers such as you see at home, who put on a uniform for training days, and then take it off and go back to their business again. But these are soldiers all the time, and do nothing else but drill, and stand sentinels, and learn how to fight battles. Almost all of them are wicked men, and as they live altogether in great houses called barracks, they become still more wicked. Some of them have children, and these little boys and girls, brought up in these barracks, are taught all manner of vice. Now you may easily suppose that we wish very much to do something for these poor children. We do indeed; and we have a Sabbath school on Sunday afternoon for them. But as they are taught to be so wicked, they need something to induce them to come to Sabbath school, and there is hardly any thing so attractive as a Sabbath school book to take home and read. We have now very few books to give them, and consequently not so many attend as used to. We want, therefore, very much some Sabbath school books for these poor children of soldiers. Will you send us some? These books can go where we cannot, into these same wicked barracks. Sometimes the soldiers come and ask for books themselves, and we trust that some have thus been blessed in their souls. Surely this is missionary work; for these children are in some cases little better than heathen.

"When Mrs. D. asked the other day, Where shall we get some Sabbath school books for our scholars? Mr. A. said, Write to Watertown, and they will send you some. What can you do for us? May we look for a little box ere long? Pray for us, dear friends, and the Lord hear your supplications in his mercy.

"Your grateful and affectionate friend,

"S. E. Waldo."

CHAPTER XX.

Removal to Piraeus—Visit to Athens—Letter to the Board—Persecutions of Dr. King—To the Thanksgiving circle at home—Last hours of 1846.

As they were expecting a teacher from Scotland in the course of a few months, to take the charge of those Jewesses now in the Corfu mission school, by which the number of their pupils would be so much reduced as hardly to require the services of two, it was thought best that Miss Waldo should visit Athens, or rather Piraeus, the port of Athens, for the purpose of consulting with Mr. and Mrs. Buel, and seeing what prospect there might be of her being more useful with them. The particulars of her journey are given in the following letter

TO HER MOTHER.

"*Piraeus, July* 2, 1846.

"My dear Mother :—Will you not be surprised when you see the place of my date? You have been so long accustomed to Corfu, that this will look like a strange face. Well, dearest mother, here is your Emmy, within sight of that once renowned city, to whom the whole world looked, as the seat of learning and the arts, the home of the gifted and the brave. Here I am, surrounded by the ruins of ancient greatness and glory, now no more. Wherever my eye turns, it meets with objects replete with classic associations, and awakening emotions not to be described. But before I indulge my still excited feelings in an account of some of the wonders I have seen, let me tell you how I came here. Mrs. Buel very kindly invited me to spend a few days with her last May, but circumstances did not then allow me to. At length, every thing being favorable, I yielded to her re-renewed and earnest solicitations, and the advice of our own family, and left home June 20th.

"Was I not rather adventurous to travel unaccompanied by any one? I did dread it a little, but a gracious Providence protected me, and attended my way with mercies. From Corfu to Patras, I was the only lady on board the steamer; but the captain was very gentlemanly and attentive; and at Patras, we were joined by a pleasant Greek family,—a young bride and her husband, with a sick cousin, whom they were accompanying to Athens for change of air. We left Corfu at 1 o'clock, P. M., and reached Patras at 4 A. M. It looks like a hot place, rather low, but has some fine houses and pleasant country seats. We left Patras at noon, and stopped at the pretty village of Vostitza on the gulf of Corinth, a romantic little spot which took my fancy more than Patras, although I was told it was rendered unhealthy by the badness of the water. It is built on a high cliff, which rises abruptly from the sea, perforated with large subterranean passages, which communicate with the town. Large parties of the Vostitziotes came off in boats to the steamer, bringing and taking passengers. Their intelligent countenances and manly forms struck me as bearing a striking contrast to those of the Corfuotes. From Vostitza we came to Lontraki, so called from warm springs found there, supposed to afford a beneficial bath for invalids. We anchored here at 9 P. M., and slept on board. In the morning we went on shore. From the depot we had a fine view of ancient Corinth. You may imagine my feelings as I gazed on the very city where Paul lived a year and a half, and to whose inhabitants he had preached the glorious gospel of the blessed God, with the sweet assurance from the God he served, 'Fear not, Paul, I have much people in this city.' To think he had looked on the same skies and rocky hills, had sailed on the same broad gulf, and looked on the very landscape that lay before me, was an inspiring thought. I breathed forth a prayer, that I too might possess a portion of that spirit which glowed in his bosom, which made him almost forget to observe the beauties of art and nature that met his eye, as he traversed the streets of that fair city once called the eye of Greece.

"At twelve we got into the carriages which transport the passengers and baggage across the isthmus to Piraeus. This is rather a dangerous route, although across an open plain; for the whole surrounding country is infested with mountain robbers. Only three days before this, they had attacked a party, who had been on an excursion to Southern Greece, and were returning with the horses of the king. As we had some public money with us, we went guarded, and I think you would have been amused to have seen our company,—four or five old rattling carriages drawn by gaunt, bony horses, that looked as if they never ate a peck of oats, preceded by four Greek officers, mounted on fine, high spirited steeds, and armed to the teeth with pistols, swords, &c. In this way we went galloping over the sandy plain, now and then halting, as we drew near some dreaded spot, to take a moment's reconnoitre, and cast a trembling glance at some neighboring thicket, to see if it concealed any of the fierce brigands.

"Mr. B. kindly came up to Calamachy to meet me at the depot there. Right glad was I to see a fellow countryman again, and relieve my tongue by speaking English once more, as I had spoken Greek and Italian all the journey. We had a pleasant sail of four hours, and at eight in the evening, anchored in the ancient port of Athens, Piraeus. Mr. B. has a very pleasant residence here, cool and airy, and a very pleasant circle of Greek friends, a number of whom I have already seen.

"Last week we went to Athens to visit the schools, and heard and saw much to interest. There is far more love of learning here than in Corfu. The girls seem like those at home, and I heard some spirited recitations from dark-eyed Athenians. Being somewhat indisposed from the fatigue of my journey, and the extreme heat, I was unable to visit the ruins of the Acropolis. That rich feast I enjoyed yesterday. I stood on the platform where Demosthenes, ages since, had stood and thundered forth in burning eloquence his soul-stirring orations. No wonder that the flame of Greek patriotism kindled in his bosom, as, from that lofty summit, he looked out on a scene of rare beauty. The clear sky of Attica over his head, the lovely vale at his feet, the noble hills everywhere bounding his horizon, save where the blue Archipelago shut it in, all, all was calculated to stir each patriotic feeling, and awaken heroic ardor.

"But more subdued and holier feelings possessed my heart, when I planted my feet on the rocky summit of Mars' Hill, and heard the echo of that voice that once there proclaimed to the superstitious Athenians, the

Unknown God. Alas, could he now return, he would find the God of the Bible still '*Unknown*' in modern Athens. He would see a people still in all things too superstitious, and would still have occasion to repeat the proclamation, 'God now commandeth all men everywhere to repent.'

"How can I describe, dear mother, the delight I felt while viewing the chaste beauty of the temple of Theseus, or the awe that came over me as I drew near the gigantic Parthenon, or the admiration spontaneously called forth by the finished perfection of Erectheon. These were the works of distant ages. The glad throng that once frequented these temples, the triumphal processions that once passed through these gates, where are they now? So shall we pass away and be as a forgotten dream. Yet when these massive pillars, that have stood for ages, shall have crumbled to dust, and the earth itself shall be dissolved, our deathless spirits will live on, and on, surviving the wreck of all material things, themselves immortal and imperishable. O what a mystery is our being! How awful the trust committed to us, the keeping of such a soul! It is too great a trust for us. Let us give it into the hands of our mighty Redeemer who alone is able to keep us until the last day; and then, amid dissolving worlds, we can lift up our heads and rejoice that our salvation draws nigh.

"Dearest mother, how your Emmy wishes you were at her side, sharing all these pleasures and thus doubling them. They cannot fill the void your absence leaves in my heart. They cannot make me forget that I am a stranger, far away from a land whose sky is indeed often lowering and dark, whose howling winds and rude storms contrast strongly with this sunny clime;—but the land of my fathers,—the home of liberty, truth and piety, —dear, dear New England. And that humble spot, my home, where a mother's heart glows with warm affection, where dear sisters and brothers meet in fond fraternal intercourse,—that bright fireside which even the passing stranger loves,—O, is not my heart ever there?

"Well, dear mother, perhaps I shall make this my sojourning place instead of Corfu. I am not yet decided, nor do I know how the Board may view the matter. One object in visiting Piraeus now, was to reconnoitre the field, and see what prospects of usefulness it afforded. My dear friends here are very desirous that I should come, and I know they would make my home as happy as it could possibly be away from you. I can have access to a much better class of Greeks here than in Corfu. But I cannot have as direct an influence over them, as it would be impossible here to form a regular school. The government will not tolerate any school in which the Greek catechism is not taught by a priest; and that, our principles would not allow. But our missionaries have permission to teach English here; a large number of young persons wish to learn it, and through this door we can gain access to them. The domestic duties of Mrs. B. do not allow her to meet the requests of the people here, and to do so, a teacher who can devote herself wholly to the work is necessary. I feel that it is a field requiring much heavenly wisdom and holy determination, and I cannot but shrink in view of my own unfitness. Pray for me, dear mother, that God would lead me in his own way and prepare me for his own glory.

"God bless you, dearest, keep you from every ill, and unite us before his glorious throne, prays

"Your own fond

"EMMY."

Her reasons for leaving Corfu are more fully detailed in the following letter

TO THE SECRETARY OF THE BOARD.

"*Piraeus, Aug.* 3, 1846.

"REV. S. PECK,

"DEAR SIR:—Your kind note of June 16th was received with wonted pleasure. Though brief, I valued it all the more for the kindness that would snatch a moment from pressing cares and multiform duties to write to one so undeserving. Thank you a thousand times for every word of encouragement it breathed, and each consoling exhortation to trust unfalteringly in that faithful Redeemer who is 'the same yesterday, to-day, and forever.' Our only hope is in him, whether discouragements meet us from home or abroad; for we know that it is no less his sovereign work to enkindle and keep alive in his church a zeal for the extension of his kingdom, than to open the superstitious mind to the cheerful reception of the truth.

"In my last, I expressed a desire to meet more fully the design of the Board in sending me to Greece. I knew it was the opinion of the members of the Corfu mission, and it most decidedly accorded with my own, that the Greek department of the school was far from answering the original intentions of the Board in establishing a mission school, and what was more that there was no probability it ever would.

"While the removal of the mission to some other station was a matter of probability, I cherished the hope that a change of locality might open to me some more useful and promising field. Salonica especially had attracted my attention as being destitute of female schools, and solicitous for their establishment. But with the abandonment of that idea, and after the decision to remain at Corfu, I often felt in a strait betwixt two as to my personal duty. I had no desire to return home if I could serve God more abroad, but I could not be willing to burden our dear church with my support, if I could not return an equivalent in service to his cause.

"Such feelings were not, I trust, the restlessness of a discontented spirit, nor even the disguised yearnings of an exile's heart for home. No, my dear sir, it was not so; for whenever I have met with any thing that seemed to say, I was not here in vain, from my inmost heart I have felt that it would be sweet to teach, to toil, to die even, in this strange land, if I might here save some precious souls from death. I have indeed often felt, (did before I came abroad, and have still more since,) that the work of a missionary was too high, too holy a trust to be committed to me,—that I was exceedingly deficient in the most important qualifications for it,—and a sense of this has often made me weep and tremble.

"In this state of mind I received an invitation from dear Mrs. B. to spend a few weeks with her in Piraeus; and a favorable opportunity offering, I left Corfu on the 20th of June with no other intention than that of enjoying the society of these dear fellow laborers for a brief interval, and visiting the principal schools in Athens, to return better fitted for my work. But after my arrival, I found some things in P. to encourage the hope that I might here find a field of labor, which, with the blessing of God, would offer better promise of success than Corfu had done. The nature of that opening you have already learned from the letters of the other members of the mission, without whose advice and approval I should have felt unwilling to act, but whose cordial assent to my removal here, has seemed a token of God's guiding providence.

"It was painful to me to feel myself thus abruptly separated from my little charge and Christian friends in Corfu; but I thought it wrong to incur the expense of my return and a journey back again in the fall, for the sake of a few months longer stay in Corfu, though I would have especially liked to aid my beloved companion Mrs. D., through this hot summer, until the arrival of the missionary teacher for the Jewesses should relieve her. But as other arrangements have been made for her assistance and relief, I have decided not to return to C. This parting is, as you may suppose, a sad one. My missionary life has been nothing but uncertainty and change, a reflection of the fluctuations which preceded my embarkation. Surely, 'coming events cast their shadows before,' in my experience. I feel especially my separation from the dear friend whose toils I have shared, and who has been a foster-mother to me, in this strange land. Her ready sympathy, her Christian counsel, her godly example, and her fervent prayers have been a precious treasure to me. I bless God that I was ever privileged with her friendship.

"I consider this undertaking as only a trial and one of uncertain issue. It may prove a failure, but that I must leave with God. I have not forgotten the caution of dear Dr. Bolles when he first spoke to me of this mission. 'The missionary to European nations,' said he, 'is above all others in danger of being diverted from his work, and of becoming insensibly interested in other subordinate objects.' And I still remember your own solemn charge on the eve of our public designation to this mission, as to the one single object we were to keep ever in view. And rest assured, my dear sir, when I find I can no longer serve that object, my connection with this mission ceases. Pray for me then, my reverend brother, that I may have grace to make this trial in the fear and strength of God. And whatever be the issue, may I be enabled to say, 'The will of the Lord be done.'"

TO MISS M. WHITING.

"*August* 4, 1846.

"Though you did not mention our beloved Seminary in your long kind letter, yet I doubt not it shares as largely as ever in your thoughts, affections, and prayers. The dear church, too, has gone through many severe trials since we parted, over which I have wept in this distant island, far away from those hallowed courts where the dove of peace so long rested. At this distance, perhaps I could not well judge of the merits of the case, nor do I wish to pass sentence on either side. Among the seceders are some whom I know as the Lord's most faithful disciples, who were sincerely devoted to his cause, and who desired to live for his glory; while among those who remain are included my most intimate and beloved friends, some of whom I have always regarded as among the Lord's hidden ones. May the Lord be with them both, and unite them to each other, by uniting them to himself. I was very happy to learn by late letters, that there was reason to hope for this.

* * * * * * * *

"Our school is indeed a motley group, including worshipers in Jewish synagogues, adorers of Catholic idolatries, devotees of Greek superstitions, and children of Episcopalians, Presbyterians, and Wesleyans, for the most part poor, and very ignorant, untidy in their habits, untruthful in word, and selfish in their feelings. To all who can read we teach the word of God daily in three different languages, and attempt to lead them to Christ. But as yet we have gathered no ripe fruit."

TO MISS S. T. BOSWORTH.

"*Aug.* 5, 1846.

"The Greek government was never more intolerant than it now is. You have no doubt seen allusions to the persecutions of Rev. Dr. King, long missionary of your Board to Greece. He published a small book, in answer to some charges brought against him, in which he took opportunity to point out some of the corruptions of the Greek church, and quoted their own fathers against them. This excited great indignation. He was accused of blasphemy, and afterwards brought to trial. He appealed from the first court which condemned him, and his trial was to have taken place in Syra, a neighboring island. Meanwhile every means was used to stir up the people against him, especially in Syra. And when two weeks since, he went there in a steamer, such a crowd had assembled on the shore, and such excitement existed in the place, that it was not thought safe for him to land.

They threatened to imprison him for five or ten years. He has been once assaulted in the streets. It is not known what will be the issue, but for the present, his trial is postponed. It is true the enlightened and better classes among the Greeks, deprecate these violent measures. But still they blame him for irritating the prejudices of the people. I esteem him highly, and he has many dear friends among the pious in Europe, where he is extensively known."

TO MRS. DICKSON.

" *Sept.* 11.

" It is Saturday evening and I can imagine how happy and grateful you feel that you have been carried through another week,—have finished its labors, performed its duties, enjoyed its privileges, and been brought so much nearer your final rest. I remember with what feelings you anticipated the returning Sabbath, and rejoiced in resting a little season from earth's weary cares, and communing with Him whom your soul loveth. How I should love to ask you of the past week. Who listened with tearful attention to the Bible lesson? Who seemed subdued and serious? Who tried your patience and faith? Is there a Jewess who seems any more willing to hear the truth? Is there a Greek who seems to have any doubt of her salvation? Who has been added to the little company? Who is about to leave? Does any one seem interested in the prayer meeting, any one concerned for his soul? The brethren, alas! how few remain! are they united and engaged? What are the prospects of the mission? What signs of promise bid us hope on? O, how often have we talked over all these interesting subjects and tried to commend them to God.

"I miss very much the little prayer and missionary meetings which I enjoyed in Corfu. When there, I used to contrast them with the privileges of home, and feel as if I were in a thirsty land. But here, cut off from all Christian society and public means of grace, I feel that I have left great privileges. Thus ungrateful, I overlook present mercies in longings for the past, until, deprived of them, I learn that they too were precious. Would that I knew more of that life of faith which draws directly from the never failing fullness of Christ, and will still be vigorous when earthly supplies are all, all cut off. Pray for me that my soul may return unto its rest.

"We hope the day of our merciful visitation is not far distant,—the hour when the Lord's right arm shall be extended here in salvation. We feel that he has come near to us, and we desire to give up ourselves anew and forever to him. We have been reading 'CHRIST ON THE CROSS,' by Stephenson; a work which has given us new insight into the depths of our Saviour's sufferings for us, and the awfully heinous nature of sin, for which naught but his blood could atone. Dear Mrs. B. is intending to send you this most interesting volume, as soon as the friends in Athens have finished reading it; and may its perusal, my dear sister, bring you sweet refreshing from above. We love to commend you, with all your work, to the great Redeemer, the ever living Intercessor. May the blessed Sun of righteousness arise on our every soul, with healing in his beams. There is a precious word, dear sister, in the book of God, a most precious word, which I love to recall and repeat. It is God's word to the backslider, '*Return.*' O, does he say, Return? and will he take us back again? Yes, the command involves a promise. He who has bidden us return, will assuredly receive. He will in no wise cast out. O, to return so wholly and heartily that I might never, never rove again."

TO THE THANKSGIVING CIRCLE AT HOME.

"*Piraeus, Thanksgiving Eve, Nov.* 26, 1846.

"DEAR MOTHER, BROTHERS, AND SISTERS:—The loved anniversary of this New England festival has brought you all most tenderly to mind, and ere it closes, I must unburden my overflowing heart and tell you all again how dearly I love you. The coming shades are gathering over us, but you have just returned from the praises of the sanctuary, and are gathering round the parlor fire. Yes, I see you all. Dear, precious mother, the light and centre of that home, now smiling in the happy enjoyment of her loved ones' presence, now dropping a tear for the far away. There stands dear C., leaning over his loved S., and caressing his little E. with a father's pride. And here is our sweet J. with her darling babe in her arms, while its father is listening to the prattle of little C., and grandma has a watchful eye on gentle E. Sister S. is turning now to this one, and now to that, to see where she may lighten a care, or show a kindness. Dear L. perhaps is singing some song of by-gone days; and P., may be, is whispering in mother's ear, 'Don't you wish that Emmy was with us, mother?' Aunt M. has no doubt joined your circle and thinks of the dear brother who once rejoiced in these scenes.

"Dear, precious ones! How I would love to see you all. How would I delight to softly lift the garden latch and slily enter that old door, and be with you ere you were aware. I know you have thought of me, I know you have remembered her who three years ago (how long it seems) was with you all. She did not know then as she now does, how dear you all were, how sweet a home she had, what loving hearts she was about to tear herself from, what a cold world she was to enter.

" But this is a day of *Thanksgiving*, not of regrets. Yes, and I do give thanks. I do praise God that I ever had such a home,—that he has preserved it from sickness, sorrow, and death, these three years,—that he has blessed me with so many sweet tokens and assurances of the unabated, devoted love that still throbs in your hearts for your unworthy Emmy. And I do thank him for all his goodness to me in a strange land,—for all the fostering care of my beloved Mrs. D., for all the kindness of dear Mr. and Mrs. A., for the privilege of teaching some dear youth in Corfu about Christ, for the pleasant home I now enjoy, for the thousand comforts that are strewn in my pathway, the mercies that in rich profusion, his infinite love is daily bestowing. Yes, and I thank him for every trial, every pang of anguish, every hour of sorrow. Every stroke has been in mercy, every cross was laid upon me in love. Yes, gracious Father,

' For all I thank thee, most for the severe.'

If I never see any fruit of my feeble labors here, I shall still feel that it was ordered in mercy that I should come, that I might learn to know myself.

" Shall I ever join that dear circle again ? is a question that will intrude itself. Shall I ever again join with them in those sweet festivities ? God knows, dearest ones, he alone. His will, not ours, be done. But O, there will be a great Thanksgiving day, a gathering of an innumerable family, even the family of the first-born, whose names are written in heaven. A father waits in that heavenly mansion to welcome home his long wandering children, to wipe every tear of sorrow away; to welcome them to his arms, and bid them be forever blest. No coming separation mars the pleasure of that meeting; no thought of sickness, change, or death, casts a shade on those smiling countenances. No taint of sin is there. Say, my beloved, will you join that circle? Will you share in the thanksgivings of that redeemed company, 'who have washed their robes and made them white in the blood of the Lamb?' To be absent from you now, saddens my spirit, but to be found wanting in that great gathering, O it will be bitterness.

"God bless you all. How much my heart craves for you this night. How it yearns for you. How it would pour itself into your bosoms. Dear ones, do you not feel Emma's spirit with you? Yes, she is near.

"Farewell, dear ones, fare ye well.

"EMILY."

TO MISS M. A. WRIGHT, OF ATHENS.

"*Last Hours of* 1846.

"MY DEAR SISTER:—Your last dear note deserves many thanks; indeed, my dear sister, your friendship is a sweet privilege to me, and I trust may be a sanctified one.

"To you will I give a few moments of these last hours. How solemn the thought that we stand on the threshold of another year. The past has gone never to be recalled, with its record of mercies and privileges, of wanderings and sins. The neglected opportunities it offered we cannot again enjoy,—the transgressions that marked its hours we cannot undo. O, what so becoming to us as to bow in the dust before God, lamenting our many backslidings, and applying to him anew for pardon and cleansing in the open fountain. These are always serious hours to me, would that they had been of more lasting profit. Looking on many broken resolves, and unfulfilled purposes, and feeling more than ever my own utter weakness, I would cry, Work thou in me, O my God, for in me dwelleth no good thing."

CHAPTER XXI.

Home feelings—Incidents in School—Arrival of a box of Sabbath school books from America—Good Friday—Procession of the Tomb of Christ—Visit to Mount Pentelicos.

THE commencement of the year was always a solemn season with Miss Waldo, particularly after she joined the Greek mission. As it was on the first of January she bade farewell to her native land, the return of that day ever after recalled to her mind with great vividness the scenes of early life, the endearments of Christian friendship, and all those thousand associations which cluster around the name of home. On the third anniversary of that day she wrote as follows

TO MISS S. P. CARTER.

" *Jan.* 1, 1847.

" Sarah, love, is your heart with Emmie to-day? Are you thinking of that last sad farewell, that last burning kiss, that last agonizing embrace? Yes, I doubt not, love, amid whatever festivities you may spend the day, one answering chord will vibrate sadly to the memory of your absent Emmie. Her heart is sad to-day, for it turns back to those parting scenes, it yearns for those loved and left. Three long years have fled since I heard your voice. How long! I have been sad, but you were not near to dry my tears. I have been happy, but you were not at hand to share my joy. I have been anxious and perplexed, but I could not turn to you for counsel. I have been lonely in spirit, but you could not come to me to cheer me. I have looked on nature's beauties, but your eye could not follow my delighted gaze. I have admired the remains of art, but they were still unknown to you. Yet there has been one sweet spot, one place of meeting, love,

> 'Though sundered far, by faith we meet
> Around one common mercy-seat.'

O how often may I have been blessed in answer to your fervent supplications; and perhaps some precious upliftings of a Father's reconciled countenance, have been granted you in answer to my unworthy prayers. Here then let us continue to meet, until rich grace shall have made us meet for our eternal reunion. May we not be disappointed in that expectation. May we not then experience the anguish of eternal separation. My only hope is in the atoning death and imputed righteousness of the dear Son of God. I feel that I deserve to perish, I have undone myself, but in him is my help found.

"I have been reading with great interest, '*Christ our Law*,' by Caroline Fry, and in the clear, strong views she takes of his justifying righteousness, I have found much comfort. If the work of salvation were at all my own, if one step depended solely on me, I should despair; but because it is all of grace, from the foundation to the top stone, all through, and in Christ, there is hope even for me. O the depth of the riches of redeeming love! Self is my great foe and enemy. It asserts its claims on every occasion, and leads me into many a snare. O that it were crucified, and buried beneath the Cross."

TO MR. AND MRS. J. CARTER.

"*Piraeus, Feb.* 2, 1847.

"MY DEAR MR. AND MRS. C:—How often the memory of all your parental kindness brings the warm tears to my eyes,—and fills my heart with the tenderest emotion. Your house was like a second home to me where I never felt myself unwelcome, and which I always left with increased attachment for its dear inmates. Your kind concern in my welfare, your unfeigned friendship, your counsel and your prayers, have bound you closely to my heart in the bonds of an affection which neither absence nor distance can sever. How often I picture to myself that snug, warm parlor, where I have spent so many a quiet winter evening,—that pleasant basement where so many a prayer meeting was held—and most of all that dear little bedroom of my beloved Sarah's, where the links of our love were so closely riveted. Nor do I forget the noble vine that graces the portico, nor even the little bed of fragrant pinks or gay tulips; all is marked on memory's tablet with the accuracy of a daguerreotype. And that last Sabbath, that hasty farewell visit at noon, that parting prayer for me,—O I can never, never forget them.

"More than three years have passed since then, and, though the weeks fly by as if winged, yet when I think of you, it seems more than three times three years since I saw you. There is something inexpressibly painful in the sudden severing of all those ties which have bound us to life,—to all we hold most dear. It seems at first as if mother, sisters, brother, friends had all died at once; as if some mysterious and awful calamity had cut them off at a stroke, and left the homeless wanderer like the scathed tree of the forest when the fire has laid low its fellows. And when letters from them restore them again to you, if I may so say, it is but a partial, temporary restoration; and as the soothed spirit turns again to the scenes around it, the aching sense of separation comes home all the more keenly, as the common expressions of ordinary intercourse contrast with the warm gushings of affection contained in these letters from the early loved.

"But you will think I am unhappy, my dear friends, —that I regret, or would recall the sacrifice. O no, I am not, only the very writing of your names at the commencement of this, brought in such a tide of home feelings, that I have just given loose to them, and written as my full heart prompted. If I have changed since I left you, and I feel that I have,—if a sadder shade has fallen on my heart, these have not been the cause. It is because I have learned more of the desperate wickedness of a most deceitful heart. It is because I am so unfit for my responsible station. The trials of a missionary I had thought of and prepared for, but the necessary graces of the spirit, the previous heavenly training, the strength of faith, the unceasing conflict of the missionary, these, dear friends, were what I had not sufficiently estimated; and the painful sense of deficiency in these respects often sends me weeping to my closet. O, it is a great thing to be a *real* Christian. Have I been? Am I? are ever returning questions. There is a blessed Hiding Place, a precious, spotless righteousness, which can cover our nakedness, a blood that cleanseth. O, that is my only hope.

"But God has been very good to me, my dear friends, since we parted. His tender mercies, O, how great. His good hand is still upon me here. I have a very pleasant home with dear Mrs. B. and her kind husband. I have also a little flock around me here, to whom I hope to do good. A part of them come to learn English. They translate from the Bible, from 'The Young Christian,' from 'Todd's Evangelical Lectures to the Young,' &c., and through this medium I try to communicate instruction to them. Another part come to learn needle-work and fancy knitting; these are collected into a Sabbath school on Sunday.

"Shall I copy my last Sunday's journal for you? 'January 31. A very windy, tempestuous Sabbath, so that we expected no children at the Sabbath school. Were agreeably disappointed by the coming of thirteen interesting girls. Two of these had committed to memory the ten commandments and an entire chapter in Matthew; others had learned more or less verses. The lesson was the tenth of Mark, commencing at the seventeenth verse. Labored to show them the necessity of supreme love to God, and the consequent guilt and perdition of all who love any inferior object before him. Illustrated it by the case of the rich youth who would not sell all. As is usual among the Greeks, all asserted that they loved Christ. Endeavored to convince them of their delusion, by showing them that love manifests itself in desires to please the loved object, &c. One little girl could hardly restrain her tears. All were attentive.'"

TO HER MOTHER.

"*Piraeus, Feb.* 4, 1847.

"DEAREST MOTHER:—Your last letter of December 16, awakened mingled feelings of joy and sadness; joy and gratitude that my beloved ones were spared while others were in a moment stripped of their heart's treasures, and sadness because you were sad, dearest mother, because you felt lonely and dejected, because you missed the absent and departed. But it must be so in this world, mother dear; such is life. We cannot escape the common lot. Thanks to God that we have been spared much of human misery. How many years we were an unbroken circle, full of health and life! And when sickness had laid its heavy hand on dear father, how many years was he spared to bless us! And then, too, when death first came, when the first chasm was made, how much mercy was mingled with the cup! And since that bereaving stroke that left us so lonely—that took from us our guide, our counselor, our kind and loving father, O has not God been good, very good? Did not his kind hand prosper me, a mere girl, in my four years teaching in Boston? Did it not raise up a kind and affectionate husband for our sweet J.? Did it not succeed the efforts of our dear C. in business, and bless him with domestic joys? Has it not supplied your every want, educated dear sisters, and watched over your far away Emmie, preserving her in perfect health and strength unto this day? Shall we not say, beloved mother, 'Bless the Lord, O our souls, and forget not all his benefits?' Let us dwell on these; and let us think, dearest, of those richer blessings of the heavenly inheritance. Let us think of an atoning, interceding Saviour, a blessed Sanctifier and Comforter, a loving, heavenly Father, a heaven of perfect rest, and let us pray that we and ours may enter into that rest.

"Since I last wrote you I have had several things to encourage me in my work here. Beside my English classes, I have an interesting class of ten or twelve who spend three or four hours of the afternoon with me, sewing or knitting. They have all come of their own accord; and as we can talk or read to them while they are at work, and as all attend Sabbath school, we feel glad in this addition to our labors. Any thing that will give us access to the people, particularly to the young, is pleasing to us. Our Sabbath school is now quite interesting. O that we could see some of them convicted of sin, and sensible of their need of a Saviour. How we feel our own powerlessness when we attempt to produce this conviction. This is what we cannot do. We can give moral instruction, we can point out what is right and wrong, but to make even a child *feel* that he is a sinner we cannot. There we must bow before the sovereign grace of God."

"*Feb.* 24, 1847.

"To-day I had a very interesting conversation with my boys who are very intelligent, communicative lads. Something led me to remark that the church with us is composed only of those who commune, they asked with great surprise, But do not all commune; This led to a long and serious conversation on the nature of the Lord's Supper, and the qualifications requisite to the right observance of it. It was very interesting to see these dear youth, with the most fixed attention, and earnest manner, listen and speak on these important subjects, on the right knowledge of which their salvation depends.

"I must tell you a little incident which occurred day before yesterday. One of the lads who had been a little vexed with his companion for proving him to be wrong on a point upon which he had been very positive began to amuse himself by causing others to laugh while we were reading, and as they seemed more disposed to be diverted than instructed, I closed the book, and said, 'Since you are only making sport of your lesson, I shall hear no more to-day.' So saying, I left them, sat down at the girls' table, and addressed myself to them. I felt grieved, for it was the Bible they were reading, and I felt particularly desirous that *that* chapter might be blessed to them. They saw that I was grieved, but I said no more, and they went silently away. What was my surprise ten minutes after, to hear the door bell ring and see them all return, the offender in advance. With a trembling voice he said, 'We are sensible, Miss W., that we did wrong and we are very sorry for it. We have come back to beg you to forgive us.' This frank and manly confession, so difficult to the proud spirit of youth, has attached me more than ever to these young lads. Of course I was most happy to pardon them all."

TO MISS C. HAYNES.

"*March* 5, 1847.

"I have been very much interested of late in one of my classes. It consists of three intelligent lads about fifteen years of age. One of them in particular is a frank, open-hearted youth, and not without feeling on religious subjects. You would be interested, could you hear the long, earnest talks we have together. They have just finished translating into English a little Greek book enitled, '*Conversations of a Mother with her Children about a New Heart.*' It treats of the subject of regeneration, that great mystery to the Greeks, in a simple, evangelical manner, so plain that it could not be misunderstood; that is, so far as the unrenewed heart can understand it. I think they have now some clear idea of its nature, but that it is something they can experience, seems to them incredible. 'Why, such a change,' said the one above referred to, 'such a living to please God, is absolutely beyond man's power.' 'Yes,' I replied, 'it is beyond his power, and for that very reason is the Holy Spirit promised to do it for, and in us.'

"Yesterday they were reading of a person who had been converted, of whom it was remarked that he at first appeared very sad and distressed, but after a short time thoughtful but peaceful. I asked what had made him sad? 'Because he was repenting,' was the reply. 'And what made him afterwards peaceful?' 'Because of the good works he began to do,' they answered. Here was an essential error with which we have frequently to contend. I then tried to show them that it was the peace of pardon through Christ. 'But how can a man know he is pardoned?' they eagerly asked. And in this most interesting manner they talked long and earnestly. O pray for these dear youth that they may be led to Christ."

About this time she received from America the box of books for the missionary school at Corfu, for which she had written June 8. Her gratitude for this expression of interest and assurance of continued prayer, is expressed in the following note

TO MRS. DICKSON.

"*Piraeus, March* 12, 1847.

"MY DEAR MRS. DICKSON:—I should like to see your pleasure, may I not say delight, when this box arrives, and its contents are examined. I am sure you will say,

Blessings on the Watertown Sabbath School Missionary Society. Really they have exceeded my expectations, generous as I knew their young hearts to be. Blessed be the Lord who hath put it into their hearts to love the Corfu school. I have been very busy unpacking and repacking, assorting papers, &c., so that nothing might delay the forwarding of the box by tomorrow's steamer, as I know you need it immediately. It contains, as you will see, about one hundred and sixty bound volumes, beside a large number of interesting juvenile papers, magazines, tracts, &c. There were duplicates of a few of the books. These I have retained, as they will be of use here. I have taken out a set of the different magazines and papers, and intend to have them bound, as they are too good to be lost, which would be their fate in their present form.

"A most kind and interesting letter arrived the same day by mail, from their late superintendent. I hesitated about sending it for your perusal, as it expresses far more esteem and confidence towards me than I am worthy to enjoy. But as I wish you to see the spirit of our young benefactors, I have concluded to send it; confident that you know my faults and defects too well, to be misled by my too kind friends. I hope you will be able in the course of the spring or summer, to write these young friends, and give them some interesting particulars of your dear flock, which you know how to do so well, but which it is impossible for me to do, now that I am removed from Corfu.

"O may the blessing of God attend this gift. May the Holy Spirit accompany the perusal of these little volumes, and may these weak things be made to confound the things that are mighty. The best of all is, that they who give, are they who *pray* for us. We are not forgotten, our dear charge are not forgotten before God."

Addressing the Sabbath school from which the books had been received, she says, "I have the greatest reason to thank you for your readiness to respond to my request, when you had so many other calls upon your charities; and I thank you for the noble generosity with which you have supplied the Corfu school. The Lord reward you for all your labors of love, and grant that while watering others, your own souls may be richly blest. I am as happy to know that you give fifty dollars to support a Western Colporteur, as to receive forty dollars for the mission school in Corfu. My cause is a very little thing. Christ's cause is the great object. I would gladly hide myself and my work, if his may prosper. Yet do not think I would have you abate one jot of your interest in the Greek mission. O that with strong cryings and tears you might supplicate the Throne of Mercy in its behalf, till this wilderness be made to blossom as the rose."

TO HER MOTHER.

"*Piraeus, April* 2, 1847.

"MY DEAREST MOTHER:—My heart has a strong drawing homeward this afternoon, and I feel as if I must converse a while with you. It is not a strange or unwonted thing to feel thus. O, no, dearest mother, your image like a sweet guardian angel seems ever near me. Every kind voice seems an echo of your own loving tones, every affectionate glance seems a beam from your own dear eyes, every thoughtful attention is a sweet memento of your untiring devotion, that fostered me all too tenderly. Ah, my mother! dear cherished name, shall I ever again hear the response to my oft repeated exclamation, my mother? Dear Mrs. B. often calls me her daughter, and the word thrills through my heart, though she is more a sister than a mother. But God is very good to me, yes, very kind and gracious. I would dwell on what I have, not on what I have not. I feel ashamed and confounded before him, when I think of the ungrateful returns I have made for all his infinite goodness. O for a heart to love him supremely, to obey him implicitly, to live alone for him. What great condescension God has shown in comparing his love to that of a parent. I remember one text especially that has often seemed most tender and precious. 'As one whom his *mother* comforteth,' saith God, '*so* will I comfort thee.' He knows all the sweetness of this tender relation, and he has been pleased to speak to our hearts in such declarations of his tender affection. And yet he is the High and Holy One who dwelleth in light inaccessible, the Infinite, the Ever-blessed. Truly there is a mystery in his love for fallen, sinful man, which these narrow hearts of ours cannot fathom. What an inexpressible comfort that we are not in a world where chance rules, but where a God of infinite wisdom and love reigns. We cannot die before his appointed hour, we cannot suffer but in his appointed way, and shall we not cheerfully say, 'Our Father's will be done?'

"To-day every thing is still and quiet around us. Silence and seriousness reign. The yards of the shipping are reversed, the flags are at half-mast. The strictest abstinence from food is observed. It is '*good Friday*,' or '*great Friday*,' as the Greeks say,—the most solemn day in all the year. And truly it is a day to awaken serious thought, and penitential remembrances, for it witnessed the crucifixion of our Lord, when he poured out his soul unto death, when he bore our sins in his own body on the tree. O, that we could see among this people some evidence that they realized the object of the great event they commemorate,—that the Son of God was manifested to take away our sins. But, alas! with them it is but an outward ceremony, that excites the passions for the hour, by the exhibition to their senses of a suffering Saviour, while it produces none of that repentance which is unto life.

"Tomorrow, at midnight, the long fast of forty days ceases; and many sit up till one o'clock that they may satisfy the cravings of appetite, and not a few fall sick from the sudden exchange from severe abstinence to overeating. The lambs are killed tomorrow, and on Sabbath morning very early they celebrate the resurrection. This, and the following five days, are great feasts, and are called by the Greeks ἡ Λαμπρά, the bright days. The Greek church, however, has nothing of the pomp and parade of the Romish church on these occasions.

"*April* 3.

"Last night we went to see the procession of the Tomb of Christ, as it is called. A gaudy sort of bier, painted blue, and decked with flowers and candles, stood in the middle of the church. On the bier, beneath the canopy, lay an embroidered representation of the dead Saviour, and at the head, a richly bound New Testament. These were kissed by the thronging multitude who, after performing this ceremony, crawled underneath the bier, imagining that they would thereby be healed of any malady which they then had. At about ten o'clock the bier, brilliant with innumerable candles, was brought out on men's shoulders and carried through the principal streets, accompanied and preceded by an immense crowd, all bearing candles. They give a peculiar waving motion to the candle, which makes them flash and flicker, and a brilliant scene it was. Ever and anon, the shrill voices of the children rose on the breeze, crying, 'Κύριε Ελέησον' 'Lord, have mercy,' and as they drew nearer, the low chant of the priests could be heard. At about eleven it is brought back to the church, and then there is a tremendous rush for the candles on the tomb or bier, as they are supposed to possess some peculiar virtue, and are a special protection to sailors in a storm. It did not seem to produce any serious feelings in the Greeks, but was only something pretty to look at, and something efficacious to worship. Ah, mother dear, what a great work must be wrought before such minds can appreciate the simplicity of the gospel."

The following letter contains an account of her visit to Mount Pentelicus.

"*Piraeus, April* 10, 1847.

"MY VERY DEAR MRS. DICKSON:—This lovely day reminds me of sunny spring time in Corfu; of the sweet, bright days when we walked together through the green lanes or by the flowery hedges, enjoying the perfume of the opening flowers, and watching the tender buds as they put forth. I remember the rich flowering of last May, when even the dark olives were bright with white starry blossoms. Yesterday, for the first time since I came to Piraeus, I saw something like the verdure of Corfu that used to delight me so much. As the Easter holidays broke up our classes, we improved the opportunity of a leisure day, to go to Mount Pentelicus. A young Greek, an acquaintance of Mrs. Buel, had kindly undertaken all the trouble of arranging, and had acquainted the Abbot of the Monastery with our intended visit. Our excellent friends, Capt. and Mrs. L. H., joined our party, and we left Piraeus at half-past seven, A. M. At Athens our friend was waiting for us, with a large coach and four; and at half-past eight, we started for our mountain trip; our Greek friend being with us on horseback. As we left Athens, the aridness of its immediate environs was exchanged for fields of grain, and orchards of fruit trees. To us, so long wearied with the sight of bare hills, baked fields, and dusty roads, it seemed enchanting. We reached the monastery at half-past ten, and a curious old place it was. I wonder if your old convent at Cephalonia ever looked like this. Through a low, narrow, and arched way, we entered the court, around which the cells are built. In the centre was a magnificent tree, in full bloom, which they called daphne, but Mrs. L. H. said it was a bay tree.

"The old abbot received us very kindly, brought us some coffee, and showed us the buildings; telling us the tale of its destruction by the Turks, and its re-construction by his uncle, the late abbot, in 1836. An inscription to this effect was written in the little church which stood on the western side of the court.

"Having rested a little, we ladies mounted the horses provided for us and ascended with them as far as the great cavern. On the left of the cavern were immense blocks of stone, I should think forty feet in height, forming a huge wall of marble, which had been broken down in the middle to obtain materials for some of the splendid temples of Athens. The cavern was quite extensive and we brought from it some beautiful crystals.

"And now began the toil; all before had been play. It was climb, climb, on and on, till we would fall down from complete exhaustion; the topmost peak ever receding as we advanced, till we almost despaired of reaching the summit. But when we reached the pass between the two highest points and could look down on the country beyond, when a wide sea of hills burst suddenly upon our view, the green plain of Marathon on their right surrounding the beautiful bay of the same name, then we were in ecstasies. O, it was a magnificent scene—wherever the eye turned, it was feasted with the most extensive and varied landscape,—hill and valley, green plain and sombre olive grove, and far away the clear blue sea dotted with innumerable islands. I shall not soon forget it. Aching at every bone and muscle, faint with exhaustion, I threw myself down beneath the shelter of a projecting rock and thought I could go no further. The rest of the party, however, were not content, but started off for the topmost peak. As I saw their receding forms, I made one more desperate effort, rose, and overtook them, and thus had the satisfaction of a full view of the Eubean Gulf.

"The descent was worse for the feet, but otherwise less fatiguing; though many a time we dropped down on the road-side, our trembling limbs refusing to sustain our weight. We dined quite in Greek style: a whole lamb roasted on a stick, and honey in the comb composed our rural repast. Mr. Buel presented the abbot with a copy of the New Testament in the original, the Old Testament translated, and other books. He had considerable conversation with him and the promise of a visit. We reached our own door at a quarter past eight, and, quite wearied, were glad to retire to our beds. To-day we find ourselves a little stiff, but not very tired."

CHAPTER XXII.

Discouragements—Means of grace—Missionary labors—Persecutions of Dr. King—Death of one of her scholars—Simonides—Order of the Demarch to discontinue their school.

MISS WALDO's plan of performing missionary labor through the medium of English classes, did not result as favorably as had been at first anticipated. Her first class was broken up by long continued illness in two of the families. Many came only for a few weeks, or at most a few months, so that the actual number who continued for any length of time, was comparatively small. It now became a serious question with her, whether Mrs. Buel could not without much difficulty perform all the missionary work which was shared between them. "I love my work," she would say, "I love the Greeks, I want to stay here and labor for their conversion; but ought I, shall I stay? I awake in the morning, and the first conscious mental action is to ask this question. I lie down at night, and fall asleep revolving it. Two hundred and forty dollars here, takes two hundred and forty from Burmah or Arracan. If it were not spent here it would be there. Is then what I can accomplish here, an equivalent to the loss of this sum to those missions? Can I hope to realize an amount of good equivalent to five native missionaries? for my salary would nearly pay five of the Maulmain assistants. This is the ever recurring question which, in some form or other, is presenting itself to my mind. If the Board were flush in funds, I should feel at ease, and would believe that a little here presented a stronger claim than more at home. But the question does not resolve itself into that; it involves the important consideration already alluded to, and it is that which makes it so serious a matter. In view of this, I have set apart the Saturdays of those weeks preceding mail day, as days of fasting and prayer, that God would prepare me to write to the Board as I ought, and that he would graciously interpose in the mean while, and open such a door as would exclude all uncertainty, and make me feel that it was indeed his good pleasure that I should remain.

"I am neither discouraged, disheartened, nor weary. But shall the laborers in one vineyard have so light and easy a task, and those in another be broken down by excessive and exhausting labor? O that there might be no necessity to agitate such questions—that all the tithes might be brought into the store-house, and the treasury of the Lord be filled. O that he would turn and save us, and make us like those that dream, that this people might say, 'The Lord hath done great things for them.'

"Sometimes, I think God may be only trying my faith and spirit of prayer, and is calling me to wrestle for the blessing he is ready to bestow. He has, I believe, visited our souls, and began a work of quickening grace within our hearts; and we do desire to give ourselves up to him to be his alone. In his loving kindness he has given us the society of a most holy, devoted Christian, whose faithful efforts, heavenly walk, and fervent prayers, have been blessed to our souls. We hear our God saying to us, 'Awake, thou that sleepest, and arise from the dead, and Christ shall give thee light.' We hope the light will come; we do trust that God is preparing us for a blessing, and therefore, though cast down, we are not in despair. This dear brother is Lieutenant H. of her Majesty's ship Rodney, which has been lying in port some seven weeks or more. I never knew a man so Christ-like. I never saw such beautiful symmetry of Christian character. I never behold such harmonious blending of all the various graces of the true believer. Though abounding in earnest effort, he is of a deeply meditative character, and, though eminently devout, there is such an unaffected meekness adorning his whole conduct, as adds a crowning charm to every grace. We do bless God for granting us the privilege of knowing so holy a man, one who lives so much above the world, so dead to sin, and so much alive to God. His prayers I shall not soon forget; they seem so much like talking with God. When we see how trying his situation,—a First Lieutenant of a large ship, not one of whose officers is a Christian, and scarcely one at all serious, it makes it most manifest that place and circumstances are no excuse for worldliness, and I feel ashamed and confounded that I have allowed such excuses for my coldness and earthliness. O that his brief stay may be blessed to our quickening and return to God."

The nature of her missionary labors at Piraeus, may be learned from the following letter

TO THE SECRETARY OF THE BOARD.

" *Piraeus, June* 9, 1847.

" Rev. S. Peck,—Dear Sir:—The returning heat of summer reminds me that nearly a year has passed since I came to Piraeus, though I can scarcely realize the lapse of time. Often during its revolving months have I been tenderly affected by a sense of the loving kindness of my heavenly Father, in giving me so happy a home in this foreign land; verily he hath remembered his covenant to the fatherless and the stranger. In dear Mrs. Buel especially, I have found a most tender friend, a most affectionate sister. I should indeed be ungrateful were I unhappy in the midst of such blessings. A review of the Lord's mercies is always more delightful than that of our own doings, but I feel that it will be profitable both for quickening and humbling, to consider the latter also.

"Some of my first efforts were for the class of young ladies who formerly enjoyed the instruction of Mrs. B. I continued with them her practice of reading and translating into Greek select chapters from the Bible. They also commenced the translation of Abbott's 'Young Christian,' which I thought well adapted from its simplicity to give them correct views, and at the same time they were occupied in translating into English an excellent little Greek tract, entitled, '*Conversations on the New Heart*,' a subject least of all understood by this nation. They were an interesting class truly, although their volatility seemed almost to exclude serious thought. But long continued illness has broken up this class, and it is not probable it will be re-collected. One only continues.

"My next class consisted of lads about fifteen years of age; less advanced, however, than the others in English. They completed the little work on regeneration mentioned above, and very many interesting conversations had we about that most interesting doctrine. The leading points, viz., the universal depravity of mankind, the necessity of regeneration, our absolute dependence upon the Holy

Spirit, and our personal responsibility, were successively considered and explained; the Searcher of hearts alone knows with what effect. They are now reading an admirable little tale published by Dr. King, from the French of the Countess de Gasparin, on the observance of the Sabbath. They have also translated half of Todd's '*Lectures to Children*,' which is not too simple for minds previously destitute of all right views of the Gospel. They have also a weekly lesson in the Gospel. The most interesting of this class has lately gone to Russia. Only two remain. Besides the seven in the above mentioned classes, I have had thirteen pupils, some for one month, some for two, some for three, and of all these but three have continued. These are interesting young persons; one especially is thoughtful and susceptible, a regular attendant on our Sabbath school, where she each Sunday repeats an entire chapter, committed to memory during the week in the midst of many other duties.

"Since January we have had a little sewing school, attended as varyingly as the English classes. Some twenty girls have at different times attended, though seldom over ten on any one day, and often less. Of late, however, this has been more regularly and fully attended; but whether it will continue to be I cannot tell. A few of the younger I am teaching to read and write. All are expected to attend the Sabbath school, and a pleasant hour is that on the Sabbath morn; then we feel most happy, most at home. The little ones are separated into an infant class, which we alternate in teaching, and seldom do we have to complain of inattention, although their minds seem to lose impressions as fast as they are made. You see, my dear sir, that my work is to a considerable extent uncertain, and desultory; and recent attempts have settled the question of the practicability of a regularly organized school, as not to be hoped for. We must be satisfied therefore, 'to draw the bow at a venture,' so to speak, and trust to the guiding Spirit to infix the arrow in some sinner's heart.

"Will you write me with all frankness, and tell me without reserve your candid opinion of my duty, assured that I have the fullest confidence in your decisions; and may the Lord Jehovah guide us by his pillar-cloud through this wilderness, prays

"Your attached friend and sister in the gospel

"S. E. Waldo."

TO MISS. C. HAYNES.

"*Piraeus, July* 6, 1847.

"My ever dear C.:—Your dear long letters of March and May have been received since my note to you of March 5,—and many thanks do I owe you for all the warm affection they breathe, and for all the information they contain on subjects of mutual interest. What can I send you in return out of my barren stock? We have no dear church here of whom to write; no large circle of friends to whom to refer; no new and profitable publications to mention; no gathering of souls; no lengthening of Zion's cords. Well, dear Caty, if all these fail, there is one dear and loving Friend; one who is Zion's glory, and her King; one who is to us, 'all, and in all,' of whom we might write endlessly, without ever exhausting the glorious theme. O, for a heart so full of him that all my conversation and all my correspondence might bear a holy unction from him.

"I have just finished reading the life and writings of

one who lived for and in him, who was determined to know nothing among men, save Christ, and him crucified; and the perusal has been condemning and soul humbling indeed. O, how little I know of him, though so long called by his name. How little have I felt of that hidden life in him of which the world knows not. How is it with you, my Caty? Is he the beloved of your soul, and do you sit under his shadow with great delight?

"I find the style of Scotch writers and preachers quite marked and peculiar, bearing very much the impress of the days of the Covenanters; especially is this the case in their views, or rather in their expressions, relative to the Lord Jesus. There is a glow, a fervor, a holy familiarity with our gracious Elder Brother, and especially, frequent, expressive, aud rich allusions to him, in his glorious character of the Lord our righteousness, which I think are wanting in our American preachers and authors, especially in New England. One reason for this in N. E. is, I think, the prevalence of that doctrine, which, despising all the glorious mysteries of faith as dreamy mysticism, would treat the great truths of the gospel with all the coldness of the philosopher, and not with the glowing feelings of the believer. And it is a natural consequence that those who oppose their errors should follow their style, and oppose argument to argument. But, alas! too often thereby the fervent love which should be the charm of gospel preaching is lost.

"The English writers too, I mean the devotional writers, dwell largely and richly on the glorious theme of Christ our Justification; but they have not that peculiar, and, if I may so say, familiar style of writing of Christ which marks the Scotch. The Scotch are peculiarly biblical in their prayers and preaching, delighting in

Scripture phraseology. And I do think there is more true piety in Scotland than in all Europe beside.

" We see no signs of the Spirit's moving among us, but we hear of his workings not far off. Six hundred Syrians near Aleppo have lately sought Protestant instruction; and though no one supposes they are converted men, yet that they voluntarily come to put themselves under the preaching of a simple gospel, O, is it not cause for gratitude to God? The work among the Armenians, too, is going gradually on. Twelve females were lately added to the infant church in Constantinople, and the little churches in Nicomedia, and Ada Bazar, remain faithful, although yet without pastors.

" Pray for me, that I may have grace to give myself wholly to the Lord and his work, and be made the instrument of bringing some perishing sinners to Jesus. In myself is nothing but sin, but in Jesus is perfect righteousness. He is the cleft rock in which the guilty sinner may hide and fear the wrath of God no more. O, to be hidden deep in him. Who that feels his innate vileness and unworthiness, can doubt that salvation is of grace, through the righteousness of another, for whose sake alone we are saved, and loved, and adopted? Is it not sweet to be loved in the beloved? That is a ground of hope and confidence on which the guiltiest may stand when lost to all hope in himself. When I see how wholly evil and perverse I am, having nothing good in me except what his own Spirit works, O, I tremble and am ready to sink. But when I see that when we were enemies Christ died for us, was made a curse for us, became sin for us, blotted out the hand-writing against us,—when I see that the Father hid his face from his only begotten, and dearly beloved, because our sin was upon him,—

when I read that the righteousness of God without the law is manifested, which is by faith of Jesus Christ,—that by the obedience of one many shall be made righteous,—then my poor, guilty, perishing soul beholds a refuge, a glorious hiding-place. Hateful in myself, yet beloved in the Son; vile in myself, but lovely in him; cast out, condemned, and undone in myself, justified and adopted in my Saviour! Precious doctrine, stumbling to the natural heart, but glorious to the soul taught of God. O, to feel its living influence. This is my burden, that I live under so feeble a sense of its constraining power, that it is so slow to draw my affections after him who I know is the only object worthy of my love and service. O, stupid soul, ever to see any loveliness in a creature which could turn thine eyes from the lovely Saviour."

In the following extracts we have some further particulars relating to the trials of Dr. King. They are from a letter addressed

TO THE FIRST BAPTIST CHURCH, CHARLESTOWN.

"*Piraeus, August* 2, 1847.

"DEAR BRETHREN AND SISTERS:—Your most kind and fraternal letter of December 18th, did not reach me until March 10th. Be assured, my beloved brethren and sisters, of my grateful sense of all the affectionate interest you express in my work, and in myself. Your love has ever been most dearly prized, although I am most deeply conscious of my utter unworthiness of such a blessing. But though there is nothing good or lovely in me, yet in that precious righteousness of the dear surety in which I would hide my sinful, naked soul, there is infinite beauty and loveliness which can attract even the love of the sin-hating God, and consequently the love of all his people. That precious doctrine of *substitution* was never so clear, so glorious as now. A deep sense of sin and hell-desert made it impossible for me to find rest, except in that Rock of ages cleft for me,—that bleeding side whence flowed the cleansing fountain. The Lord our righteousness, precious name, it is all my trust.

" Recent circumstances have shown us by what an uncertain tenure, humanly speaking, we hold our position here, and that consequently it becomes us to do with our might what our hands find to do, as we may soon have no more opportunity to labor here. None of you can be strangers to the persecution which our devoted missionary brother, Rev. Dr. King, has been enduring here for a year or two past; for both the secular and religious press seem to have felt the liveliest sympathy in his trials. After the first weeks of excitement following his return from Syra had passed, Dr. King resumed his preaching as before, but in his dwelling house, not in his chapel; and was comparatively undisturbed, as those of you who have heard Dr. Baird speak of the state in which he found matters here would infer. Indeed Dr. B. and others thought and said that the worst was over. But we who know what Greeks are, shook our heads at these sanguine hopes, and time has shown with what reason.

" For some months past, Dr. K. had been frequently threatened by a violent fanatic named Simonides who had insulted him on board the steamer in which he returned from Syra. He, however, begged Dr. K's pardon before leaving the boat, and afterwards called at the house, and frequently enjoyed the hospitalities of this kind-hearted missionary. But in April last, he sent him a threatening and insulting letter, and gradually proceeded to such lengths as to break up the religious service of Dr. K. on the Sabbath. This called for the interference of the law, and Simonides was called to answer for disturbing a private dwelling. But so little did he care for the law, and so well was he supported by priests and fanatics in the back ground, that the Sunday before his trial, he went again with others to the house of Dr. K., armed with heavy sticks, and after the service, proceeded to abuse and threaten him and his family. He was, however, tried, and sentenced to ten days imprisonment, and costs; the mildest possible sentence, compatible with any regard to the law. But no sooner was Simonides released, than he published in one of the semi-weekly papers an article entitled 'The Orgies,' in which he describes a series of Bacchanalian rites which he pretends to have seen performed at the house of Dr. K., as religious ceremonies, viz., those of marriage and baptism. A fabrication more abominable and outrageous cannot be conceived; and yet the Greek community of Athens, a community boasting of their intelligence, could believe this monstrous compound of obscenity and malice, and rose up as one against a man who had lived nineteen years among them a blameless life; who had relieved their bodily distresses, educated their youth, circulated many useful books among them, and whose only crime was that he preached a pure gospel to all who would hear him. Can you believe it, my dear friends?

"They bade Dr. K. cease preaching, or at least prevent those who came to hear him from entering his house. The request was too absurd to be listened to for a moment, and Dr. K. indignantly repelled it. But the city was fired with excitement; they threatened to kill him, to burn his house, to drive him from the city. The government said it was impossible to protect him, and begged him to withdraw, lest blood should be shed in the attempt to defend him. And so this good man was forced to leave his beloved family and go he knows not whither. The government said he could return after the excitement had passed; but there is very little reason to believe that he will ever be allowed to reside here again.

"You can easily understand, my dear brethren and sisters, that among such a people we have no security save in God, who holdeth the tempest of human passions in his mighty hand, that it can only rage when, and so far as he pleases. A similar calumny may be circulated against us any day, and we may be sent away as summarily. But we shall not go before God wills, and that is enough for us to know. When we are thus sensible that we can put no trust in any one around us, that there is not a bosom that throbs with any sympathy for our work, when the feeling that we are alive in the midst of secret enemies comes over us, it is then a precious truth that 'God is our refuge and strength, a very present help.'

"It is sweet to us to remember to-night, that thousands of prayers are ascending to God for us, and for our work, and for the great cause of missions. It was soothing to feel as we gathered round our family altar, and joined in the great concert of prayer, that we were not alone. We felt the answer to petitions offered up in distant lands. O, remember ever to bear us company on this day of prayer for missions. And it would be an unspeakable comfort to us, if such of you as can, would set apart a little season daily to remember the Greeks particularly, and to ask, especially, 1st, 'that utterance may be given us, that we may speak boldly as we ought to speak the truth of God; 2d, that this nation may be turned from their lying refuges—their confidence in the mediation of the virgin, in the prayers of saints, and in their own works, and 3d, that those under our instruction may be made wise unto salvation; the Word being mixed with faith in those that hear it. And may the God of Israel give you grace to wrestle and prevail.

" Yours in a precious Saviour,

" S. E. Waldo."

TO THE CORRESPONDING SECRETARY, REV. S. PECK.

" *October* 9, 1847.

" The past three months have been more full of interest than any I have spent abroad, and will ever form a memorable epoch in my missionary experience. The violent persecution excited against our dear brother missionary, Dr. King, terminating as it did in his unlooked for departure from Greece, under the most painful circumstances, could not but be deeply felt by us all. Our cause is one, our enemies the same. His experience to-day, might be ours tomorrow. It was our privilege to mingle our tears and prayers with our afflicted brother, and to soothe the last hours he spent in Greece with all the alleviations of Christian sympathy.

" During this brief interval, a sad event occurred, which cast a gloom over our little flock, and was afterwards turned to account by our enemies, in their attempts to excite a prejudice against us. This was the death of a little country girl who had been in our school only about two months, and whom we had hoped to train up for usefulness and for God.

"On Friday the 13th of August, poor Marigo left us in full health, and in all the light-heartedness of childhood, to return home from school, and in a few moments after was a lifeless corpse. Fleeing in fright from a dog which had sprung upon her, she fell into a deep well, and as half an hour passed before she was extricated from it, no life was remaining when she was brought to the surface.

"We did not know of the accident until nearly an hour had passed, and when we reached the house to which she had been removed, she was past all human help. I shall not soon forget that sad scene. The lifeless body of my little pupil extended before me, the wild and frantic shrieks of her aunt with whom she had lived in the town, the pale and terrified faces of many of her little schoolmates, who stood around her, and the awful thought that her soul had entered an unchanging eternity, all left an impression on memory's tablet, not soon to be effaced. We did all in our power for the poor family, and they seemed to feel our kindness; but the priests used every means to embitter their minds against us; telling them this was the judgment of God upon them for allowing her to come to us heretics, and asking them how they would answer to him for it.

"The following week, on the afternoon of the 20th, three young men called on Mr. Buel, to ask him to teach them English. Two we knew, the other was a stranger, calling himself N. Kosmopoulos, from Athens. Having made arrangements with Mrs. B. for his own lessons, he remarked that he had a little sister, twelve years of age, whom he wished to send to our school. Mrs. B. told him we had not a regular school, as the Government did not license us—that we only had permission to teach

English. Needle-work as a matter of course, we had a right to teach. He replied that he would like to have us teach her whatever we taught others—that she was then in Athens, but he was intending to remove to P., and would bring her with him. His answers to the interrogatories of Mrs. B. were not satisfactory, but she finally consented to receive her. Of the sister we never heard more. He himself, however, came on that and the following evening, to receive his English lesson from Mr. B., and when leaving on Saturday, asked if he should come on the following evening; to which Mr. B. replied that he should be happy to see him at his Bible class. He accordingly came. The subject under discussion that evening was the Pharisees, and all the young men listened with respectful attention, save the stranger. He soon manifested uneasiness, and at length broke out into impatient and disrespectful remarks, and questions evidently intended to entrap Mr. B.

" After the class had broken up, we overheard the other members of the class remonstrating with the new comer on his improper deportment, but no one dreamed that he was no other than our arch-enemy Simonides. This fact we ascertained the following morning, and of course he came no more. We learned from others that he boasted of the deception he had practiced, saying, ' he should publish articles which would drive us from the country, as Dr. King had been driven; and that he was circulating numberless groundless reports, calculated to injure us. Nothing, however, was published; and he satisfied himself with reporting that he had sent Mr. Buel to Malta. Whether he was in any way the procuring cause of the order from the Demarch, of which Mr. Buel writes you, we cannot tell; but it is not at all improbable that he had some hand in it.

"This order is a more serious matter than any of the unauthorized attacks of Simonides; and when it was seconded by the Demarch in person, a month after, we felt it time to consider what we should do. We have never asked permission from the government, as you well know, to give instruction except in English, because we knew it would only be granted on condition that we gave the requisite pledges as they express it, that is to have the Greek catechism taught in our school.

"Some parents, however, had urged us to teach their children some elementary branches, as reading, writing, arithmetic, and grammar. After frequent refusals, on the ground that we had no permission to do this, we at length yielded to the repeated and earnest solicitations of some twelve families, who assured us that the government would never trouble themselves about so small a matter. Had the government let us alone, we might have had as large a school as we chose. But the Demarch's order came. We knew that by a strict interpretation of the law, we might be condemned for teaching Greek without a license, and we therefore resolved to suspend all lessons except in English and needle-work, always excepting Bible instruction, to give which we ask *no man's* permission.

"On Sunday, the 26th ult., we told our pupils after Sabbath school, that there would be no school on the following day, but that we would call on their parents and explain the matter. We did not know what would be the result of this suspension of the customary lessons, and we could not but feel some sad forebodings lest it would scatter our dear little flock. But we knew who had all hearts in his hands, and how often he had made those things to be for the furtherance of the gospel, which his enemies intended for its overthrow; and we therefore cast all our care upon him. It was our united prayer, ere we went out on our visits, that he would go before us, and turn the hearts of the people towards us; and graciously did he listen to our unworthy supplications.

" We met with the warmest reception from every parent, all testifying their deep regret at what had occurred, and begging us to allow the children to continue to come, declaring that they would rather take the trouble to teach them their lessons at home, than send them to the other school. The next day our little school room was well filled, and instead of lessons, as they sat and sewed, we read the Scriptures and other good books. Three only left, and three new scholars came. On our present plan we have more instruction from the Scriptures than ever before. How long things will go on thus, we cannot tell; but the Lord's past mercies encourage us to leave all at his disposal, who has so graciously sustained and guided us hitherto. This persecution has shown us that we have the affection of children and parents, and that our enemies are not the people, but the priests.

" I cannot tell you what a sweet comfort it has been, during these times of difficulty, to feel that God's dear people were praying for us. In writing, months ago, to a dear missionary society, it was specially requested that they should make daily prayer for us that we might be delivered from unreasonable and wicked men. At that time we were not particularly exposed; but many signal interpositions of Providence of late have seemed to be answers to such prayers,—and we desire that thanksgiving also may abound to God on our behalf, from all those who have pleaded for us in secret places."

Three days after the date of the above letter, they received peremptory orders from the Demarch, requiring them to disband their school within twenty-four hours, under penalty of fine or imprisonment. Of this event Miss Waldo thus writes:

"*October* 13.

"The dreaded blow has fallen at last, and what a blight has it thrown over all our bright prospects. Yes, withered lies my gourd, and my fair hopes lay low. But yesterday, and all was full of promise. Now in a moment, all is sadness and discouragement. But God has not changed, and here I rest.

'E'en the hour that darkest seemeth,
Will his changeless goodness prove;
From the gloom his brightness streameth—
God is wisdom, God is love.'

"But it was a sad scene truly when I told my little flock I could teach them no more—that they must no more gather around me with their smiling, happy faces, to listen to instruction from my lips. Poor little ones, they could not understand that it could be a crime to teach them how to be useful, and happy,—how to be converted and saved. They looked at each other, and at me, as if to be assured that what they heard was not a dream. Who now will care for their souls? Who will warn them of the consequences of impenitence and unbelief? Who will speak to them of an able and willing

Saviour? Who will guide them in the paths of virtue, in the ways of peace? O, must they, must they perish?

"Truly God's way is in the deep. I would be still and know that it is His doing who giveth not account of his matters. I know I was never worthy of the sweet privilege of instructing these erring little ones, and that I may most justly be deprived of it. But O, for them, my scattered flock, for them my heart yearns. Spirit of all grace, teach thou them. In their benighted homes, visit thou their souls with light from on high, and reveal unto some of these babes the saving truths their priests and their nation reject."

It was under these sad circumstances that she addressed the following note

TO THE SECRETARY OF THE BOARD.

"*Piraeus, October* 20, 1847.

"REV. S. PECK,

"VERY DEAR SIR:—Shall we receive good at the hand of the Lord, and shall we not receive evil? It has long been my privilege to write to you of the Lord's mercies, and shall I murmur that I have now to speak of his judgments? I know that he doeth all things well, and I do not doubt his wisdom or his love; but my fond hopes are blighted, withered lies my gourd, whose budding promise had gladdened my heart in this weary land.

"The account Mr. Buel gave you, in his letter of the 10th inst., of the vigorous manner in which the Demarch was following up his attempts to disperse our school, may have prepared your mind in some measure for the sad intelligence. We had feared it, and prayed that it might be averted, but, when the blow did indeed fall, and a peremptory order came from the Demarch commanding us to close our school within twenty-four hours, under penalty of imprisonment or fine, we felt that a grievous stroke had smitten us. We saw there was no way of escape from the requirement of the government, no resource but in submission to the stern command. And I could not conceal from myself the fact, nay, it was this which gave poignancy to my sorrow, that this was not a passing persecution merely, which would subside and allow us to resume our work; but it was the final settling of the question whether it was possible to have any kind of mission school here. It was the stern application of law which cut off the hope of all future efforts of this kind, at least while the present constitution is in force. True, we know that this enforcement of the law is only a pretext to conceal their opposition to our religious instructions, for we have been told again and again, that the government would never trouble us, if we would not teach the New Testament; but nevertheless the law can be so construed, and we cannot resist it. Surely we can only walk by faith in days such as these; knowing that our enemies can do no more than is given them, and that the interests of Christ's kingdom are far dearer to him than they can be to us. I occupy myself for the present with my few pupils in English, with reading, study, &c. We were cheered on Sunday by seeing twelve children present.

"Begging your prayers that I may not yield to despondency in this dark and cloudy day, I remain

"Yours in sadness, but submission,

"S. E. Waldo."

CHAPTER XXIII.

Feelings on giving up her school—Visit of the Count and Countess de Gasparin—Trial of Mr. B.—Her views on various points connected with the Greek church—Memorandum of pupils at Piraeus—Close of the year 1847.

It was a great trial to Miss Waldo thus to see her little flock scattered without the hope of ever being able to gather them again. A few extracts from her correspondence at this time will present to us her feelings in her own language.

"*Oct.* 29.

"Life is not always measured by the numbering of weeks and months; we seem to live more in a few brief weeks in some periods of our existence than in years before. So much of deep and intense interest has been crowded into the short period that has elapsed since I wrote you last, that my mind is confused, and I know not what to write. Memorable days indeed have they been to me. And O, it has often been a sweet relief to feel that you were praying for me—that you were imploring for me the strength, the grace, the guidance, I have so often needed. Sweet is the love of those who meet at the mercy-seat. Have not our spirits often commingled there?

"You speak, dearest, of the darkness of the prospect here, and you will have learned, ere this reaches you, that our sky has not brightened. Yes, my love, the Lord has laid his afflicting hand upon me and touched me in the tenderest part. My bright hopes of usefulness here have been blighted, and I sit in sadness viewing the wreck. Yet I do not murmur. He hath not dealt with me after my sins. It was he who gave me so much happiness the past summer, and it is he who hath taken it away.

'His mercy made my garden bloom,
The sun shone bright and I was gay,
His equal mercy spread the gloom
That darkened o'er my little day.'

"He doeth all things well, only let my soul read aright the lessons he is teaching me; only let his chastenings work the peaceable fruits of righteousness, and I ask no more. He doth not willingly afflict even his wandering and wayward children, but in love he chastens them for their eternal profit.

'Sweet to lie passive in his hands,
And know no will but his.'"

"*Oct.* 30.

"Your sympathy, my beloved sister, was most grateful to my burdened heart; and though it made the tears flow faster, they were tears which relieved an oppressed spirit, never so tenderly alive as now to every expression of sympathetic regard. It is my heart's desire that God will bless to me his present disciplinary dealings, that they may purify my nature, elevate my affections, strengthen my faith, and humble every feeling of pride. O, to lie low at his feet, abased and prostrate, under a deep sense of my unworthiness and innate vileness; I would not have one stroke the less, one drop of bitterness withdrawn from the cup of chastening, but I only pray that I may be sanctified thereby, and that all may work the peaceable fruits of righteousness. In the midst of much sadness, I feel sweet peace of soul in committing my way to the Lord, and in the undoubting assurance that he will do all things well.

"Two Sabbaths have passed since we disbanded our school. On the first we had twelve, on the second ten, which was more than we expected after what had occurred. The government have sent no reply as yet to the remonstrance of Mr. B. Whether they mean to let us alone now, or whether they are devising new plans to secure our removal, time will develope. We are cast down but not in despair, persecuted but not destroyed. While Jesus lives we need not fear. Of late I have thought often of that verse,—'He shall not fail nor be discouraged till he have set judgment in the earth.' Shall we be faint-hearted then while our Captain assures us of final victory?

"My English pupils are very few, nor do I expect there will ever be pupils enough in English to call for the labors of a special missionary. Mr. and Mrs. B. could easily do all that I have to do without any great fatigue. And I do not and cannot conceal from myself that the dispersion of my little flock settles the question of my future usefulness here, and sixteen months' trial must be sufficient to show how far the teaching of English may be made the means of communicating evangelical instruction. Yet I turn away from the future; I cannot anticipate the painful duties to which it may call me; I can only leave it with God and say in the sweet words of a favorite hymn:—

'Thy various messengers employ,
Thy purposes of love fulfill,
And 'mid the wreck of earthly joy,
Let humble faith adore thy will.'"

TO MRS. DICKSON.

"*Nov*. 20, 1847.

"It is ten o'clock Saturday evening, the first quiet hour I could command to write you—but late as it is, the deeply interesting events of the past week cannot be left for another mail; and I hasten to tell you some of the scenes through which we have passed. On Sunday, as usual, we had the privilege of teaching a few dear children. I think we had twelve girls and four boys. They came rather later than usual, and I was beginning to fear none would come. This thought was so painful that I went to spread the case before Him in whose hands are all hearts, and while still pleading for his gracious remembrance of us in our low estate, a little company came. Dear Mr. L. being with us closed the school with prayer. He preached for us in the afternoon, and when he left us on Monday, we felt that it had been good for us to meet at a throne of grace.

"Hardly had they gone, when a clerk of the police called and asked to see Mr. B. on private business. Mr. B. was out, but he communicated to Mrs. B. the intelligence, that it had been decided upon by the Ministry of Public Instruction to serve a writ upon Mr. B. for violating the school law by teaching children upon the Sabbath. This gentleman came as a friend, as he said, to forewarn Mr. B. of the intended prosecution, that he might avoid it by giving a pledge to the Demarch to refrain from teaching the gospel in future. He tried to excite our fears by representing a trial as a dreadful thing, which would disgrace Mr. B., and expose him to insult and violence. He said that he jeopardized his own interests by giving us this information, but his high regard for Mr. B. had induced him to do so. In the meantime Mr. B. had accidentally met with the Head of Police who informed him of the same thing.

"We saw then what was before us, and we felt that God was our only refuge. Mrs. B. and myself had a sweet season of prayer on Monday noon, and in the evening we all united in commending our case to God—desiring that he might prevent the threatened trial if it might be his will, or if not that we might have grace to glorify him therein. On Tuesday Mr. B. was occupied in drawing up a petition to the King, representing the injustice of the measures commenced or purposed against us, and begging his interference. On Wednesday morning the summons came, ordering Mr. B. to appear before the Police Court to stand his trial on a charge of assumption of teachers' duties, in that he assembled boys and girls on Sundays and on feast days, teaching them the Holy Gospel, and distributing books without permission. The trial was ordered to take place on Friday morning at ten o'clock. On Thursday, Mr. B. called at the Palace with his communication to the King. He was very kindly received by the secretary to the Chamberlain, the latter being himself absent from Athens at this time. The secretary took the communication immediately to the King and Mr. B. returned home.

"But meanwhile we had enjoyed an unexpected pleasure,—a comfort which we felt to have been sent from God in the midst of our anxieties and trials. One needs to be in trial to know the sweetness of such consolations. You have heard of the good Count and Countess de Gasparin, the noble and zealous defendants of Protestantism in France, and not mere Protestants in name, but devoted, heavenly-minded Christians. These dear sympathizing friends did the Lord send to cheer us in our despondency. They spent nearly an hour with us in the absence of Mr. B., expressing the liveliest sympathy in our difficulties, and telling us for our encouragement that no strange thing had happened unto us, but in their own dear France the same things were constantly occurring, and yet the gospel was triumphing.

"Friday came, the day of trial. We did not fear violence or any serious issue at the time. Mr. Buel is universally respected, and we have the affection and good will of almost all in Piraeus. Yet we did feel alone in the midst of enemies. Judge then how tenderly we were affected when the Count drove up half an hour before the trial, saying that he had come to accompany Mr. Buel to the Court, feeling it a privilege thus to express his Christian sympathy and regard for any persecuted servant of Christ. This noble son of one of the proud peers of France, the elegant, the accomplished Count, walked humbly by the side of our dear brother, with all the meekness of a lowly disciple. Indeed, there is a sweet, child-like spirit manifest both in himself and the Countess which show them to be taught of God, Israelites indeed in whom there is no guile. These excellent persons have been traveling three or four weeks in the Peloponnessus on their way to Jerusalem ; nor had we heard of their return, until they called upon us, having letters of introduction from Dr. King.

"The trial was short. The clerk of the Demarch deposed that he had seen ten or twelve children come to us on each Sabbath morning, and that they received books from us. Two of our little S. S. scholars were then brought forward, and testified that they came with ten or twenty others, more or less regularly, were taught the gospel, and received books to read, which they brought back each Sunday and exchanged. I suppose the poor children were either threatened or bribed to be witnesses, and did not dare refuse. Mr. Buel's lawyer made a very good defence, proving that all that had been deposed did not make Mr. B. liable to the charge preferred against him. But what could his words avail when the sentence was to be given by one who, it was said, had express directions from the ministry in Athens to condemn Mr. B., and who would probably have lost his office had he acquitted him.

" Mr B. was accordingly found guilty, and fined fifty drachmas, ($8.33⅓,) the lowest possible amount; which showed that the enmity was towards our teaching, not towards us. Indeed, Mr. B. was treated with the greatest respect, and nothing like personal malice was shown during the whole trial. The condemnation was really brought against Mrs. B. and myself, for nothing was deposed by any of Mr. B's Sabbath scholars, nor was any proof of his teaching brought forward. So we were the offenders, as his lawyer declared, and not Mr. B. But Mr. B. will probably appeal, and we beg your earnest and united prayers that the decision may be reversed by the judges of the Court of First Instance. Not that the fine is any thing of course ; but because this decision makes it impossible for us ever to have a Sunday school again, at least until there is an entire change of administration."

The suspension of her school did not however entirely interrupt the missionary labors of Miss Waldo. Beside laboring in a variety of ways for the good of the lower classes around her, she had formed a personal acquaintance with several intelligent Greeks whom she spared no pains to enlighten on the great truths of religion. The following extracts from letters addressed to one of this class of correspondents will illustrate the character of this part of her labor.

* * * *

"Need I assure you of my sincere sympathy with a friend who is obliged 'to labor his cheerless way through a society whose principles he cannot approve?' I should not be worthy of the privileges I have enjoyed in my own loved land, if my heart did not beat in unison with every struggling spirit that sighed and panted for a freer, purer air than he can find in this tainted atmosphere. Because I was born and nurtured in the land of freedom and piety, the home of high and noble thought, of pure and holy feeling, I have not therefore learned to despise my less favored brethren of the human race, who, though they may boast of a fairer clime, and sunnier skies, lie shrouded in moral darkness, their better nature neglected, abused, and corrupted.

"It is no cause for boasting, but only of gratitude to the Giver of all mercies, that my childhood's home was in dear New England. Would it were in my power to confer on every human being the same inestimable blessings showered on me. Would that every heart that yearns for freedom, truth, and God, might call such a land his home. And yet the elements of all that makes such a land the favored one it is, every man may have in his own bosom. And, however barren the world about him, he may form around himself a green oasis, which if watered by the dews of God's rich grace, may be to him a little Eden.

"Alas! my dear sir, in my own blest land, there are

many miserable, wretched beings, all whose privileges fail to render them happy. For could Satan be carried to the abodes of the blest in heaven, his dark, rebellious spirit could find no joy amid all its light and love. The songs of the redeemed would be like harsh discord to his ear, and their pleasures altogether distasteful. And so a heart that is not at peace with God, that has not learned to draw from him its highest, purest joys, will ever feel an aching void, that earth's most delightsome scenes, its sweetest pleasures, were they all his, could never remove. And so on the other hand the heart that has learned that earth's sweetest fountains of happiness are but broken cisterns, and has turned for satisfaction to the Fountain of living waters, the ever blessed God, such a heart has within itself sources of happiness of which outward circumstances cannot despoil it.

"Men do not believe this, I know. Perhaps you do not. You may imagine, with others, that, were some yet unattained blessing within your grasp, your happiness would be complete. Men follow such hopes as the deluded traveler does the Mirage of the Desert, but it is only to reap a bitter disappointment. Believe me, my dear sir, the attainment of no earthly good, be it the purest and noblest, could ever fill the cravings of the immortal spirit within you. God has given you a deathless soul. He has not suffered you to imbrute and smother its aspirations as the multitude around you. He has formed that soul to find its rest only in himself; and as well might the young plant be green and bloom without sun and water, as that soul of yours be truly happy without God. He must be the object of your intensest love, his service your highest delight, if you would know what true happiness is."

* * * *

"Your remarks about human systems, I accord with sincerely, and lament most heartily that the church of Christ has so little of that unity for which he prayed. Yet while it is self-evident that all cannot be right, it is equally certain that truth is and must be *one;* and therefore for *truth* let us seek. Can we not unite in a friendly search after truth, and mutually examine the ground on which we stand, that we may know whether it is solid rock or sliding sand, seeking guidance from Him who is the Way, the Truth, and the Life?"

* * * *

"You speak of Masson's Apology, and since you choose that as an expression of your views let us take it up. Mr. M. first controverts the Rev. C. Andrews' statement that any system of missionary operations founded on *non-interference* will end in disappointment. Now before this can be proved it must be settled what is *hoped* for; for the word disappointment is a relative term and always supposes something *expected.* If a missionary only expects a pleasant residence in Greece, an agreeable circle of friends, the introduction of few improvements in the external condition and habits of the poorer classes, the instruction of the young in arts and sciences, the publishing and diffusion of useful and elementary works, then I agree with Mr. Masson that such missionary operations will not end in disappointment. But if the missionary expects the moral regeneration of the nation, the return of the present church to primitive purity, then I do most positively declare, that non-interference operations will end in complete disappointment, and never will, and never can realize such expectations. As well might John the Baptist have expected the Jewish nation to reform without preaching to them,—'Repent, for the kingdom of heaven is at hand.'

"Is the Greek church right or wrong? If right she needs no apology and no reform. If wrong, to tell her so is interference; to do, or to advise any thing for her correction or improvement is interference. And what is a missionary, and what are missionary operations but a *name*, if they are limited to less than this? No, my dear friend, it must be either interference or no missionary. To talk of *missionary* operations and non-interference, is playing with words. Political operations, social operations, school operations, these may be without interference, but missionary operations never! 'But Greece has her own preachers,' continues Mr. Masson. Yet who does not know that the moment a Greek priest begins to preach reform, he becomes an object of suspicion and persecution. It is not the man that excites opposition, it is the doctrine, it is the truth. Never will the Greek church be restored to her former purity without a struggle, a hot, a bitter struggle. It cannot be otherwise. It is not in the nature of man; it is not in the nature of truth.

"You beg to distinguish Greek Christians from Pagans and Jews, as not to be addressed by the same portions of God's word, but as standing on quite a different foundation. This is a most serious point, my dear friend, and I pray God to guide my pen while I speak of it, that I may not err. I freely admit there is a general sense in which we apply the term Christian to nations and communities. We technically call all Christians who profess belief in Jesus Christ, as the foretold and anointed Saviour of mankind. But there is a high and holy sense in which I use the name Christian (and all who hold like sentiments with myself do the same) quite different from this general and nominal application. We regard mankind, not as divided into Christians, Jews, Mohammedans, and Pagans, but as separated into two great classes, the regenerate and the unregenerate, the impenitent and the penitent, the natural man and the Christian. The Bible addresses men as such, and not as belonging to different sects; and we must read the word of God in this light or we shall derive very little benefit from it. I am not to ask, Does the Bible speak to me as a Greek or an idolater? as a Baptist or an Episcopalian? for I shall find nothing suited to my case. But the question is, Am I of that great class who are children of wrath, who tread the broad way, who mind the things of the flesh, in a word, who like Nicodemus have never yet learned what it is to be born again? Or am I, by the grace of God, a new creature, saved by grace through faith, having put on the new man which after God is created in righteousness and true holiness?

"If I belong to the former class, (and my own conscience and inward experience must decide) I am not a Christian, be I named Baptist, Presbyterian, Greek, or Catholic, though I hold the most orthodox creed, and possess the most amiable character. If, with humble gratitude to God, I may find in myself the evidence that his infinite mercy has made me one of the latter class, then I may appropriate to myself the precious name of Christian.

"With such views of the deep and solemn significance of this appellation, do you think I could give it to a community of worldly, God-forgetting persons, because they profess belief in Christ? It were too dishonoring to that sacred title. I know the time when I was not a Christian. Though then, in my self-ignorance, and little acquaintance with the gospel, I should have been indignant to have been denied the appellative. Christ was then to me but a name,—a great and glorious person, a spotless holy being, indeed, but not my only hope and trust, my heart's choicest treasure, my single plea for pardon and acceptance with a holy God, my Lord and sovereign Master, my First, my Last, my *All in All.* O, no; he was little in my thoughts, and less in my affections; I did my own pleasure nor thought of bowing my will to his; I had been baptized in his name, professed belief in him as the Christ, but I was not a Christian.

"And if now the inward consciousness of far different feelings towards him, far different views of my relations and obligations to him, strengthens the hope that God's grace has regenerated my heart, still I fall so far short of that resemblance to him I ought to possess, that subjection to his supreme authority in every word, and thought, and act, which is my bounden duty, that it is with trembling and doubting I call myself a Christian. I apply then to you, and to others, no severer test than I lay down for myself, and this you cannot call bigotry or sectarianism. God's word does not take for granted that any man is of course a Christian. It gives certain tests and evidences, and then leaves every man to apply them in the fear of God."

Her interest in her scholars continued long after she ceased to be their teacher. In the commencement of her teaching, she adopted a method of noting down the most prominent traits in the character of each, a plan which she undeviatingly continued both with Sabbath and day scholars. She often spoke of the benefit she had derived from this plan, particularly as it enabled her to follow each with her prayers long after they ceased to be under her particular care. The following is an extract from her memorandum of pupils at Piraeus, the letters of the alphabet being substituted for their names.

" *A.*—A thoughtful, intelligent lad; left in about two months for Athens.

" *B.* and *C.*—Docile and affectionate children, without a religious idea.

" *D.*—An excellent scholar, but of a most earthly mind, incapable of any noble feelings, knowing little and caring less for the Bible.

" *E.*—A lad of fine and generous feelings, frank and noble, but with no application and little energy. Deeply interested in religious inquiry, holding in contempt superstition, and scorning all dissembling in religion.

" *F.*—A boy of considerable address, but artful and insincere, ready to seem any thing when interest required it.

" *G.*—An amiable girl of pleasing manners and kind feelings, but of little character.

" *H.*—A lovely creature, full of heart and good humor, but so much under a vain and worldly influence, that better feelings and soberer thoughts are stifled.

" *I.*—A delicate girl, trying to drown the memory of sickness and disease, and shut out the serious thoughts they bring.

" *J.*—A poor girl, of good mind, but utterly selfish;

abandoned her lessons when she found she could not make them profitable.

"*K.*—An humble lad, the most serious I have met with, sensible of his sinfulness, and anxious for his soul, but withal wedded to superstition.

"*L.*—A sweet, serious girl of most exemplary deportment, and often manifesting tender feelings. O, may she be gathered into Christ's fold.

"*M.*—A noisy, light-headed girl, quick to learn, but with a head full of vanity."

The following are her reflections at the close of the year.

"*Dec.* 31.

"This is the last day of the closing year. Shall I ever forget 1847? Old age must strangely dim my faculties ere I shall cease to remember its never-to-be-forgotten events. How checkered they have been! I remember last New Year's, how we gathered our little flock around us, and presenting them some little token of our affectionate interest, received from them the promise of more regular attendance, and better attention to the word of God. How happy and hopeful we were that day. And then when sickness broke up some of my classes, and the attendance was so irregular that I began to feel it was hardly worth my salary to continue me here, what longing desires I had for more work; and how I rejoiced, in the spring, to see one after another added to our little company, a wider door opening before us, and all confirmed by that dear letter from Mr. Peck bidding me go on and doubt not.

"And what happy soul-reviving days we spent in the society of that holy man of God, Lieut. ——! What a Bethel to our souls! Then those sweet tidings from my dear sister of a work of grace begun in her soul, under circumstances calculated to fill my heart with gratitude and praise. And then the clouds gathered, and the tempest came that swept away our persecuted brother, Dr. King. Soon followed the sad death of my poor little Marigo. And then the clouds grew darker, and the first order from the Demarch was sent, and Simonides' treacherous, ill-omened visit awakened our fears.

"But September—shall I ever forget September, 1847—that memorable month when I first cherished the hope that God was leading my dear friend to himself, was forming in him that new man which after God is created in righteousness and true holiness,—that month when his heart and hand were offered me, and when the intensity of the mental conflict which the non-acceptance of them caused, first revealed to me the strength of my own attachment? Yes, September is graven in lines deep and ineffaceable on my inmost heart, and whatever be my future lot, the feelings, the thoughts, the conflicts of that month will never be forgotten.

"And stormy days have passed since then, and cloud on cloud has gathered over our sky. The disbanding of our school, the prosecution, the trial, and that bright ray of Heaven's own sunlight, the visit of the Count and Countess de Gasparin in the hour of our need; are they not memorable too? And these last closing scenes of cloud and sunshine, the bitter and the sweet of these few weeks past, have been in keeping with the varied experience of the year whose last sands are running. O, may mercies and judgments alike chasten and purify us, and work together for good to our souls. What cause for the deepest self-humiliation does the retrospect awaken. How many duties neglected. How many opportunities unimproved. What want of zeal and love, of faith and holiness. O, may the blood of sprinkling cleanse me, and the righteousness of Jesus cover me.

> 'Other refuge have I none,
> Simply to the cross I cling.'"

CHAPTER XXIV.

Gives up all hope of doing more in Piraeus—Excursion to the pass of Phyle—Leaves Piraeus for Corfu—Important question of duty—Her views in relation to it—Decides upon going to Zante—Her marriage—Passage to Zante.

THERE seemed now very little prospect of her performing any further missionary labor in Piraeus, at least any which might not just as well be performed by Mr. and Mrs. Buel; and it became a serious question whether she ought to return to the United States or seek some other field of labor. Writing under date of Jan. 27th, she says, " With all my intense desire for the continuance of this mission, I must say that I think there is no reasonable prospect of usefulness for me. It is now more than three months since I dismissed my little school by the Demarch's orders, and the little that I have since had to do in the way of teaching English, could not satisfy me that it was my duty to remain. I have only quieted myself during this long interval by the belief that something decisive would result from the measures commenced against us, and still more by the hope that we should yet obtain permission from the government to teach. But that hope I now think fallacious, although it seems impossible to obtain a positive answer from the Bureau of Education."

A few weeks after this she obtained an interview with the Director of Schools, told him her wishes, and asked what would be required of her. He told her that as she was a foreigner she would be exempt from teaching their catechism, but that she would be required to give a pledge that she would not teach her own catechism. On Miss Waldo's replying "We have no catechism but the New Testament," he told her sternly that she would not be allowed to teach the New Testament, as that would be teaching her own dogmas. "This," says Miss Waldo, "he very positively and emphatically repeated with slightly different words, and thus set forever at rest the question whether we could conscientiously establish a school in Greece. I left, with mingled emotions of sadness and satisfaction; of satisfaction that the question was settled and duty made clear, but of heart-felt sadness that I must abandon all hopes of resuming my loved employment here.

"In the meanwhile it is proposed that I should go and assist Mrs. Dickson, who has been in very feeble health all winter. The school in Corfu is in a prosperous condition, having a good proportion of Greeks of respectable families, and I should be most happy to aid my beloved friend, Mrs. D., in her onerous duties for a time. But I do not wish to plan, or purpose, or ask any thing, for I dare not trust my own heart. Yet, I trust I shall have grace given me to accord cheerfully with whatever is thought best by my dear associates, and shall see in their plans the guiding finger of God."

Before leaving Piraeus she visited several places of interest, among which was the celebrated pass of Phyle. Of her visit to this place she thus writes:

"*April* 18.

"Let me tell you how a kind Providence watched over us in a little excursion we made the other day to the famous pass of Phyle. This remarkable pass in the Paynes range, is formed by an immense mass of rock thrown up across a deep ravine, rising about five hundred feet perpendicularly, on two sides, from the valley beneath. The summit of this rock is crowned with the ruins of an old castle, supposed to have been built before the days of Heroditus, though no trace of its origin has been preserved. Its design was to defend this only pass from Beotia into Attica. Here the famous Thrasybulus routed the thirty thousand under whose oppression Athens then groaned.

"Mr. and Mrs. B., Mrs. H. and myself started from Athens in a carriage, at 9 o'clock, A. M., and Mr. H., Capt. S., and Lieutenant C. of her Majesty's ship Spartan, followed on horseback. Our plan was to go by carriage to the village of Kassia, and thence with mules or donkeys up to the old castle. But we had no idea of the difficulties in the way, or we should never have attempted it. We were obliged to leave our carriage about half a mile from the village, as no carriage could climb that rocky path. We walked on as far as the village, expecting to obtain mules or donkeys there. But on arriving there, none were to be had except a donkey belonging to Mrs. H., which had been sent out in the morning. Two mules, however, were promised; but as we had no time to lose, the gentlemen proposed that we should take their horses, which were very gentle, and they would follow with the mules as soon as they were ready. But how to ride with gentlemen's saddles was the question. However, by shortening the stirrups on one side, and sitting well on to the horse, we found we could manage, although the want of a pommel made it very difficult for us to keep our seats when the road became precipitous. To add to our dismay, when the mules appeared, they proved to be such vicious beasts that even the gentlemen could hardly manage them, and they said it would be very unsafe for us to mount them. So there was no alternative but for us to keep on our way. I tremble now when I think of the steep acclivities we passed, where one misstep would have plunged us all down into a deep ravine of some two hundred feet. Many an inward prayer did I offer to the God of my life as I passed these dangerous spots, and sometimes an involuntary scream would escape me as I found myself half off my horse.

"After a hot ride of an hour we reached the old monastery, and dismounted for a short rest. The Abbot, whose appearance was as wild as that of the surrounding scenery, received us kindly, and offered us all his scanty board afforded. But we could not stop long, and remounting were soon on our way for the castle, another half hour's ride. We had completed about half of this, and I was beginning to feel quite fearless from having passed so many dangerous places in safety, when suddenly my horse's foot slipped on some yielding earth, I lost my balance and fell directly over his back. The suddenness of the fall left me no time to think; still holding the reins in my hand, I pulled the horse round, and the ground sloping, I rolled under his feet. I remember nothing but a vague consciousness of his foot over my head and the thought that I should be trampled to death. But the noble creature stood perfectly still, and when he felt my head, raised his foot again immediately, and held it up until I was relieved; for my friends were instantly at my side and extricated me. Providentially I fell on my face and his hoof came down on the back of my head, which was in part protected by my bonnet. But though he stepped so lightly, it seemed to me for a moment as though my skull must break, and I felt the impression of his hoof for a week afterwards. Never did I so fully realize those words of the Psalmist, 'Who redeemeth thy life from destruction.'

"On rising, I found that I had lamed my back so that I could not walk without extreme pain, I was therefore forced to remount. But my fears had become so much excited that I soon preferred the pain of walking, rather than to ride in such fear. It was then proposed that Mrs. H. should take my horse, as her donkey had become somewhat tired. But taking fright at something just as she seated herself in the saddle, he threw her quite over his back. Providentially Lieut. C. caught her in his arms, so that she did not sustain the least injury. At length we reached the castle, and saw the splendid view from its summit, which Byron thinks the finest in Greece. Thankful were we to reach it, and a very pleasant hour we spent in that wild spot. On one side we looked down a perpendicular declivity of more than five hundred feet.

"We dined at the old castle, and having rested from our fatigue, prepared to descend. A safe mule was found for me and I came down without difficulty. Mr. B. was, however, thrown from his mule, and Mrs. B. from her horse, though providentially both escaped without any severe injury. It was eleven o'clock when we laid our tired limbs upon our beds, grateful to the God of our lives that he had preserved us from death. Much as I enjoyed the excursion, I never wish to make another such."

TO REV. W. C. CHILDS.

"*Piraeus, April* 19, 1848.

"MY DEAR PASTOR:—Accept my heartfelt thanks for your affectionate interest in my work, your sympathy in my trials and enjoyments. We both have the same enemy to contend with, namely, the unrenewed and carnal heart of man. The forms of its opposition, the developments of its innate enmity to God, may vary with different climes and nations, but the essential principle of rebellion is still the same. Yet I sometimes think the unsuccessful labors of a Christian minister at home, far more disheartening than the fruitless efforts of a missionary abroad. The former labors for those who are surrounded by innumerable saving, and awakening influences, and his labors are concentrated on a comparatively small number. If he sees few or no souls converted to God, has he not far more to bow down his spirit, than the missionary alone in the midst of a community surrounded by every thing that can blind, mislead, or harden them? Surely the one needs faith to support him no less than the other. Our joys too, are essentially the same if we are the people of God, for he is the fountain of his people's joy.

"You speak of pleasing associations with apostolic times in this land where once that gospel won such trophies to Christ. Alas! my dear Sir, the painful contrast it now presents embitters all these associations, and makes us exclaim, 'How has the gold become dim, and the most fine gold changed!'

"We have passed through many anxious and sorrowful days. To me especially the breaking up of my little school was a most painful event, and the more so as it seems to have shut up the door of usefulness to me in Greece. I am just now on the point of leaving Piraeus to go to the assistance of Mrs. Dickson in Corfu. That dear sister is in feeble health, and I feel it my duty to relieve her of some of her cares and labors, until the Board decide what is to be done with the mission. We shall be alone at Corfu this summer, as brother and sister Arnold will be obliged to leave the island for a change of climate for a few months; both Mrs. A. and her little boy having suffered from the humidity of the atmosphere of Corfu. I trust the church will remember us in a special manner, that the Lord may graciously take such weak things as we are to confound the mighty, that all the glory may be his."

Miss W. left Piraeus for Corfu about the middle of April. A few days before leaving, addressing her mother, she says, "Once more, and probably for the last time, I date you a letter from this dear home,—not my girlhood's home 'tis true, that dear spot which concentrates in itself all that is most loved and loving,—but yet a sweet sojourning place has it been to your wanderer, and sad thoughts will come over her as she proposes to bid it farewell. My little bark had found such a pleasant shelter in this quiet haven, that it is loath to launch out again on the stormy sea of life. But if the heavenly Pilot guide, I need not fear, though our way be through the floods, for he has promised they shall not overwhelm me. With him at the helm, all is safe. Ah, there is no permanent anchorage for the soul till we reach the haven of eternal blessedness. There only is unchanging rest and joy. To the dear friends here I must soon say, adieu. Yes, to God we must commit each other. Blessed thought, that we are in his hands. These simple lines, which I learned when a child, have frequently come to my mind with soothing power:

> 'Art thou my Father? I'll depend
> Upon the care of such a friend;
> And only wish to do and be
> Whatever seemeth good to thee.'"

Writing to Mrs. Dickson about the same time, in reference to the dear friends she was about to leave at Piraeus, she adds, "I am amazed at the goodness of God towards me in the matter of friends. From time to time has he blessed me with the most true, faithful, and devoted friends, whose hearts, whose minds, whose prayers have been my choicest earthly treasure. I look back on the dear teacher who first spoke to me about my soul, and who watched over me with maternal anxiety and tenderness during the three years I was under her tuition; I recall the touching devotion of my beloved Sarah C., the strength and purity of whose affection, I never expect to see surpassed; I remember the kind solicitude, and lively sympathy which you, my dear foster-mother, showed for me a fatherless stranger; I think of the sweet affection of my own darling sister, Mrs. B., of the pious friendship of my dear Miss W., not to speak of many others, the good and the true who bless me with their affection, and I can only exclaim,

> 'These are thy gifts, O heavenly Father, thine
> This precious boon of love.'

"I often think it cannot be myself whom these dear ones love, but a fancied being to whom they impute excellences which I know too well are not my own. And then I think they may love me in Christ, though I am all vileness in myself, as I would hope that the holy and blessed Father accepts and loves me in his dear Son my righteousness. O that his blessed image might indeed be reflected in my soul."

For some time previous to her return to Corfu, the mind of Miss Waldo had been more or less agitated with the question whether the providence of God might not be preparing a field of usefulness for her in some other part of Greece. Among the friends whom, in this land of her exile, she had learned to esteem and love, was one whose qualities of mind and heart seemed all she could desire in a companion, but who did not for some time give her all the evidence she desired of having been truly and thoroughly regenerated. And beside this, though his mind had been greatly enlightened, and he longed and labored for a reformation in the Greek church in which he had from infancy been nurtured, yet he had not seen his way clear to leave all and come out on the side of the Lord. These were with her sufficient reasons for positively declining the offer of his hand. But as she afterwards had increasing evidence that he had been truly born of the Spirit, and was earnestly seeking direction in regard to his personal duty, especially as her affections were enlisted in his favor, she could not but watch with prayerful interest his progress in divine things. Her views and feelings on this subject may be seen from the ollowing brief extracts:

"From the time when, by the grace of God, I turned from the pleasures of a gay world and publicly professed myself a disciple of Christ, I felt that I could no longer have companionship with the unrenewed in heart, with the worldly, the impenitent, but that my friends must evermore be the children of God, the few who walked the narrow way, who were not of the world. Time and experience have only strengthened this conviction, for every departure from it has planted a thorn in my bosom. It is not that I feel myself so holy, so sanctified, that contact with the world would be pollution to me, but for the very contrary reason, because I am so weak in faith, so prone to err, so ready to yield, that my only safety is in fleeing temptation and surrounding myself by every influence that can elevate, strengthen, and sanctify. If then I need to hold fast this decision of my better judgment in ordinary friendships, judge how all-important it is in choosing a companion for life, a bosom friend, a second self. I cannot, dare not, trust my heart to one who has not himself been made a new creature in Christ Jesus, who has not come out from the world, and separating himself from the multitude, has entered the strait gate, the narrow way that leadeth unto life."

* * * * * *

"There are certain feelings characteristic of the renewed soul which always develope themselves more or less distinctly in all the truly regenerate. Of these the most prominent is self-renunciation, that is a renouncing of all self-dependence, self-confidence, and self-righteousness, arising from a profound view, an inward consciousness of the extreme sinfulness of the heart; and connected with this is an entire reliance upon, and a supreme attachment to Christ as the only and all-sufficient Saviour. These I have looked for with all the anxiety of true affection, but have closed many a letter in sadness because it seemed to deny me the longed for evidence."

* * * * *

"Affection may blind your eyes to the real magnitude of our differences, and because they are confined to a few particulars, they may seem to you small, but you forget that they are on a great point, and therefore become great differences. Our tastes and predilections are, I think, very similar, and many sweet sources of earthly enjoyment might be opened to us, of which we might freely partake with united hearts; but if in those most hallowed and intimate of all emotions, our religious feelings, we are not essentially one, there would be a canker-blight on all our happiness. We differ in country, education, habits, and mode of life, differences not trifling, nor to be disregarded; yet these are comparatively small distinctions which true affection might accommodate and reconcile. But religious differences cannot be thus disposed of. They are not at the control of the affections. While, therefore, these points of difference remain, affection must be sacrificed to religion, and we can only pray for each other."

At a somewhat later date, in reply to a letter giving some account of a gracious change in his religious affections, she thus writes:

"I cannot describe the feeling that thrilled through my bosom when reading of your heart's humble hope of salvation through faith in Christ Jesus. I cannot indeed be sure that you are regenerated, nor would I for worlds encourage you to cherish an unfounded hope of your soul's safety. I rejoice that you say, 'not without doubting,' for you cannot search and probe your heart too closely on this great matter of regeneration. You may err on other points, and yet be in no serious danger, but a mistake here is fatal, is soul-destroying. We cannot remember too often what He has told us, who alone knows what will be the revealings of the judgment-day, that many will say, 'Lord, Lord, have we not prophesied in thy name?' to whom he will answer, 'Depart, I never knew you.' O, may he deliver you from all self-ignorance, and grant you the inward witness of his Spirit that you are born of God.

"Yet while from my inmost heart I bless God for what he has wrought in your soul, and while I feel that to be united by living faith to the same Saviour, is infinitely more important than to belong to the same communion, I dare not say this is enough. I do not mean to say that there can be no conjugal happiness without a perfect coincidence of sentiment. On the contrary I agree with you that this is very difficult, if not impossible. I can easily imagine a case of as perfect happiness as is admissible in this imperfect world, where the parties concerned are of different denominations. A Wesleyan for instance might marry a Presbyterian or an Independent, and feel that he only stepped within the pale of a sister church, whose members on all essential points were of his own faith. But I could never regard the Greek as a sister church, but as a lapsed communion, which has shut herself out of the sisterhood of Evangelical churches, by the adoption of most fatal errors."

About the time of leaving Piraeus, she thus writes to a friend:

" Much as I at times suffered from the inward conflict between affection and duty, I never wavered in my purpose to marry only in the Lord. And it is only now when I have reason to believe that the Lord is teaching him, and is leading him in his own right way, it is only now, when to all the natural loveliness of his character, is added the charm of sincere piety, that I feel to hope our attachment may be owned and blessed of God. But I bless his name that I can from my inmost heart give this whole matter entirely up into his hands. There have been moments when the struggle has been severe, and the tempter would fain have awakened rebellious feelings in my heart; but thanks to infinite grace, this has past, and from the depths of my soul I can, and do say, 'Not my will but thine be done.' O, it is sweet to feel that our times are not in our own hands; that though 'the lot is cast into the lap, the whole disposing thereof is of the Lord.' My heart's desire and constant prayer is, that God will lead me in the path most promotive of his glory, and my own sanctification."

Mr. J. York, the person above referred to, was a native of Corfu, residing in Zante, where he had long had the charge of a flourishing school. For many years he had been a sincere inquirer after truth, and through the influence of our missionaries was gradually brought to see and feel his need of a thorough renovation of heart through the operation of the divine Spirit. Previous to the time of which we are now speaking, a blessed change seems to have been effectually wrought in him by the sovereign grace of God, by which he was gradually led to renounce all for Christ, and willingly to consecrate his future services to him.

Watching the leadings of divine Providence, Miss W. at length decided that the Lord had called her to share with him the labors and trials, the joys and sorrows of life. She had already requested of the Board that she might be at liberty to close her connection with them, as she saw no prospect of rendering them any service which could justify them in continuing her support. The following extract is from a letter to the Board, written after her decision to go to Zante:

"*Corfu, May* 20, 1848.

"For the past six months I have cherished a trembling hope that another door would be opened for me which would realize my undiminished desire to devote myself to the instruction of Greek youth. It has been a time of sore trial to me. My soul has been cast down and disquieted within me, and my only refuge and solace has been a throne of grace. Through the tender mercy of God, light has now shone on my darkened way, and I do praise him who has been the 'help of my countenance, and my God.' I have consented to enter a field of labor, where, though I shall no longer be under the kind superintendence of the Board, I hope to continue the same work for which you sent me forth. I have decided to go to Zante, to share the labors of one already introduced to you by my associates in the mission. Having been called by the grace of God to leave all for Christ's sake, his one purpose and desire is to live for his glory, for the promotion of his cause, and the dissemination of his truth, particularly among the young in the responsible situation of teacher. Trusting that we have God's blessing on our union, we hope your approval will be added, to that accorded by the dear members of this mission; and though I shall not be called your missionary, it is our united and earnest desire to be missionaries in the full sense of the word."

Her summer was spent at Corfu, with Mrs. Dickson, assisting her in school, and endeavoring to perform such missionary work as circumstances would permit. Her mind seemed solemn and thoughtful in view of her anticipated union. Conscious that she had sought the guidance of her heavenly Father, she saw his hand indicating the path of duty, and was happy to feel herself directed by the leadings of his providence. Addressing a friend, under date of May 5th, she says,

"I feel more and more that it has all been of God, and while I never felt more sober and serious, I have seldom had more inward peace and comfort in God than in this step. It is my earnest prayer that God will make me the worthy companion of my dear J.—the strengthener of his faith, the joy of his home, a help, meet for him. I have the full sanction of dear Mrs. D., whose affectionate interest, and kind counsel are most grateful to my feelings. She acts the mother for me now, and I am anticipating a happy summer with her. I am very happy in the school; indeed my sky is quite sunshiny. Praise the Lord with me."

On the 18th of August, 1848, she was united in marriage with Mr. J. York, at the Lord High Commissioner's palace, by Rev. Mr. Warner, Civil Chaplain of Corfu; and on the following day left Corfu for Zante. The particulars of her marriage and passage to Zante, are given in the following letter

TO HER MOTHER.

"*Zante, August* 23, 1848.

"MY EVER DEAR MOTHER:—Your rover has at length found a nest where she can fold her weary wings, glad to end her wanderings in this fair island home. Yes, dearest mother, though far away from all I have known and loved, yet with my loved and loving husband, and among his kind, kind friends, I feel that I am at home, though all is new and strange about me. If I could only have you all near me, my darling mother, brother and sisters, I should indeed be too happy. There must be always some alloy, some drawback to all earthly joy, or these weak hearts would love the world too well. Even now how we cling to it! How strong hold have creatures and creature good upon our souls!

"Your precious letters, whose non-arrival had disappointed me so much when I closed my last to you, came two days after from Piraeus, where they were sent, I suppose, by mistake. How gladly would I have wiped away those '*bitter tears*,' my dearest mother, which you shed for your Emmie, and have whispered in your ear that she was no less your own loving child, because she had given her heart and hand to another; and had promised to share his home, his labors, trials, cares, his hopes and joys. No, dear mother, conjugal affection can never quench the flame of filial love. I think of you ever with the fondest, tenderest feeling.

"Shall I first of all tell you something of the last week, an era in my life whose every minute event and feeling is indelibly engraven on memory's tablet? One week ago, my dear J. arrived in Corfu with his mother, who tenderly embraced me, as I welcomed her to C., and, while her warm tears fell fast upon my cheek, said with true maternal feeling, 'Love my J.; make him happy, and may God bless you.' No thought of herself seemed to cross her mind, every wish of her heart seemed to centre in this beloved son, whose happiness was the one thing she desired.

"Our wedding day did not prove a sunshiny and cloudless one, though we had expected it as a matter of course, as the time had hardly come for the first rains. Yet the sun occasionally broke through the dark clouds, and scattered them for an hour or two. Will our wedded life be as often clouded, and the sunshine of our earthly happiness be as often obscured? God knows, and into his hands we commit ourselves.

> 'Whatever come, if he will bless
> The brightness and the gloom,
> And temper joy and soothe distress,
> We fear no earthly doom.'

"'Hope in God,' is our motto. This has sustained through the trials of the past, this is the foundation of our happiness now, and this encourages us to fear no evil in the unknown future.

"At eleven the carriages were at the door, and our little company rode to the Palace. Mr. and Mrs. Arnold, Mrs. York, Mrs. Dickson and ourselves, only six in all, beside the clergyman. The marriage service, according to the Episcopal ritual, is simple and impressive; and with my whole heart, dearest mother, I promised to love, honor, and obey him whom I then took to be my 'wedded husband,' and as fully did he affirm his purpose to '*love, honor*, and *cherish*,' your Emmie. Our plighted troth, given in the presence of God and man, we wish daily to renew 'till death do us part.' It was a solemn but a happy hour. How I wished you could be there, and my dear sisters, brother and friends. You were all in my mind. Not one was forgotten. The clouds broke away in time to allow most of our friends to call, and it was late before the last visitor had left, and trunks were packed ready for an early start on the morrow. What a night of thunder and storm, I shall never forget it. It was still wet and cloudy, when we bade adieu to Corfu on Saturday morning. Our dear friends came down to the quay with us, and we parted with mingled tears and smiles, hoping soon to meet again.

"Our passage was disagreeable on many accounts. The steamer was old and small, and rocked from side to side all day. I was more sick than I had ever before been on board a steamboat; still not too much so to enjoy the sailing among the Ionian Isles. We stopped at the little island of Paxo, for a few moments only. In the afternoon we reached Santa Maura. This is a dull, sad looking place. The houses are built of wood, on account of the frequent earthquakes with which the island is visited; and, being unpainted, are dark and gloomy externally. It is a strange place, altogether unlike any thing I ever saw. At day break we were at Argostoli, one of the principal ports of Cephalonia. It is a new town, quite regularly built for this part of the world.

"I was too anxious, however, to see Zante, and too much engrossed with the thought of meeting my new relatives and friends, to give much heed to any thing else. You may imagine with what feelings I first saw the dim outline of this green isle, and as we drew nearer how I looked at this, and that beautiful site, so familiar to my dear J., who pointed them out as the steamer passed them. These emotions grew intense as we entered the harbor, cast anchor, and saw the boat pushing off towards us, which contained our brothers and friends. They were soon on board, and warm congratulations and fraternal kisses were exchanged. A new welcome awaiting us at home from the sisters and pupils of dear J. I could not be long among hearts so kind, and not feel myself at home. Especially when I came into my own room, and recognized the chair in which I had so often sat; the desk, the wardrobe, all familiar objects for years,* the feeling of strangeness was almost forgotten.

"We have a large airy room opening on an immense terrace, which runs the whole length of the house, and could easily contain one hundred people. It is delightfully cool, and supplied with every thing I could wish. Indeed every thing had been arranged as much as possible for my comfort. The house is very large, as it needs to be to accommodate so large a family; besides, the two schools are in the house. I have a sweet girl for assistant in the school, in whom I can have all confidence, and who is most ready to do any thing in her power. In Mrs. York I have a most kind and affectionate mother, who makes me think constantly of dear grandmother F. She is just such a one as your dear mother was. What is more than all, I have a dear husband, the tenderest, fondest, truest, and noblest, that woman's heart could desire. We are most happy in each other, and in the

* Her furniture had been previously conveyed there.

fond anticipation of being made useful to others. Could you ask for more for your Emmie ?

" The island is exceedingly beautiful, quite different from Corfu ; it has a more laughing, smiling loveliness, if I may use the expression ; for the dark olive which covers Corfu, though graceful and beautiful, gives a sombre cast to the scenery there, quite different from that produced by the rich green of the luxuriant currant vineyards. We are just now in the midst of the vintage."

CHAPTER XXV.

Her situation at Zante—Letter to the Thanksgiving Circle at Home—To Miss S. P. C.—To her Mother —To Miss C. H.—To Miss M. D. B.—To Mrs. D.

Miss Waldo was now called to occupy a new position in society. She was no longer the missionary supported by foreigners, but the wife of a native teacher—the head of a family—a component part of the community among whom she labored. We are still dependent on her correspondence for an account of the joys and trials of her new situation.

TO MRS. DICKSON.

"*Zante, August* 26, 1848.

"My beloved Friend:—I can hardly believe it is but one week since I bade you adieu; so much has transpired since, that I seem to have lived a month in a week. Not that time has hung heavily. O no, never did the golden hours glide so brightly by. Never was life so full of sunshine, never was this heart so happy. You remember, perhaps, what I said once in answer to your request that I would write you fully and freely. I told you if I was happy I would, otherwise I would bury in my own bosom every grief, for no one should ever learn from me that I was an unhappy wife. Blessed be the Father of mercies for the abounding love that has filled my cup with blessings, and crowned the innumerable favors of the past, with the precious gift of my beloved J. Yes, my dearest friend, I am a most happy wife. My fondest expectations are more than realized. I can only exclaim, Bless the Lord, O my soul, and forget not all his benefits. The more I know of J., of his past exercises and his present feelings, of his hopes, his aims, and his purposes for the future, the more I rejoice in the providence that has linked my destiny with his. My one hope and prayer is that I may have grace to be a help *meet* for him. Pray for this, my dear Mrs. D.

"I found only six boarders in the house, the rest being absent in the country. It was with peculiar emotions I looked on the dear girls who would look up to me in the future as their instructress, their example, their counselor, and guide. We need no common share of wisdom and prudence to direct us. How sweet is the promise, 'If any man lack wisdom, let him ask of God, who giveth to all men liberally, and upbraideth not, and it shall be given him.' Greek parents will naturally look with suspicion on almost every movement of ours; and the temptation therefore becomes strong to yield to their prejudices, that we may avoid giving offence. To be faithful to God, and true to our own convictions, and at the same time to avoid wounding unnecessarily the feelings of our friends—this is an undertaking that calls for divine help. This is my only cause of anxiety.

"Mr. C., J's head teacher, has kindly taught the pupils who have been in attendance this week; but on Monday J. will return to his regular duties, and I shall see less of him. But I shall have enough to employ my time and thoughts, and we feel it is time to begin to work. Life must not be spent in fond dalliance, God has wisely and justly ordained that our sweetest joys should turn to bitterness, when they are misused, and indulged in to excess. While we bless our merciful Father for all the sources of enjoyment he has opened to us, we desire not to rest in any creature good, but to make him our portion. I feel the need of guarding against that spirit of self-indulgence, so likely to be awakened by the constant devotion, the unremitted attentions of my loving J. They are most sweet to a heart that has long felt lone and desolate in the midst of a cold world ; torn from the fond embrace of an affectionate mother and sisters. But there is danger I know in its very sweetness—danger of becoming selfish, and of forgetting that woman especially, is called upon to minister, and not to be ministered unto. So to forget my high calling, were indeed an ungrateful return for all the loving kindness that has spared and blessed my forfeited life.

' Yes, unto God I would devote
The remnant of my days.'

" *Monday afternoon.*

" Here I am, dear Mrs. D., in my school-room once more, engaged in my wonted employment. I have had a good many anxious thoughts to-day, as I have begun to realize more clearly what I have undertaken. A painful sense of weakness and insufficiency quite weighed down my heart this morning. But the sweet promises of God's word, and the sympathy and encouraging assurances of my dear husband, have inspired me with fresh hope and confidence. May the everlasting arms be ever beneath me, or I shall surely fall."

"*Zante, September* 15, 1848.

"I need not tell you, my dearest sister, what you already know, that your affection is a blessing I prize most highly, and that I love to recall the hours spent with you, the scenes of trial and of joy through which we have passed together. I love to think that you still pray for me; and especially when Wednesday eve comes, will I feel that you are near me in spirit, and that your prayers ascend with mine to the throne of all grace, that I may be kept from temptation, and led in the path of duty. Never had I more need of such petitions, my dearest sister; never had I so much to lead me astray—so many obstacles to surmount, in attempting to serve God. Yet I find him the same ever-present, ever-gracious Saviour, as willing and ready to hear the cry of his weak and erring child here in this land of darkness and sin, as in the favored home of my girlhood.

"Nor do I pray alone. My beloved husband's prayers are joined to mine, and we cherish the same desire to be led by God's own hand in ways well pleasing to him. He is never more dear to me than when explaining the Gospel to the children, or bowing the knee with them in prayer to Him who alone can renew and save them. But we are watched very closely and jealously, and now more so than ever, since the populace have been so excited about K. The past week has been an anxious and trying one, and we have often asked each other, What will be the end of all this?

"You will easily understand that, connected as we are with K., in the minds of the people, this tumult must affect us intimately. We would not shrink from the cross, we only wish to know what is duty, what the

Lord would have us to do. Poor K. looks to us as his only sympathizers, and we would fain do something for him. May his afflictions be sanctified to his soul, that by them he may be brought to Christ, and know him as his only Saviour."

TO MISS C. HAYNES.

" *September* 22.

" Could you see me now, dear C., I hardly know whether you would laugh or start. A Greek school-room is so entirely different from every thing we are accustomed to, that you would hardly recognize our assembly of children as entitled to the name of a school. Perhaps you will say, But why don't you reform ? Yes, dear, I hope and mean to do so. But '*patience;*' as my dear husband says. To attempt at once to enforce our stern discipline, would disgust the children, and drive them all from us, and so we rather prefer to work gradually and win them by kindness.

" I have entered on an entirely new life, wholly unlike all I had before experienced or known. Strange habits, manners, mode of life, all is so new and strange, that I am often bewildered, and feel as if I were in some dream land, and not actually, *really*, living and acting. My dearest J. is all the world to me. No one around us understands our feelings, no one shares our hopes and aims, no one cares for the one object that interests us. Though all are kind and affectionate, we are in a peculiar sense *alone*, in the midst of a multitude. How sweet to find *that one friend* all your heart longs for. How sweet to find that heart beating in unison with every throb of your own. How sweet to share its fullest confidence, to enjoy its tenderest regard, and be blest with its warmest love.

" I have sacrificed much in making Zante my home it is true; but I have in my darling J. more than an equivalent. We have many trials from without, as you may suppose; but we are not anxious, we commit our way unto the Lord, and we believe he will direct our steps."

" *November* 18.

" This has been a very busy week, and every hour has been fully occupied. On Monday the first of the month, (O. S.), we changed our school hours, so as to have but one session, from nine to half-past three, with only an intermission of half an hour, from half-past twelve to one o'clock, when all take a slight lunch. At four we are ready for our walk, and return at five, when dinner is on the table for us. We spend a pleasant hour at the social board; and could you look on us then, you would see a happy set of smiling faces around our large dining table. When the children have been good, we allow them fifteen or twenty minutes recreation after dinner, in which we take a kind interest. Then all repair to the school-room, and after prayers, sit down to prepare their lessons for the next day. I like this new arrangement very much, though I find it rather exhausting for me. When I get more accustomed to it, however, I hope I shall be less fatigued. I am very much interested in my classes, they are attentive, and ambitious, and making all the progress I could expect. I have become much attached to several of my pupils, and can see a sensible improvement in some of the more fractious and troublesome.

"But when shall we see that inward renovation effected, which is the only sure foundation of moral loveliness? This must be God's work; a precious thought, which at once encourages and humbles us. All human probabilities are against us, but if Christ undertake for us, we are sure of success. We hope that some of the seed sown beside all waters, may, in an hour unknown to us, be quickened into spiritual life, and prove the salvation of some lost sinner. We frequently talk over plans for increasing our usefulness and improving our pupils; but all our plans we commit to Him who has hitherto led and guided us, and who has assured us, if we commit our way unto him, he will direct our steps."

TO THE THANKSGIVING CIRCLE AT HOME.

"*Thanksgiving Evening, Nov.* 30, 1848.

"DEAR ONES AT HOME:—Do you not feel that Emmie's spirit is with you to-night. Surely her heart is with you all, and her fancy busy in picturing you once more in that dear old home. This will probably be the last Thanksgiving you will spend there.* How I wish we could have joined your festal circle for this last time there. But if we are spared to come to you, it will be a Thanksgiving day, wherever spent. We have thought and talked much of you, and have just been praying that Heaven's richest blessings may rest on each one of you, and that our loving Father may hear our united prayers for an early reunion.

"We feel that we have peculiar reason for gratitude in reviewing the past year, for it has witnessed the answer to the prayers and wishes of years. It has realized our

* Her mother was at this time expecting soon to remove from the homestead.

fondest, sweetest hopes, and opened to us new and precious joy. When we remember the pangs, the fears, the anxieties of the past winter, and then recall the goodness which changed them all to joys, sweet, and tender as earth can offer, we feel that words fail to express the gratitude we owe our merciful God. Our happiness to-day has been greatly increased too, by a merciful interposition of Providence, which has delivered a brother-in-law of J. from impending evil, just when we were ready to give up hope,.and has thus changed the gloom and tears of his devoted wife into smiles of joy.

" Indeed we are happy to-night. Happy that we have a Father in heaven to whom we can go in every difficulty; happy that we have a Saviour to intercede for our sinful and erring hearts; happy that we have a dear mother, brother, and sisters in America, who love us, as well as those here who bear the same appellatives; happy in the affection of tried and true friends who love us, and pray for us; and happy, very happy in each other. Do you not share our happiness, and shall not our thanksgivings ascend together to the Father of our mercies? Let us not murmur at the little that is withheld, but be astonished at the much that is given; for what do we merit but his chastisements, and his displeasure? Alas, that I have lived twenty-nine years in this world of probation, and done so very, very little for Him who has loaded me with blessings."

TO MISS S. P. CARTER.

" *Zante, Dec.* 7, 1848.

" MY DEAREST SARAH :—The barque Stamboul leaves our port tomorrow, for Boston direct, and thus affords me an excellent opportunity for sending a box home. I am disappointed that she is in quarantine, and I cannot go on board. She has been the home of so many dear missionaries, that I feel as if there were something holy about her. The sainted Mrs. Von Lennep, came out in her. I have hastily glanced over her Memoir, as I have not yet had time to read it leisurely. She seems to have been a simple-hearted, affectionate creature; and there is a manifest growth in grace apparent in her writings, which one loves to see. How mysterious her early death, and how sad her bereaved husband's lot. Of the other books sent by the Jasco, I have only read '*The Withered Branch Revived*,' which interested me exceedingly."

After expressing her opinion of some other works, which had been sent to her, she adds:

"Perhaps you think I ought not to censure the tinge of romance in these works, when I have seemed to be influenced by this spirit in my life, if its peculiar events and changes can give a guiding clue. It certainly never entered into my youthful dreams, wild as they sometimes were, that I should be what I now am. And yet I do not think I have been influenced by the spirit of romance in any step I have taken; unless it be romantic to love ardently, and to follow the promptings of that love. I sometimes feel as if I had been asleep, and had dreamed the strange events of the past year—that it cannot be reality that I am the wife of a foreigner.

"We often say that it is strange we should be so alike in all our tastes and feelings, brought up so differently as we have been. Yet the discipline to which our souls have been subjected, has not been so very dissimilar. We were both brought up in error, both have tasted the anguish of feeling that we must separate from those we loved most dearly, and give pain to those we would give worlds to make happy. Both were early left fatherless; both chose a teacher's profession, and love the work. Both of us have a distaste for worldly society; love a quiet and retired life, and fancy there never was a happier couple in the world than ourselves.

"I don't suppose you have the least idea of society here, for it is utterly unlike all you have ever known. The present generation, godless as they are, must have had very godly ancestors, for the name of God is ever on their lips. If a child is ill and recovers, the uniform remark is, 'God interfered and it recovered.' At every agreeable circumstance mentioned, all exclaim, 'Glory be to thee, O God.' If a person is left without any company, he is said to be 'alone with God.' Other innumerable expressions of the kind are in use. On the other hand when any thing vexatious occurs, they exclaim, 'O the sins that I have,' or, 'The Lord have mercy on me a sinner.' When you bid any one good-bye, he says, 'Go in the blessing of God.' The constant use of such expressions, and they are universal, might at first lead one to suppose he was in the midst of a most religious people. But alas, their hearts are far from God, and the name so lightly, and profanely uttered, awakens no feelings of awe, penitence, or love, in their hearts."

In a letter to her mother by the same box, after specifying how she would have various articles appropriated, she adds,

"It is a sort of painful pleasure I feel in sending these little tokens of love to you; for I think they will go, but I cannot. Dear hands will touch them which I would give, O how much? to clasp. Fond eyes will look on them, which I long to look into. O, that I could wrap myself in these folds, and be carried to the dear home where they will be borne. And then, my darling husband sees the gathering tear, and hearing the half-suppressed wish involuntarily murmured, says, 'Shall I send you, Emmie?' But when to my 'O yes,' he asks, 'And for how long a separation?' my clinging heart cannot detach itself from this treasured object of its fondest love; and I can only say, 'I cannot go without you.' The good Lord hasten it in his time. If it be his blessed will, we hope the day is not distant when some good ship will bear us over the waves, and bring us to New England's rock-bound coast.

"They say the Pope is taken prisoner, several Cardinals beheaded, and Rome revolutionized. Vienna too, beautiful Vienna lies in ruins; and how many other cities of the old world have seen their fair palaces and cathedrals demolished since this year commenced? When January 1st, 1848, ushered in the new year, how few dreamed that it would witness the astonishing revolutions which have made it a never-to-be-forgotten year in the annals of Europe. Did Louis Philippe foresee its close? Did Pius IX? Did the crowned heads of Europe, whose thrones have almost tottered to their fall since February last, did they anticipate it? One only knew. One who ever knows all that *has been*, *is*, and *will be*. In his almighty hand are the destinies alike of nations, and of individuals, and to him let us commit our unknown future, with the trusting confidence of little children; fo he doeth all things well.

"Our school is going on pretty well, and we find ourselves constantly occupied. I always find it easy to win children's hearts. There is an ever fresh interest in teaching, which relieves the tedium of elementary instruction; I mean the new developments of character which every day affords, together with the study of character and of the motives which will influence different minds. There is very little regard paid to motives by parents here. To secure the present object is the one thing thought of, and if this be secured, it matters not how, be it by threats or caresses, by cheating or falsehood. I find that affection will work wonders, and is the best constrainer in the long run. Is it not so with us all? Does not our merciful God himself thus win the hearts of men? Is it not Christ lifted up, the manifestation of perfect love and pity, that draws all men unto him? True there are terrors in God's law, awful threatenings, not to be disregarded; these alarm the soul, and break the spirit, but they never of themselves can bring the sinner with the broken-hearted contrition of the prodigal to say, 'Father, I have sinned against heaven and in thy sight.' O that we felt the amazing love of God as deeply as the fond love of the creature. But how great the disproportion!"

Under the same date she thus writes

TO MISS C. HAYNES.

"MY DEAR CATY:—Do not look scornfully on this tiny sheet, though it is so out of proportion to your generous one. I would fain take a large one, had I time to fill it. And what shall I write you about? I am not in a land of Missionary, Bible, and Tract societies, of Sunday schools and prayer meetings, of books and lectures, and means of grace. Naught of all this.

"Picture to yourself a bright green island, rugged mountains shutting in a most fertile plain, the combination of all that is beautiful; verdant currant vineyards, interspersed with pretty white country seats, and here and there clumps of olive trees. Turn around, and you see a towering hill, surmounted by a fort or castle, and down the steep sides, and at its base, lies the city stretching along the shore, some two miles in extent. Here is the home of your old friend Emmie. In a house belonging originally to an Italian Count, built in the style of the Venetians more than seventy years ago, in a large airy chamber looking out on the harbor, sits your quondam friend penning this epistle to you. It is a holiday, and we have no school, but the voices of our boarders are heard in the next room, chatting away in a language you could not understand, but which is almost like my mother tongue to me now. A dark-eyed gentleman, ever and anon comes in to address some questions to me, a stranger to you, dear C., but who calls me his dear wife. Can you make out a picture of Emmy in circumstances so unlike those in which you once knew her?

"But, dear C., the longer I live, the more I feel that it is not the outward, but the inward that constitutes our chief happiness; and that a happy heart makes a happy home, in whatever land, amid whatever scenes. I only wish I could see some turning to God from the midst of this people. Up to this time for a number of years, there has been not a single clergyman in Zante, of any denomination. But we hope soon to enjoy the preaching of the gospel if the Lord will, although not as we could wish, from a Baptist. Still if it be the gospel, we shall rejoice; for I think far less of sects and names than formerly.

"Many thanks, dearest, for the Memoir of Mrs. Shuck, and that sweet book of Dr. Clark, 'The Withered Branch Revived.' This last spoke to my heart; for alas, I knew too well what backsliding was. The Lord grant that I may indeed be reunited to him, and bring forth fruit to his glory.

"Accept Mr. Y's kind regards, and believe me ever

Yours, EMMIE."

TO MISS M. D. BALFOUR.

"*Zante, December* 7, 1848.

"MY DEAR MARY:—It was very kind of you to think of your old friend when so far away, and so long absent too. You seem to have no idle hours, although you have not assumed a matron's or a mother's duties like most of our old schoolmates. A single lady at home, that is, in the United States, can easily find many paths of usefulness in which to tread, many ways of doing good and being happy. But here it is far otherwise; and it is thought a great calamity if no husband can be bought for a lady. I say *bought*, for when a gentleman wishes to marry, the first question is, Who will give the highest dowry? And influenced by that, the gentleman accepts, and is betrothed to a lady whom he may never have seen, though this last circumstance is not so common now as formerly.

"I do not wonder that you feel so deep an interest in 'the West.' Every true-hearted New Englander must feel that he owes his first and highest energies to the work of enlightening that vast portion of our country. Much as there is to fear from Romanists, I cannot but hope it will yet be won for Christ, and the strong holds of the man of sin taken by Him who is stronger than he. Satan, alas! seems to reign triumphant here, and God's servants are almost discouraged by the obstinate unbelief and superstition of this people. Yet with God all things are possible.

"And now, dear Mary, adieu. Remember me to your family, and believe me yours ever,

"S. E. W. YORK."

TO THE FIRST BAPTIST CHURCH IN CHARLESTOWN.

"*Zante, December* 22, 1848.

"DEAR BRETHREN AND SISTERS:—You have probably ere this been apprised from other sources of the important and interesting changes through which I have passed since I last wrote you; how, when on the eve of recall and return to my native land, a new door of usefulness was opened for me among those to whom I was sent out, and a companion granted me in the precious work of teaching the youth of these dark corners of the earth,—one whom the Lord was pleased to enlighten and prepare for this important service. This step was not taken until after much thought, and earnest prayer that God would allow us to do nothing which would not be for his highest glory, and the advancement of his cause. We do feel that it was his hand which brought us together from the ends of the earth, and entrusted to us these poor stray lambs, that we might labor together for their ingathering into the fold of the good Shepherd. My change of name and connection, therefore, has not changed my work, and I still beg an interest in your prayers, my dear brethren, for myself and my dear companion, that we may be faithful to the trust committed to us. I shall no longer need your contributions, as my wants are otherwise supplied, but I need your prayers more than ever.

"We have made this island our home, not because it is lovely as the garden of Eden, a bright, and sunny land of fragrant flowers and luscious fruits, but in the hope that we can make ourselves useful.

"We have, however, many enemies. How could it be otherwise? The gayety, the ungodliness, the superstition, and the wickedness, that surround us, raise mighty barriers against our feeble efforts, and sometimes we have been ready to faint like sinking Peter when the roaring waves surrounded him.

"Shortly after my coming to Zante, an individual here named Kynegus, a candidate for the priesthood, became the object of popular odium and violence. He had long been known to cherish Protestant sentiments, and had thus been a marked and suspected man for a year or two past. On returning from a visit to Corfu last September, a sort of half witted monk came with him, who professed to wish to become a Protestant, and went about Zante publicly making ridicule of the patron saint of the Island whose relics are worshiped here. The populace, of course, were at once enraged both with the Monk and Kynegus, his constant companion. The Bishop ordered the Monk to leave the Island, and Kynegus to lay aside his clerical dress. The latter refusing to do this, was taken by the police to the Bishop's house, attended by an excited rabble who threatened even his life. There his long hair was cut off, his sacred dress taken from him, and a secular one given him, amidst the shouts and derisions of the mob. At midnight, when a shower of rain had dispersed the rabble, he was taken home. He has lost his situation as teacher, and is chiefly dependent on the kindness of those who sympathize with him. It is wonderful that he has held his ground with so much firmness, for though his mind is much enlightened, his heart does not appear to have been savingly renewed. We hope, however, that the truth for which he has suffered so much, may yet make him wise unto salvation, and that his daily life may be consistent with its sacred requirements.

"These events, of course, have had a bearing upon us, and have added much to the opposition we have had to encounter. But God has been pleased in a measure to make even our enemies to be at peace with us; and we have the privilege of praying and reading God's word with some dear children daily. We have nine boarders with us, and about fifty day scholars, for whom we bespeak your most fervent prayers.

"Once more accept of my warmest thanks for your kind support, continued for more than four years. May your funds in the future be devoted to one more worthy to be your representative in heathen and benighted lands, and may they be doubled, yea increased ten-fold in this good work. And in the midst of abundant means of grace and precious Christian privileges, remember us in this land of Mesech, where we sojourn in the hope that we may be made instrumental in causing this moral wilderness to blossom as the rose.

"Will you not sometimes write to your attached, though unworthy sister,

"S. E. W. YORK."

TO MRS. DICKSON.

" *Zante, December* 31, 1848.

" MY DEAR MRS. D. :—Is your absent friend Emmie at all in your thoughts to-day ? Do some memories of her mingle with the thoughts that doubtless occupy your mind on this closing day of the departing year ? I doubt it not, and my heart longs this evening for converse with you as in by-gone days. How sweet it would be, this quiet Sabbath eve, to retrace together the past year, to talk over all its varying scenes,—the dark clouds with which it entered, the bright rainbow of hope that afterwards gilded them, and the sweet quiet sunshine of happiness which has gladdened its close.

" What an eventful year to my beloved husband, not in a temporal sense merely, but especially in a spiritual point of view. Blessed be God for the experience it has given him of the preciousness of the truth, and the privilege of bearing the cross for Christ's sake. Blessed be the grace that enabled him to make a decision so painful to his affectionate heart, because it was almost a death blow to his family and friends. Blessed be the living Spirit who has been gently leading him the past year in the path of life and peace.

" Last Friday, which was a day spent by the Greeks in honor of a certain saint, he was telling me how entirely his feelings had been changed in regard to this creature worship. Years ago he would have been shocked at the idea that it was otherwise than meritorious to join in this ; while now his heart ached for those blinded by such delusion, and it seemed strange to him that any could put their trust in such things. There was a time when he even thought the Greek church needed no reform, and that it would be wrong to admit any improvement, which would be a departure from the regulations of the church. He told me how doubts would sometimes spring up in his mind, about the right of rendering such homage to a man; but that he hushed all such thoughts as temptations from Satan, to pry into what did not belong to him. But gradually, step by step, did God lead his mind out of this spiritual bondage, to see that there is none other name given under heaven whereby we can be saved, but the name of Jesus.

"Yes, dear Mrs. D., long shall we remember 1848,—those sweet summer months we spent together so quietly, so happily,—all your tender and lively interest in my welfare, your maternal affection, your kind counsels, your earnest prayers. The Lord reward you, and bless you with his own love.

"How naturally the review of the past leads us on to anticipations of the future, especially when the boundaries of the old year have been passed, and the new year entered upon. How little do we know of its coming secrets. I try to realize its uncertainty, and that ere its close, I may be in my grave—in eternity. But still my thoughts will busy themselves with life and its projects. New plans, new arrangements, occupy many of my few moments for reflection, and I fear that I do not keep heaven in sight as I ought. Pray for me, that I may be prepared for all the will of God. And may Jehovah Jireh provide graciously for you, and grant you to see his guiding hand in every change that may befall you."

"*March* 3.

"I can hardly realize that we are so soon to see you face to face, God willing; surely Christian society, and Christian privileges will be more dearly prized than ever before; and I trust more truly blessed to me for that reason. Yet we have great occasion to bless a faithful God that he doth not hide himself from us here, but doth fulfill his promise that where two or three are met in his name, he is there in their midst. We were enabled to spend yesterday, agreeably to the intention mentioned in my last, as a day of fasting and prayer; and we both agreed at its close, that it was the happiest day we had ever spent together; yes, one of the happiest in our lives. Like that happy day I spent with you last May, we found that the more we prayed, the more we had to pray for, and the more we enjoyed prayer. The Lord grant that we may keep our vows, and remember our covenant with him to live henceforth for him alone. We trust he will bless our coming unto you, and cause us to sit together in heavenly places in Christ Jesus. May he meet us in both his ordinances, and fill us with his love. We anticipate much in enjoying the Lord's supper with you.

"I feel the need of relaxation, for my nerves are getting irritable with the constant tension to which they are subjected. From my first waking moments, until our boarders are asleep, I have no rest, there is something to be said or done constantly, and ten hours of teaching would not be more exhausting. Indeed I am frequently in the school-room from nine in the morning till six in the afternoon.

"It is a sweet mercy to my soul to have my dear companion fully one with me, and that not from any attempts of mine to persuade him to it, but purely as the result of his own deliberate, thorough, and prayerful investigation of the whole subject. I resolved from the first that I would not mention the subject, as I knew he wished to feel unbiased in his examination, and I too desired this. Our school will doubtless be injured by this step, and we may have to leave Zante, but J. has counted the cost, and is prepared for any thing. Not that he does not feel. O, no. A sensitive heart like his must feel keenly the grief and disapprobation of friends. But his heart is at peace in God."

" *March* 9.

" I have just finished reading the Memoirs of Crocker, Mrs. Van Lennep, and Mrs. Shuck, and have read all with the deepest interest. Each has its peculiar charm, but Crocker's makes one feel what it is to be a Christian. What a lovely character he possessed; what a sweet, subdued spirit was he governed by. To what subjection to God was his will brought, &c. O, for grace to possess that heavenly temper, that broken heart, that subdued will. I could hardly believe it possible that one woman, and she young and delicate, could do all that Mrs. Shuck did. Her domestic cares and missionary labors were enough to break down three strong women."

" *June* 3.

" What blessings are these sweet Sabbath days to our tempted souls, our care-worn spirits,—these holy intervals when we can collect our scattered thoughts, and see where our souls stand. Alas, my earthly nature grovels here below, and I have constantly to mourn over divided and languid affections. We have both of us been much impressed this afternoon in reading an interesting chapter from 'Christ on the Cross;' at the comparison between man's heart and a garden. For as a garden after years of wholesome and careful culture will yet produce only weeds if left to itself, so the natural product of man's heart will be only sin, even after years of watchfulness and self mortification.

"I have found a little leisure lately for Cheever's Bunyan with which I am delighted. This introduction throws a new light over that beautiful allegory, as it gives a clue to many of its most interesting passages. We have also been reading Elijah the Tishbite, together, with much interest. How sweetly simple is Krummacher's style. Would there were more of such preachers in Germany."

CHAPTER XXVI.

Visit to Corfu—Baptism of Mr. York—To Miss S. T. B—To her mother—To Rev. S. Peck—Encouragement in their work—Her religious feelings—Hopeful conversion of one of her scholars—Prejudices of the people—Residence at Acrotini.

AT the time of their marriage, Mr. York, though he had fully come out from the Greek church, had not formally connected himself with any other. He wished to consider the subject carefully, and to have his mind unbiased by any worldly considerations. Mrs. York, who approved of his course, scrupulously avoided every thing that was calculated to influence his mind, or prevent him from following the simple teachings of the Spirit. It was therefore a matter of sincere rejoicing to her, when she found that his mind was fully made up to connect himself with the little Baptist church, and that he contemplated visiting Corfu for that purpose, during their April vacation. The particulars of this visit are given in the following letter

TO HER MOTHER.

"*Zante, May* 2, 1849.

"MY DEAREST MOTHER:—How many interesting scenes have we passed through since I closed my last of April 9th. I was then finishing my preparations for our visit to Corfu, which we had anticipated for so many weeks with such peculiar interest. We bade adieu to our young family at 10 o'clock in the morning of the 10th, and went on board the steamer Ionia. We were hardly out of sight of the city when I became at first faint, and then deathly sea-sick. Dear J. had a mattress brought upon deck for me, and did every thing possible for my comfort and relief. But nothing could avail. I could not lift my head up for a moment. We reached Corfu at a quarter past 11, P. M., and it was near midnight when we knocked at Mr. Arnold's door. They soon opened to us and gave us a warm welcome.

"We found Mr. A. quite delicate, having been reduced by frequent bilious attacks. Mrs. A's health has improved, and Mrs. D. is looking remarkably well. It was indeed delightful to join that dear family circle once more. We felt ourselves refreshed, comforted, and strengthened by the sweet Christian fellowship which united us, and long and deeply graven on memory's tablet will be those two weeks spent in Corfu. Our own feelings in view of J's profession of his faith, were solemn and peculiar, and we felt it a sweet relief to pour out our full hearts before God that all might be to his glory.

"On Thursday evening our little church assembled, a small company indeed, only six in all; for of all who have at one time or another belonged to our number in Corfu, these only were left. The rest were all scattered hither and thither, in England, Africa, and I know not where. Dear J., as is the custom in our churches, related his Christian experience—his first early impressions—his seriousness occasioned by the sickness and death of his brother George—the inquiries commenced by our correspondence and leading to an examination of his religious belief—his first anxious concern about his own salvation—his subsequent change of heart, and his after decisions, examinations, and purposes, together with his present hopes and feelings. It was somewhat trying to him to speak thus before others of his heart's inward feelings, for he is naturally reserved, and very slow to speak of himself. But he felt it to be duty and the Lord helped him.

"He was accepted as a member, and his baptism was appointed to take place on the following day. That sweet Friday, the 13th of April, shall I ever forget it? The clouds, which had been pouring out their contents for two or three days previous, broke away at early morn and we started for Paliocostritza at 8 o'clock. This is a romantic, retired spot by the sea-side, thirteen miles from the city, much resorted to in summer for its cool and healthy air, and for the advantages it offers for sea-bathing. There is little there beside a monastery, perched upon a high promontory some two hundred feet above the sea, and a few straggling cottages.

"We had a delightful ride of three hours, and alighting at the foot of the hill, sent up the carriages with the servants and children, while we waited below. After a few moments preparation, all was ready; and prayer having been offered, my dearest J. was baptized in the smooth, bright waters, in the name of the Father, Son, and Holy Ghost. A few peasants only were present, but God and angels witnessed these vows. My own feelings were intensely excited, but after all was over, and dear J. and I had found a quiet corner where we could retire to pour out our full hearts to God, I grew more composed, and we spent a sweet quiet day in that lonely spot, returning to the city at sunset.

"On the following Sabbath, the right hand of fellowship was given to my dear husband, and we united in the commemoration of our Saviour's dying love. To J. the extreme simplicity of the service was most impressive, far more so than all the imposing ritual with which he had been accustomed to see it administered. To us it was a most interesting hour. May we ever feel its hallowed influence.

"The next week we spent mostly in visiting old friends, and in delightful intercourse with our dear brother and sisters. The days flew rapidly by, and on the morning of the 22d we bade them a tearful adieu, and after thirty hours arrived at Zante. I found all our little family so glad to see us again, and all so kind and affectionate, that I could not but be happy. Many kind providences united to make us feel that we are in a loving Father's hands, and we committed all our way to him with renewed confidence and peace. We feel more and more every day that it is blessed to cast all our cares on him who careth for us far more tenderly than we could care for ourselves."

TO MRS. DICKSON.

"*Zante, April* 28, 1849.

"MY VERY DEAR MRS. D.:—It is always sweet to feel that we are loved, that there are those in this cold world whose hearts throb in affectionate unison with our joys and sorrows, and I have bidden you adieu again, with a deepened and precious consciousness that, all unworthy as I am, I am dear to your heart. I had indeed had proofs of your affection often and long before; but there was something in the brief and hurried intercourse of this interesting fortnight, which left an inexpressible sweet and tender feeling towards you, my dear *foster-mother*. O what a treasure is sincere Christian friendship, what earthly boon can compare with it! The quiet hours spent in such communings of heart with heart, how do they outvalue the charms of worldly society, be it most brilliant and attractive. This last week has been a very happy one. I sometimes feared when in C., that I should return less contented; but, now that I am at home, I find myself full of grateful, peaceful feelings, for which I bless a gracious God."

TO MISS. S. T. BOSWORTH.

"*Zante, May* 9, 1849.

"MY BELOVED SARAH:—Among the many sorrows which have saddened your heart the last year, I fear one has been traceable to your Emmie's long, and seemingly culpable silence. If it was a comfort to you, amid other trials, to be assured of her remembrance and affection, it would be no less a grief to think that she too had forgotten you. Yet no, my Sarah, not forgotten, not ceased to love, though I have allowed months, yes, more than a year, to pass without answering your last dear letter, which begged so earnestly for an early reply.

"Your last was received when my heart was agitated by a tender conflict in view of the uncertain termination of a long and interesting acquaintance, which had ripened into a most tender attachment. I was then preparing to leave Piraeus to spend the summer in Corfu, assisting Mrs. Dickson, with the prospect of meeting him who had become so dear to me, and of deciding either to give him up forever and return to America, or to accept his hand and heart. You have already learned the particulars of that meeting and its issue.

" That summer passed most quickly, quietly, and sweetly away with my loved sister, Mrs. D., and on the 18th of August I became the wife of Mr. J. Y. and sailed the next morning for Zante, our present home. Here I found myself at the head of a school of forty misses, seven of whom boarded in the family—and the cares and labor consequent on such a position demanded every moment and every energy. Will you, dearest, forgive your Emmie after this confession, and love her as dearly as of old, assured that she cherishes the same fond affection for yourself—that no change of name, relations, or situation, can alter her attachment for her long-loved, long-tried friends.

* * * * *

" Though in a strange land, among foreigners, foreign in every thing to all I have been wont to love and cherish, though my life is one of labor and care, yet still I am most happy. My husband is my little world—a world of happiness, peace, and love. The smile of our heavenly Father is our life. The love and grace of our tender Saviour are our hope and comfort, and the gentle teachings of the Spirit our means of grace. We are engaged in an arduous but most interesting work, precisely that for which I came abroad, the education of Greek youth. Though laboring against much prejudice, suspicion, and opposition, we have much to encourage us. Pray for us, for we are alone; yet not alone, for our God and Saviour is with us.

"And now, dearest, about yourself, for I have been thus egotistical only because I thought you would wish it. Are you still teaching? Is your health comfortable? The Lord give you patience and endurance, love. The Lord strengthen and cheer your fainting, worn spirit, and give you a happy issue out of all your troubles, maturing you for the inheritance of the Saints in light. O how sweet will be the rest of heaven, darling, to your storm-tossed soul. How soon in that eternal weight of glory will these light afflictions be forgotten. Look up, then, faint one, look up. Thy Redeemer counts every tear, hears every sigh, and though he smiteth thee, yet remember 'the very hand that gives the blow was wounded once for thee.' O, my darling sister, how gladly would I take you to my heart and home were I near to you. Do write very soon and tell me all.

"Ever your devoted

"EMMIE."

TO HER MOTHER.

"*Zante, Aug.* 4, 1849.

"Why have I no letters from home this month? The English steamer has come and gone, and naught for me. Perhaps they have gone to Corfu again, as they used to do, and if so, I shall not get them till after this is mailed. I trust you are all well and happy still, though it always makes me somewhat fearful when a mail passes without bringing me my precious packet from home. The Lord have you all in his holy keeping, and prepare us for every change that may await us.

"We know life's current cannot always glide thus smoothly on, and yet how difficult it is to anticipate ill. I hardly presume to look forward to such a year of happiness as this has been, which marks our first of married life. The 18th inst. will be the anniversary of our wedding day, and with most tender, grateful, and happy feelings do we celebrate its return. Every month as it passed has added a new, and stronger link to the viewless chain that binds us, and called forth a new song of gratitude to the gracious Providence that brought us together from the ends of the earth. O how unworthy am I of all the deep, and quiet happiness which I have tasted in this relation. How unsearchable the goodness of God.

"Many blessings have been poured upon us during this happy twelve-month. Those who looked on us coldly and unkindly at first, are now our very kind friends. Our school has increased and prospered beyond our expectations, a great change is manifest in our dear boarders, who have become to us almost as our own children, a change which we feel to be of God. A plain-hearted, evangelical minister of the gospel, has come to preach here the precious gospel of our salvation; and though of another sect, yet his catholic spirit makes us brethren. And now more recently we have had two dear brethren in Christ added to our number, whom Mr. Arnold baptized at Corfu on the 4th ult. I cannot express to you our feelings at our first little prayer meeting after their return to Zante. It seemed almost too much.

"We feel greatly encouraged to hope that the time to

visit this people graciously has come, in that God has so remarkably restrained the wrath of man in behalf of these two brethren. They have been permitted to return quietly to their homes, and resume their wonted duties, apparently undisturbed. Many have received them very kindly, saying that no man had a right to interfere with another's conscience. The Lord keep these young disciples, and preserve both them, and us, from the snares that are daily laid for our feet. O how much divine aid we need to be able to live 'blameless and harmless, the children of God without rebuke.'"

TO REV. S. PECK.

Zante, Sept. 4, 1849.

"MY EVER DEAR SIR:—Your most kind and cordial letter of March 6th, was most gratefully received, and although humblingly conscious of my unworthiness of your warm approval, and esteem of my poor labors for the Board, yet the assurance of your satisfaction with my course, and your continued regard, was most comforting to my heart. Yet dear as the approval of earthly friends must ever be, there is an approval still more precious and satisfying, yes, infinitely more so. I mean the smile of our heavenly Father, the evidence that our ways please him. Rich have been the spiritual mercies which he has granted me in this foreign land, and sweet have been the tokens of his love to our souls the past year. He hath made even our enemies to be at peace with us, granted us unlooked for success in our work, and permitted us already to see results which we expected only after years of effort.

"My husband's baptism, the result of his own unbiased examination of God's word, (for in this matter I would not interfere to burden his conscience with the fear that he had not acted with a single eye,) this his profession of faith in Jesus, was, I need not assure you, an occasion of heart-felt joy and of grateful thanksgiving to God, who had thus made us wholly one; first in himself, as we humbly trust, and then in his truth and ordinances. We live but for one object, are engaged in one work, which we view in the same light, and seek to attain by the same ends. And though we are thus separated from all around us, yet in the perfect union of our own sentiments, plans, and feelings, we find strength.

"Our little household too, of interesting youth committed to our care, afford us much cause for gratitude and hope. Our day scholars, of whom we have a goodly number, are affectionate, diligent, and attentive. But it is in our boarders, who are always with us, that we see results most gratifying and encouraging. When I first came to them they were giddy girls, who never seemed to have a thought beyond what they should wear, how they should kill time, and amuse themselves, even at the expense and annoyance of those around them. A book was never seen in their hands except when a lesson must be learned. Kind feelings, kind words, and kind actions, were what they seldom thought of calling into exercise. How my heart sank within me, when I assumed the charge of such children, and what days of sadness were my first Sabbaths with them. How could I teach those to love the truth, who breathed an atmosphere of falsehood? How could I persuade those to love the sacred rest of the Sabbath, whose only idea of this hallowed day was that of a gala-day for extra merriment and fun? How could I ever get access to hearts which looked on me with cold suspicion, as a heretic who would tempt them to apostatize from the only true faith?

"But what a change have we been permitted to see within the space of one short year? One of them, we tremblingly hope, has turned her face heaven-ward, and begun to tread the narrow path. From being a harsh, selfish, ungovernable being, she has become a meek, gentle, serious girl, whose greatest happiness seems to consist in making others happy. Her bible and her religious books are her delight, and the Sabbath her happiest day. Her friends attribute the manifest transformation in her, to her personal attachment to me. But to us the hand of God is manifest. Indeed all are changed. Their word may be relied upon, and they seem to fear a lie. They are kind and affectionate to each other, and only too ready to do every thing for me. They are never so happy as when we sit down to read or talk with them of serious things. Our Sabbaths are now sweet, quiet days, which they too seem to enjoy, sitting down with a tract, or the Bible, or even the younger ones to play Sabbath school, as they say. We feel that we have some encouragement to labor, and are willing to spend and be spent in such a work.

"But more than this, God has given us two Baptist brethren. We have held sweet counsel together on Sabbath evenings, as we mingled our prayers with those of these young disciples, talked over their trials and persecutions, and sought counsel and light from the blessed word of God. How little did I think when I first came to Zante that in less than one year we should enjoy a prayer meeting with native brethren. And though they leave us for Corfu, yet we can never forget these few precious seasons of prayers and Bible study, and our hearts are full of hope that these are but the first fruits of a harvest of souls which shall be gathered in to Christ."

TO MISS S. P. CARTER.

"*Zante, Dec.* 30, 1849.

"MY EVER LOVED SARAH:—On this quiet Sabbath eve, I would sit down to spend a little season in converse with you as I would if I were by your side, in that dear little chamber where we have spent so many happy Sabbath hours. You asked me in your last, of my personal religious feelings, of which indeed I have spoken little in my hasty letters of late. My feelings you know used to be of a very impulsive character, and I was in consequence prone to extremes. I have now a more steady enjoyment of hope in God's pardoning love, and a more peace-giving faith in Jesus' precious sacrifice and righteousness than I ever tasted before. On the other hand, I have such a variety and weight of cares, that leave scarcely time or thought for heavenly things. First my husband, then my babe, then six girls whose morals I must watch over, whose minds I must educate, whose manners I must improve, whose health I must look after, and whose wardrobe I must provide for; next a school to oversee, and lessons to prepare, a large house to try to keep in order, and all the commonalities of life. You will say this is too much. We often feel so; not that it is too laborious for the body, but it is too wearing and distracting to the soul. We are now especially, earnestly seeking and praying for divine direction to know how we can so arrange our affairs, as to secure to ourselves more time for prayer and reading.

"The hopelessness of success in our labors without God's interposing grace, has led us the more to him. I feel more the sweetness of that dear name 'Our Father'—feel more the nearness of God, and the reality of his living Providence. I know more what it means to cast every burden on him. I see more how entirely I must depend on Jesus for *sanctification* as well as justification, and that he must be all in all to my poor sinful soul. My greatest inward struggles are with earthly mindedness, and impatience of spirit. Since my sickness particularly I have found a sweetness and meaning in God's word, quite peculiar, and no book is so precious, indeed I read almost nothing else. Cheever's Bunyan I have enjoyed very much, but have not yet finished it, though I commenced last May. 'Christ on the Cross' I am reading with J. on Sunday afternoons.

"But, O, dear Sarah, I want to feel the love of God filling my soul, my cold insensate heart, that ought to glow and burn with most intense ardor of affection for my sin-atoning Saviour. What loads of sin have I laid upon him! What bitter anguish has he tasted for me! O, where is the burning love which such redeeming mercy calls for."

TO THE SAME.

"*Zante, March* 3, 1850.

"MY DEAREST SARAH:—How solemnly do we feel the presence of God when we see the tear of contrition flow, and hear the sigh of a burdened heart, oppressed with the weight of its sins; and O, when we see that burden removed, and peace in believing imparted, how do we feel to exclaim, 'This is none other than the house of God and this is the gate of heaven!' It has been permitted us to see this. One of our beloved pupils who has been for some time decidedly serious, has been led, I trust, to cast her whole soul on Jesus and find peace in him. She had been sick for some days past, and on Friday I noticed that she was weeping. I stopped and asked her what was the matter. At first she answered, Nothing. But when I asked again, Are you crying because you are unwell? She answered with much feeling, 'My soul is not well.' I told her it was indeed sinful, and had need of the Great Physician; but, as she was suffering from violent headache and fever, I added, Do not be excited as it will increase your indisposition. She immediately replied, 'But my soul is worth more than my body.' Most certainly it is, said I, and I did not mean to dissuade you from caring for your soul, and seeking for its salvation immediately. I then tried to direct her to Christ, our only hope. In the evening I found her sense of sin deep and tender. Yesterday she was more peaceful and said she felt that God heard her prayers; but to-day she told me, 'I feel very happy, God and heaven are constantly on my mind, and I feel as if Christ was very near me.' Her Bible and hymn book are her constant companions. O, what a thought, dear Sarah, that salvation has indeed come to our house, that there has been joy in heaven over one of our dear charge. Praised be redeeming grace.

"Mother tells me how much you enjoy with your little F., and I can easily imagine the delight with which you watch all his developments of mind and heart. In what a blessed atmosphere of piety will that dear boy grow up. But my darling babe, O, how different the influences that will surround him. We must keep him wholly out of the world if we would have him safe, and that is a bad education, because it unfits him for active life and intercourse with the world. But I am comforted by thinking God gave us a child, knowing all our circumstances, and he can therefore enable us to glorify him in the training of that child. Besides, I am convinced that it is not place nor circumstances which will keep a child in the ways of uprightness, but God's restraining grace. Pray for my precious boy when you ask God's blessing on your own pet.

"We feel a more tender anxiety for our dear child, because all our friends look upon him as one shut out from God's blessing, by not being baptized, and as certain to be lost if he die in this state. We desire therefore that they may see that God will bestow his blessing even on an unbaptized child. There is not an unbaptized child in the island beside himself, except those of too tender an age, nor did any one here ever hear of such a thing before as leaving a child unbaptized. Our friends here regard him as left in a state of nature, unsanctified with baptismal waters, and were he to die I know not what would comfort them. But this we should leave with God, for he knows all these circumstances. O for an implicit faith in him. How much easier is it to say we trust in him, than really to have no misgivings in our faith.

"I don't know that I have ever referred to our sainted Sarah B.,* since her release from this vale of tears. How sweet to think that Jesus has forever wiped away all tears from her eyes, that she will sorrow no more and sin no more. I felt rather disposed to praise and bless God than to weep, when I heard she was no more. Should not our hearts be drawn more heavenward as our dear ones are gathered there? Dear Martha Wason too has gone to her rest. Dear sister! thy conflict is over. Thy trials and sufferings are at an end. Glory be to God for another ransomed soul brought home to its Saviour. Yes, they are going, Sarah, our dear ones are leaving us, and who knows when our turn will come."

The dear babe referred to in the preceding letter, was born at Zante, October 14, 1849. Mrs. York was taken dangerously ill soon after its birth, and continued quite sick for some weeks. A wet nurse was therefore procured for the child, which for various reasons they were obliged several times to change. Speaking some time after, of her trials on this account, she says, "How many tearful and anxious hours had I for my dear child, and how keenly I felt my own inability to provide for its sustenance. But God was better than our fears, yes, than our hopes, and sent us an excellent creature, our dear Maria. I shall always love that simple-hearted peasant, and feel grateful that she supplied my maternal deficiencies so faithfully and affectionately. May God bless and reward her."

* Miss Sarah T. Bosworth of Providence.

TO HER MOTHER.

"*Zante, June* 3, 1850.

"DEAREST MOTHER:—Again I have had to bear the disappointment of *no letters.* These homesick days especially, I do so long for those dear messengers of love from my far away native land to cheer my heart. The feeling against us here is getting stronger daily. About ten days since, an article was published in the Zante newspaper, urging that an examination should be made of the girls' schools, especially in religion. This was intended solely for us, and every one so understood it. An application was also made to the municipal officer having charge of education, to have such an examination instituted. But he refused, saying that our school was a private one, and that the government had no right to interfere. Several members of the municipal corps have assured us that we need feel no uneasiness, as nothing could be effected in this way by our enemies.

"An indirect influence, however, is manifestly felt, for our school is reduced to about one half of its former number. We have expressed our entire willingness to have any friendly examinations into our school arrangements, although we would not submit to any civil interference, since we knew it would be illegal. Our friends feel all these things very much, and since our consciences will not allow us to make all the compromise they think advisable, they would feel relieved to have us give up the school, which is equivalent to leaving Zante. Not that they do not love us. We have every proof of the contrary, but that they cannot bear to hear the world censure us. J. has most to bear, as he is far more censured than I am; yet God gives him courage and even joy in suffering for Christ's sake, though no one was ever more unwilling to wound the feelings even of a mere child. But he has heard a voice saying unto him, 'He that loveth father or mother more than me is not worthy of me;' and that love for the Saviour which hath redeemed him, enables him to lay all, even the dearest earthly object, on the altar of Christ. Pray for us, dear mother, that we may be faithful to our master through evil report as well as good report, and thus be enabled to confound all our enemies. If the Lord be for us, who can be against us? Better is the reproach of Christ, than the treasures of Egypt.

"The national feeling is growing stronger and stronger in these islands; and the dislike to every thing English, government, education, religion and every thing that characterizes the nation whom they regard as tyranizing over them, has become a deep-rooted feeling, strengthened by the political events every day occurring. The English policy towards the islands has only exasperated the feelings of the inhabitants, and made them almost madly bent on union with Greece. You can hardly fancy the enthusiasm with which every thing relating to Greece is regarded; and the feeling is nurtured in the hearts of the rising generation, as we in New England stir up the patriotism of our children by dwelling on Revolutionary scenes. All this bears strongly against us, as religion and nationality are one thing in the eyes of this people, and an apostate from the church is regarded as a traitor to his country.

"*Acrotini, July* 6, 1850.

"Will you not think we have very kind friends when I tell you that I am again enjoying the quiet of a sweet little country residence belonging to our friend Mrs. Burff? It is an English cottage, made of wood. Many years ago, an English officer resident here, dissatisfied with the houses in Zante, wrote to England for a cottage. And sure enough they made one, packed up all the parts, timbers, planks, doors, windows, portico, &c., and shipped it to Zante. Here it was perched on this long promontory, called Acrotini, and a little garden cleared away around it. In course of time, the officer leaving, it fell into the hands of Mr. B., who keeps it not as a residence, as his family prefer living in town, but for an afternoon's resort for his lady and children. As they are now absent on a four month's tour to the continent, they kindly gave us the use of it. It is about a mile and a quarter from our school. Nurse and baby stay out here. Every morning I go to school, donkeyback, and walk out in the afternoon with J., and the boarders who return home to sleep. This you can imagine is not a very comfortable arrangement. Beside the warm ride in the morn, I am separated from my child all day, and my husband all night. But for dear Georgie's sake, who suffers dreadfully from the musquitoes in town, and for nurse's, who is accustomed to the mountain air, and was beginning to sicken from the heat of the city, I have consented to it. Beside I feel myself refreshed by the quiet and cool air, and strengthened for my daily duties. It is but for a month or two we shall live so, and we trust that the benefit will compensate for the sacrifice.

"We have had a sad and touching lesson lately of the

vanity and uncertainty of all earthly things, in the sudden death of the eldest daughter of Count Roma, a distinguished Zantiote. She was a beautiful girl, who had scarce numbered eighteen summers, when she gave her hand, one short year ago, to a wealthy young Athenian, who almost idolized her. She was a loving, amiable creature, the pride of her parents and eight brothers, the inseparable companion of an only sister, the pet of all Zante. She became quite a star in her new home, and in the devoted love of her husband, the doting fondness of her mother-in-law, and in the enjoyment of luxury and elegance, she was the envied of thousands. To complete her happiness, an infant child was added, which struggled a few days for life, and then slept in death. The delicate mother was kept in ignorance of her loss; but when the mother's heart became too clamorous in its longings, and she entreated them to bring her child, fearing to tell her, they brought her another infant. But the mother could not be deceived. 'This is not my child,' she said, and never spoke again. A fever set in, and in a few hours the frail lily withered and died. God grant it may be a lesson not lost on the wide circle of the bereaved.

"Just as I was leaving for my country home, the postman came with my letters, which had been sent to Corfu with Mr. Arnold's. How can I express to you the deep feelings they awaken, the thousand thronging emotions their perusal excites. O, it is sweet to be so dearly loved by such a precious mother, such darling sisters, and true friends; and to know, too, that my treasures here are dear to you. I do not wonder that J's sweet, beautiful children win all hearts, but I rejoice that they do not exclude my own sweet boy, whose pretensions to beauty are indeed less, but who is a dear little dove for all that. He is not very dark, but still would form a contrast to his fair cousins, who I hope he will yet see. I love to hear of dear J's maternal virtues, and long to press again to my bosom this most sweet sister, so dear to us all. God grant the fulfillment of our fond wishes in his own time. I could but smile at her remark that 'time had touched you all lightly.' She who sees you every few months can hardly judge. But I, after years of absence, can best tell what havoc he has made. Still, as she says, we can keep the heart young and so never grow old."

CHAPTER XXVII.

Popular violence—Feelings on leaving Zante—Voyage to Trieste—They proceed to Dresden—Sickness and death of their babe—Visit to London—Meet her brother at Haddersfield—Sail from Liverpool to America—Arrive in Boston.

WHILE Mrs. York was thus laboring even beyond her strength, and cheerfully denying herself the most innocent gratifications of life, for the sake of enlightening and benefiting the dear youth of Zante, their enemies were zealously plotting some way to interrupt the school, and silence the lips of these faithful teachers. God, who in the accomplishment of his own wise and gracious purposes sometimes suffers wicked men for a season to triumph over the righteous, was pleased to permit their foes at this time to carry their plans into execution. The result is given in the following letter

TO HER MOTHER.

"*Zante, July* 18, 1850.

"MY DARLING MOTHER :—Little did I think, when I wrote you last mail about our coming home to you, what distressing events were soon to compel us to take our departure hence. We knew indeed that we had many enemies,—that the priests were uniting their strength against Protestants, but we had not believed that such acts of personal violence and insult to ourselves also, were preparing.

"Last week all the priests in Zante, some sixty in number, signed a petition to the Bishop, accusing two of our brethren, P. and K., of proselyting, and begging him to take active measures against us. Some of those who presented the petition said that Mr. York's name ought to have been included. The Bishop applied to the Regent and municipal officers to take vigorous measures against P. and K.; stating that there were suspicions against Mr. York, but they had no proofs. The latter wrote to the Senate of Corfu, and to the President here, as the presiding English functionary is called, and it is said that it was decided to exile P. and K. for six months, as the High Police have a right to do this without any previous trial. At any rate, P. was deposed from his situation of public teacher, which he had held for years.

"The next day, K. was summoned by a policeman early in the morning to present himself at the police office. K. told him that he would willingly comply with the order, but that the police must know that for him to go out by day, which he had never done since his former persecution, would certainly excite a disturbance, and he begged the police officer to go and ask permission for him to come in the evening. Before the man returned, however, the rabble had got hold of the matter, and collecting about the house, soon broke in, thirsting for his blood. His poor mother, who was dangerously ill, fainted; but the blows given to her son aroused her, and, opposed as she is to his sentiments, for she is a thorough devotee of her own church, the mother in her prevailed over the Greek, and she threw herself between him and his enemies, receiving the blows on her own aged form. K., escaped with difficulty to an adjoining mill, where he found a brief refuge until the police arrived. Meanwhile his house was ransacked, his papers, including private letters, all seized and carried to the Bishop, and every thing destroyed in the house, within reach of the mob. The police at length arrived with a boat, to take him by sea to the prison, but as the mill was some distance from the sea, the poor man was exposed to the fury of the mob, who assailed him with large stones and every sort of missile. The person who protected him as far as he could, by taking him under his arm and covering his head with his coat, told us afterwards that he was covered with his blood.

"When he was fairly off, the mob left for P's house, in an opposite part of the town, into which, however, they could not effect an entrance, as it had been previously well closed. Some of our friends heard the tumult, but never dreamed of any danger to ourselves, knowing the high reputation of the family. But some hired servants, when the work was done at P's, called out, 'Now for the Yorks.' Several voices answered, 'No, no. Why should we hurt York? What has he done?' Others answered, 'He is a Protestant,' &c.

"I had heard the shouts of the mob, and felt anxious for our poor friends, whom we commended to God. I saw that J. was agitated, and eat nothing at dinner, but he did not tell me he apprehended any attack on our house. About half past one o'clock, I was sitting in my room writing a note, when I heard voices nearer, and going to the half open windows, I saw a band of ragamuffins coming round the adjoining theatre. Just then one turned the corner towards our house, and cried out, 'Come on, come on.' The rest seemed afraid and held back, when he tauntingly exclaimed, 'What are you afraid of? Come on. Do you fear the Yorks?' My brother-in-law, who was in the third story, could not believe that violence was intended, and spoke to them in a kind conciliatory manner, but in vain. Indeed, supposing him to be J., they began to shout, 'There he is. There he is. Come down, you rascals. Come down, you who pay the proselytes.' For it is reported, and generally believed, that J. pays all the so-called Protestants, whom our enemies declare to be about a hundred in number. They say he gives the teachers, P. and K., five shillings a day, and the others one, and that he gets the money from America.

"We dragged brother S. from the window and closed all the shutters as the mob began to throw stones. The windows of the boys' school in the lower story were all broken, as the shutters were inside. They attempted to burst the large gate which opened into the court, but providentially it had been well shut and barred, not five minutes before. Not knowing however what pitch their violence might reach, we collected all the family, and what children were in the house, into one room, and barred the doors inside waiting for help.

"Meanwhile Mr. C., J's brother-in-law, seeing our danger, went to the police office for assistance, but no one was there, as they were in the other quarters of the town. He sent, however, whomsoever he could find, until more effectual help arrived. At that hour, when all gentlemen in Zante are asleep, and before a friend of ours knew any thing of our danger, the mob, unable to do any thing more, went to the house of C. Here similar scenes were acted over as well as at three other dwellings, where those, who were thought disposed to Protestantism, resided. At length, about forty having been arrested, order was gradually restored to the town.

"But how shall I describe to you the almost frantic distress of J's doting mother, who had always gloried in the love and respect universally accorded to her children. To have them now reviled, hooted at, and insulted by a mob, was more than she could bear, and her sobs and lamentations filled us with anguish. O, mother, what a pang rent my heart at the thought that, though nothing was said, yet all the family must feel, that I was the cause of all this misery to them,—that but for me, J. had never become a Protestant, never been reviled for changing his religion. It seemed as if my heart would break. But no one uttered a word of reproach. They only said, 'You must go. You cannot stay in Zante. We shall all be ruined if you do not leave.'

"In the afternoon our house was filled with sympathizing friends who warmly remonstrated against the base measures the priests had used to excite the people against us, and a revulsion of feeling began in our favor which has been strengthening ever since. Our friends called a meeting of all the parents of our pupils, who united in signing a declaration that we had never taught the children any thing against their religion. One only complained that the books we used, such as 'The Dairyman's Daughter,' 'Mary Lothrop,' &c., contained nothing about the saints. A warm testimony was given to J's faithfulness and devotion to the good of the children. The Director of Schools especially spoke with much feeling, offering to give us any satisfaction we desired for the aspersions brought against us.

"J. thanked them for all their kindness, both on the present and previous occasions; but said the experience of Wednesday had taught us a lesson we could not misinterpret; that personal ease and safety were not a consideration with him or with me, and, were *we* only concerned, we would willingly go on and suffer any thing in the cause of truth; but that we did not think it right to peril the lives and happiness of our mother, brothers and sisters, and that we then, and there, resigned the school to brother S. and sister A. who had it before. Many tears were shed, and kind remonstrances made. The scene was indeed affecting, and an influence went forth from the meeting which will do more we hope for the cause, than could ever have been effected had things not reached such an acme.

"So we have mingled praises with tears, and have found how true is that Scripture, 'Surely the wrath of man shall praise him and the remainder thereof he will restrain.' But the situation of our unfortunate friends is widely different. My husband's uniform character for high integrity, self-devotion, and faithfulness in his work, the gentleness and discretion with which he has always tempered his zeal for the truth, and still more the long and wide-spread influence of the family, have turned the tide in our favor."

As their way seemed for the present hedged up, Mr. and Mrs. York thought best to improve this opportunity for visiting her friends in America, designing to spend some two years or more in the United States and then return and again resume their labors in Greece. Writing to Mrs. Dickson under date of Aug. 19, Mrs. York says:—

"These have been trying yet precious days, such a

sweet mingling of mercies with trials, such kind and gracious leadings of Providence, such a tender and fatherly provision for our necessities, such a sweet union of heart between ourselves, and comfort in casting ourselves on a faithful God, we should perhaps never have experienced had this cross not been laid upon us. Never was my beloved husband so unspeakably dear to me as now, and as we yesterday commemorated the second anniversary of our marriage, we felt how much deeper, purer, and stronger, was the love that bound us, than even the glow of first affection. We made it a day of special prayer for further guidance in the path of duty. I do indeed feel much in view of our intended journey, and my heart often sinks within me in prospect of it. But our trust is in him whose all-wise providence has made it necessary. He has been pleased to take from us the means of support here, and we cannot remain. We must leave as early as the first of October. My dear husband has felt himself called upon to memorialize the government, in behalf of the trampled rights of conscience. He wishes to leave nothing undone to secure religious toleration here, knowing that God can use even unwilling instruments to accomplish his purposes."

Their first plan was to take a vessel direct for the United States; but on further consideration it was thought preferable to return by the way of Europe, and take a steamboat from Bremen to New York. With this intention they took passage in a steamer for Corfu, on the 24th of September, in company with many friends, among whom was Rev. Mr. Arnold, who had been to Zante to administer the ordinance of baptism. They reached Corfu on the following day, where they waited a day and a half for another steamboat which was to carry them to Trieste. Here Mrs. York had the pleasure of seeing for the last time her dear friends and associates, Mrs. Dickson and Mrs. Arnold, whose sympathy was peculiarly refreshing to her. On the afternoon of the next day they embarked for Trieste, and for the first time, felt alone; for they were leaving the Ionian Sea and entering the Adriatic, surrounded altogether by strangers. They had, however, a most pleasant passage; the weather was beautiful, and the sea so smooth, that very little motion was felt even on deck.

They reached Trieste on the 28th, where having rested two days, and prepared themselves for their land journey, they took the diligence to Gratz, a beautiful city, half way between Trieste and Vienna. Here they remained three more days, and made further preparations for their journey, which was to be by railway to Bremen. The change of temperature at this place was very remarkable, and the weather very disagreeable. On the evening of the third of October, they left this city and reached Vienna early next morning. At this city their little boy was taken ill, but after taking medical advice he seemed so much better, that on the 7th they proceeded by railway to Prague. Here they again called a physician, and having rested a few days, and been assured from him that they might safely continue their journey, they proceeded on as far as Dresden; not in the cars, however, as they had at first intended, but for the sake of securing many conveniences for their sick babe, they took a steamer down the Elbe. The water was remarkably smooth, and the child lay quietly on the sofa all day.

It was Saturday evening when they reached Dresden;

and finding they could not overtake the steamer without traveling on the Sabbath, they determined to remain there until there should be a decided change in their child. Writing from this place to her mother she says: "Our expenses are, of course, greatly increased, but our child's welfare is of the first consideration with us; and we trust to a gracious Providence to provide for us in the future. O, that God may spare him at least to reach New England, that we may not be called to the agony of burying him in a foreign land. Yet not our will but his be done."

Notwithstanding their utmost care, the sweet babe continued to sink, and on the morn of the 20th its spirit returned to God who gave it. The mother's feelings on this occasion are expressed in the following note.

"*Dresden, Oct.* 20, 1850.

"God has smitten us sore, has laid us in the dust. Our darling, our sweet babe, sleeps in death. This morn has closed his agonizing sufferings, sufferings which made even our fond, doting hearts beg that he might be released. Too truly did my fond heart feel that he was too sweet for earth. Through all his sickness he has been the same patient lamb, even when pain wrung forth agonizing shrieks. O what greater torture for a parent's heart, than to witness the agony of his helpless babe. God grant we may never, never forget this discipline, but feel its sanctifying influence to life's last hour. My heart was indeed too earthly and needed a heavy stroke, to sever it from the world. My precious husband, though almost heart-broken, is my sweet comforter and earthly stay, and we do feel our God a present help in this hour of bitter need.

"Sickness and death among strangers, where we can scarcely make ourselves understood, O, how agonizing! Yet blessed be the Lord for the mercies mingled with our trials. We had kind, skillful physicians, and a most excellent nurse, and as a last resort a wet nurse, but all could not avail. For ourselves we mourn no common loss in the death of such a sweet, loving, submissive child. But, blessed be God, for him we rejoice, now eternally safe with his Redeemer."

While in London she wrote some reminiscences of this dear child of which the following are the closing paragraphs.

"O, that Sabbath morning. Shall I ever forget the heart-rending scene? Worn out, I laid down for a few moments, and when I returned a half hour after, I thanked God that little cry was hushed, the flush on his fevered forehead had died away. Those sweet eyes, which had become blood-shotten from his screams, were calmer, and the breath came fainter and fainter, that was soon to cease. Yes, I thanked him, though the hot tears flowed fast, as I saw myself about to become childless, for my darling was going to his rest, where he would suffer no more forever.

"But O, the aching void when that little form was removed from our sight, and that voice which had been our sweetest music, was heard no more. At first I could not identify that wasted corpse with my bright boy; but gradually the expression of suffering departed, a sweet smile rested on his pale face, and I love to remember him as he lay there amid the flowers which sympathizing strangers had garlanded around him. We bought a little spot for him in the Lutheran Cemetery, near to where other little ones who had died like him in a strange land, were laid; and there amidst sweet flowers and trees, we committed dust to dust, ashes to ashes, in sure and certain hope of a glorious resurrection. Yet, thou art not there my darling. No, thou art a cherub with thy Saviour, a bright angel in heaven. We give thanks for thee, for thou art forever safe. No sin shall ever stain thy pure spirit, no sorrow blight thee. God give us grace to come to thee, for thou wilt no more come to us."

Having buried their sweet child, they left Dresden and proceeded across the country, through Prussia and Belgium, to the Straits of Dover, whence they proceeded direct to London. The heart of Mrs. York, stricken by her late affliction, so yearned for the dear ones at home, that she would not allow herself to be tempted by any of the sights which usually attract travelers, save that they made a flying visit to the cathedral at Cologne at early dawn on their way to the railway station. "This immense pile of building," says Mr. York, "was still in progress, though commenced in 1248, more than six centuries ago. The colossal proportions of this beautiful monument of ancient German architecture were very imposing, particularly as it was now seen by the glimmering light of a still morning."

At London they remained six days and visited several places of interest. The two objects which most particularly attracted her attention here were Guy's Hospital and the preaching of Baptist Noel. Of the latter she says, "I had expected something splendid, brilliant, and showy, but instead of this was struck with his deep humility. Never did I so much feel my own perfect nothingness, and God's infinity. The influence was irresistible; you felt yourself in the immediate presence of God. The whole house was filled to overflowing. Yet the crowded audience seemed spell-bound, and listened to his words in death-like silence."

What particularly interested her in Guy's hospital, was the fact that it was founded by the munificence of one man, in his own life-time; and that so much attention was paid to the comfort of its inmates. "It consists of a large number of buildings, including a cookery, bakery, washing-house, &c. The rooms are all well ventilated, and the greatest cleanliness is preserved throughout the wards. Its revenue has now increased to about £30,000. It affords relief to about eight hundred poor people, who have only to apply for admittance. Medical attendance and nurses are provided for them, and all their wants are supplied free of expense. The munificent donor only lived to see this establishment opened, and died the day following."

From London they proceeded to Huddersfield, where she met her only brother, from whom she had been separated nearly seven years. This interview was particularly precious to her, and called forth many expressions of grateful acknowledgment to the God of her life. He accompanied them on the next day to Liverpool, whence they took passage direct for Boston. She suffered very little from sea-sickness during their voyage, and enjoyed very much the society of two Bohemian ladies, who were fellow passengers. They arrived at Boston on Saturday evening, November 16th. Their friend, Mr. C., of Charlestown, who had been for some hours at the wharf, waiting the arrival of the steamer, was very soon by her side, and conveyed them directly to her mother's residence.

From the moment she felt that her labors were closed in Greece, her heart had yearned for the home of her childhood. In the capitals and large cities of Europe through which they passed, she had never been willing to make any stop which would occasion the least delay in their passage home; and for the last three days before they reached the shores of New England, she could hardly take food or rest. And now that she once more found herself in the embrace of her beloved mother, her happiness was almost overpowering. For some time she scarcely uttered a word but "mother, mother." She felt deeply the goodness of God in having preserved the lives of their whole family circle, and in his permitting them to meet in health after so many years of absence. It seemed as if she never could express the depth of her gratitude for this peculiar favor of her heavenly Father.

CHAPTER XXVIII.

Effects of her foreign residence—Letter to her cousin, Mrs. E. A. B.—To her aunt, Mrs. C. W.—Her sickness and death—Her usefulness—Method for reading the Scriptures—Her prayerfulness—Dependence on the Spirit—Faith in Christ—Testimony of Mr. Buel and Mrs. Arnold—Closing remarks.

A RESIDENCE of nearly seven years in a foreign country had produced quite a change in the manners and appearance of Mrs. York. Those who had known her only in her girlhood could hardly have recognized her in the lady who now charmed every one by her easy, graceful manners, her gentle mien, and the soft, sweet tones of her voice. "She seemed to me, after her return," says one, "so lovely, so sweet and gentle, her ardent and impassioned nature so subdued, her heart going out in love to all around her, interested in every thing that concerned the happiness of any one, happy to embrace as fellow Christians all who loved the Lord Jesus, of whatever sect or denomination,—O, it was truly a blessed privilege to be with her."

"Her affection," says another, "was less impassioned, but more intense. The stream had become deeper and more quiet in its flow, imparting a tranquil beauty to all around. She had learned more of human nature, and was better fitted to adapt herself to the varied society with which she mingled; while her increased spirituality gave her a power felt by all, but especially by her nearest and dearest friends. I believe that the impression made upon my own mind was less earthly than heavenly, and that even then the shadow of eternity was upon her spirit. She seemed to view her heavenly Father's hand in every thing; unseen, it led and supported her, and she ever looked upward with sweet filial confidence. Her intercourse with her friends was most delightful, both to her and to them, and if we had known how soon it would cease, a change could scarcely have been desired."

During these last eight weeks of her life, after her return to her native land, her time was so much occupied by the calls of numerous friends and with efforts to meet with different circles who were placing great dependence upon seeing her, that she had but very little leisure in which to employ her pen. Indeed the presence of those dear objects and scenes to which she was so much attached, and from which she had been so long separated, produced an excitement of so engrossing a nature, as scarcely to allow her time or thought for any thing else. Though her health seemed hardly adequate to it, yet she several times attended public worship, and was present at communion in December. She was also present at the meetings of two Ladies' Missionary Societies and addressed them. The following letter was addressed

TO HER COUSIN, MRS. E. A. B.

" *Charlestown, Nov.* 27, 1850.

" My own dear Cousin :—After a weary absence of about seven long years, through the goodness of God, I am permitted once more to return to the land of my fathers, and to the bosom of my own beloved family. The joy of return has indeed been dampened by the sickness and death of my sweet babe, in a foreign land, among strangers. Yet so many rich consolations have been mingled with our sorrow, and so many precious blessings have been spared to us, that we can but bless the Lord, and call upon all within us to bless his holy name. While death has laid low the youthful and the loved in many other family circles, I am permitted to return to the same fond mother, the same dear band of sisters, and to find them all in health and happiness. I had, too, the pleasure of seeing my dear brother Charles in England, in the enjoyment of perfect health, and well established in business.

"And then, too, I have not returned alone and lonely, but with a loved and loving companion, the dear sharer of every joy and sorrow, with whom I have ever enjoyed the purest conjugal happiness. Surely the Lord hath not dealt with me after my sins, nor rewarded me according to my iniquities, but as high as the heavens are above the earth, so great have been his mercies to my unworthy soul.

"I suppose, dear Ellen, we shall see the trace of years on each others' face. I, at least, feel many years older, for those years of absence have been the most eventful of my life. We shall have much to tell each other, though I find it most difficult to talk when the heart is fullest. I can scarcely yet realize that I am not dreaming, but am actually in the body, in dear old Charlestown once more, looking on the same scenes with which my girlhood was so familiar. How often during these years of absence have they passed before me, in the wakeful hours of night, and on the bed of languishing.

"But I cannot begin to tell you the thousand thoughts that are awakened when I think of you. Indeed my poor head is still in a whirl. I can hardly think or talk connectedly. The sorrow which only a bereaved parent can know, the fatigues of our land journey, and the exhaustion of sea-sickness, had greatly prostrated my strength on my arrival; and though I feel somewhat better, yet I am still far from well. May I ask your prayers that the Lord will graciously carry me through the hour of trial and suffering, and prepare me for all his holy will."

TO HER AUNT, MRS. C. WALDO.

"*Charlestown, Jan.* 1, 1851.

"God grant you a happy new year, my dear, kind aunt, happy in his own love and blessing, happy in the sweet consciousness that you do not live in vain, and happy in the gratitude of those cheered by your beneficence and love. I cannot come to tell you this morning, how grateful we feel, dear aunt C., for your kindness to us, but in the quietness of my chamber I can ask Him to bless you, whose favor is life. May he spare your valued life to witness many a happy returning year, bright with his smiles; and when existence shall cease to be numbered by years of time, may a more blessed eternity open before you.

"Though a tinge of sadness clouds the memories of the year just past, as we remember the sweet babe, once the sunshine of our home, now sleeping in death, yet our hearts glow in thankfulness to Him who has been rich in mercy to his unworthy children. Surely goodness and mercy have followed us, and we would bless the name of the Lord forever. In our return to the land of my fathers, in our restoration to the embrace of beloved relatives and friends, in the enjoyment of Christian society and privileges, and above all in the continued loving kindness of our heavenly Father, we feel ourselves richly blest."

This note was probably the last from her pen. On Sabbath, the fifth of January, she became the happy mother of a precious daughter,* and her friends began to hope that her heart, so lately bereaved, was yet to be solaced with earthly joy. During Monday, and the greater part of Tuesday, she was remarkably bright and cheerful, but towards evening she was seized with a chill, which, with other symptoms, somewhat alarmed her friends. Yet as applications were made which seemed efficacious, no danger was seriously apprehended until the afternoon of Thursday. She then evidently had some thought of the near approach of death, for she said to her mother, " O we have been so confident of life, but not now, not now." The mere suggestion so deeply affected her mother that she could not reply; though she afterwards regretted that she did not, as she thought it most probable that Emily wished to make her aware of her own apprehensions, and thus lead to further conversation.

As evening approached, fear increased; her physicians were called, but gave no hope of recovery, though one expressed it as his opinion that she might linger a day or two. When they had left, her husband came into the room, and she looking up to him, asked, " What did the doctors say?" "My dear," he replied, "they think your disease a dangerous one." At these words her

* This child survived its mother but a few months.

countenance immediately lighted up, and, with a heavenly expression, she observed, "O, I want to fly to Jesus." She then expressed some wishes in reference to her babe, particularly that she should be trusted only to Christians.

As she seemed much exhausted, owing to her difficulty of breathing, her husband advised her to defer any further conversation till the morning, when the doctor had expressed some hope that she might be relieved. "No," said she, "now, now is the time." She expressed some solicitude about her husband, who was so soon to be left desolate in a land of strangers. But to his remark, "Jesus can take care of me as he has done of you," she replied with emphasis, "He will, he will." "Never," said her mother, "did I see a countenance so radiant with heaven, as was dear Emmie's, during these few last hours, and never shall I forget that season of prayer when her husband knelt by her side and commended her to God. He prayed in his native tongue, of course I could not understand a word he uttered, but this seemed to me to make it the more impressive. There was such a holy fervor in his manner, into which Emmie seemed so fully to enter, so evident was it that she understood and assented to each petition, I realized as never before, that while 'all people, nations, and languages bow before him,' the Great Hearer and Answerer of prayer comprehends all with equal ease and alike blesses all. For O, it was evident that he was present, and dear Emmie seemed to be enjoying a foretaste of the heaven she was so soon to enter."

It was well she did not defer what she had to say until the morrow, for she was much nearer eternity than her friends had supposed. As her breathing became more difficult, she ceased to speak, but her countenance wore the same heavenly expression of filial trust, and inward peace; and at ten o'clock of the same evening, January 9, two hours after, her happy, loving spirit was released from its clay tenement, and earth exchanged for heaven. Her dying testimony was not needed, for her life is a standing witness to the truth.

Thus closed the earthly career of one whose motto had ever been, "a useful, not a long life." Her's was emphatically useful. Wherever she was, she never failed of finding opportunities for doing good. Whatever service was required by night or day, she never spared herself, but always seemed most happy in those situations where she found most to do. The greatest trial of her missionary life was that the government allowed her to do so little, where there was so much that needed to be done. At Zante she was more favorably situated for usefulness than she had been either at Corfu or Piraeus. She had a larger number under her immediate influence, and these were the children of the higher classes. Several of these boarded with them, so that she had a direct and constant influence over quite a large family. "Her exemplary life of itself," says one, "could not but leave a beneficial, a permanent impression, not only on her pupils, who looked on her as a superior being, but also on the large circle of her Greek friends in general. With such prospects before her, though surrounded with difficulties and pressing cares, she was happy. Hence the day which saw every thing swept away from before her by the cruel hand of persecution, was a sad day indeed. She was leaving the dear youth for which she had so successfully and earnestly labored, with no means of grace, and surrounded on all sides by sin and corruption. But having committed them to God, she found no little comfort in the hope of being permitted to return and spend her remaining days in their midst."

It was the hope of being useful which gave brightness to all her visions of the future. It was this which mainly moved her ever ready pen. It is almost incredible that she could have written so many letters amid her other onerous duties. Many of them were commenced after eleven in the evening, and we not unfrequently find two or even three long letters written at the same sitting. Several hundreds of these have been examined by the compiler, all of which were deeply interesting, and ever evince a mind set upon doing good.

Yet she never allowed her labors for others to interfere with her private duties to God. For many years previous to her death, she used a plan for reading the Scriptures, by which she regularly perused the whole volume of inspiration each year. And as she became familiar with other languages, she was in the habit of reading two or more versions in the same way. "During the two years she spent in Piraeus," says Mrs. Buel, "she, each year read the Bible through in four different languages, English, Greek, French, and Italian; one year using the modern Greek, and the other the ancient." That little compendium of Scripture promises, entitled, "Daily Food," was also her constant companion, and to few, if any, has it proved more fully what its name indicates. Truly might she say with the prophet of old, "Thy words were found, and I did eat them, and thy word was unto me the joy and rejoicing of my heart."

Prayer too was her delight. It was easy for her at any time to lift up her heart unto God. But she always made it a point to have regular seasons for devotion, and frequently set apart whole days for fasting and prayer. Not that she wholly gave up other duties on these days, or appeared unto men to fast, but they were to her seasons of sweet and special communing with God. Those who have been privileged to hear her lead in the devotions of others, can never forget the simplicity, and childlike confidence, yet holy fervor, with which she ever approached the throne of grace; giving unequivocal evidence to all that she was no stranger there. During those months of mental conflict, while deciding the question of duty in regard to going to Zante, she frequently spent whole nights in prayer, so that the servant would often inquire of Mrs. Buel if Miss Waldo was not sick, as she heard her groaning and weeping night after night.

But though scrupulous in the use of means, no one could place less dependence upon them. She fully and deeply realized her dependence at all times upon the influences of the Holy Spirit. Without that divine agency, she felt perfectly powerless, and was therefore careful to cherish no feeling or desire which could hinder the constant indwelling of this blessed Comforter. She delighted in the great principle of justification by faith,—"that blessed doctrine of substitution," as she frequently expressed it. "Give me," says she, "my own warm faith, with all its glow of feeling and life-giving vigor,—a religion of the heart, that can comfort the aching breast, calm the ruffled spirit, and speak the words of hope and pardon to the soul heavy laden with conscious guilt; that boasts not of the meretricious ornaments of eloquence and philosophy, that rests not with the cultivation of the intellect, that relies not on the imperfect works of external morality, but whose boast is a crucified Saviour, and whose preciousness consists in its perfect adaptation to the wants of a sin-diseased soul, pointing us to justification and strength, all-sufficient and omnipotent. How strange that God should have led me to feel so; once it was far otherwise. Truly may I say,

> "'Twas the same love which spread the feast
> That sweetly forced me in.'

Indeed Christ was emphatically her life. The great lesson which she learned in 1842, of entire self-renunciation, and the full acceptance of Christ as her sanctification, as well as justification, was never forgotten. Says one of her friends, referring to that blessed change, "Well do I remember how humbled in the dust she seemed, at the thought that she had ever so grieved the Saviour. Then appeared sin to her in all its deformity, and she manifested deep carefulness, and real desire to have it all eradicated, and to have every idol dethroned. I think I never shall forget the first call I received from her, after she thought she had accepted Jesus as a whole Saviour. 'Now, R.,' said she, with one of her affectionate smiles, 'Do you think that Jesus will always keep me?' With what deep humiliation did she appear to sink into the love of Jesus, desirous to live wholly to him, and redeem in the eyes of the church her former delinquencies, which, however, appeared more glaring to herself than to any one else; for very few Christians, moving in the sphere she did, live a more exemplary life. The prominent points in her Christian course, namely, a deep conviction of her sin as a professor, and the clear views she had of Jesus as a cleansing, sanctifying Saviour, will, I trust, be made a blessing to many readers, and lead some, at least, to see that there is a 'shorter way' than continually groaning, 'O, wretched man that I am!'"

It is evident, however, that she did not always enjoy that perfect peace, that constant enlargement of soul, that union with God in faith and love, which she at this time so clearly saw to be the believer's privilege. Not fully apprehending the simplicity of that life of faith, which gives itself up moment by moment, to Him who has so graciously undertaken our salvation, she at times imperceptibly slid back into that state of comparative doubt which necessarily brings the soul into bondage. Yet her mind had been too much enlightened, she had had too rich an experience of what the gospel can accomplish in the soul that exercises simple, perfect faith in Jesus, ever to be satisfied with any thing short of this. While at Corfu, during a season of comparative darkness, in the summer of 1845, she thus expressed her feelings to an intimate friend.

"How often do I feel the truth of a remark you made to me, years ago, in reference to brother ——. 'But he is in bondage,' you said. Yes, that is what I feel, 'in bondage.' That blessed freedom with which the Son makes free, O, how imperfectly do I enjoy its sweetness! I am in bondage to a sense of guilt and sin. How bitterly does the remembrance of past transgression come over my soul; in what awful contrast does it stand to the pure standard to which the gospel exhorts! Yet I know the fountain that cleanseth, I know the sacrifice that atones, I know the righteousness that justifies; and I do, O, I do cast myself a guilty, weak, and helpless worm alone on that. The precious promises and invitations of the gospel bring balm to my sin-stricken soul, and the, 'O wretched man that I am,' just changes into, 'Thanks be unto God who giveth us the victory through our Lord Jesus Christ;' and then again peace is destroyed, and hope shaken, by a consciousness, a discovery of present bondage. The inward conflict, O, how strong it often is. The flesh lusteth against the spirit, and the spirit against the flesh, and these are contrary, so contrary, the one to the other. I withdraw to the retirement of my own quiet chamber, I take the word of God, I turn my eyes to the cross, I see the salvation Jesus died to give, my heart melts, repentance is awakened, I give myself to this dear Lord, and think I ne'er will grieve him more. But I leave this quiet solitude, I am out in the world, and O, such a world as is here; the sweet savor of that hour's communion with Jesus is lost, the world gains some victory over my passions and affections, and I feel that I am still 'in bondage.'

There is so much in my feelings that I can tell only to God, that he alone can understand, that I feel a growing unwillingness to speak to others of the world within. But, dear sister, have I not said enough to show you how much I need your prayers, how much I need the grace of God to bring my whole soul into willing, cheerful subjection to Christ. Though weaker than a bending reed, I do believe that God could make me strong, that he could seal me his own, and keep the blessed image uneffaced, unmarred. Nothing else, no other power can do it. Pray that he may. Pray for my entire conformity to God, my whole-hearted consecratedness to his service, my daily joy in the Lord my strength, my deadness to the world and life to God."

The following extracts show in what estimation she

was held by her missionary associates. The former is from a letter addressed by Mr. Buel to his wife who was in this country at the time of Mrs. York's death.

"But what shall I say of the sad subject which occupies the greater part of your last epistle. I was most solemnly impressed by it. God has come very near to us in this event. This is the first instance of a death among the members of the Greek mission. The letter came in at evening, and that night was comparatively a sleepless one. As I lay in the same room, and on the same bed where our beloved sister studied and meditated, prayed and slept, days that are past and gone came crowding back, and solemn recollections of by-gone scenes kept up a tumult of thought. The past can never be recalled, but its impressions abide forever. How much reason have we to remember Emily Waldo. Here we prayed together, and were profited by her devout spirit, and encouraged by her earnest faith. Here we three communed at the Lord's supper, and thought that we realized in our own souls the Saviour's presence and promise; here we visited from house to house, and enjoyed in company the daily walk along the beach, and around these shores and hills. How many things we have said and done together that are all laid up in memory's folded hours, to appear again in eternity, fresh and distinct as though they were of yesterday. How assiduously, faithfully, and conscientiously, Emmy pursued the daily toil of teaching those little Greeks; seeking no reward but the approval of her Master and the happiness of doing good. God has owned her work as done in the Lord, and he will doubtless own and bless it more abundantly. 'Her works do follow her.'

"How I pity her desolate husband. It is the living that die when our beloved ones are taken from us. Death brings them no pang of sorrow or bitter grief. 'They sleep in Jesus and are blest.' But our dear brother has suffered a loss as great as any one can here in this vale of tears. But blessed are they that mourn, when mourning brings that comfort with which God comforteth his children. The consolations of God are the only solace for such a sorrow. I really desire to make a right improvement of this solemn providence. Emily did not live for herself, and she has not died for herself. In an important sense may it be said that she died for us. God grant that we may not let her die in vain. By becoming more holy, godly, and Christ-like; more prayerful, heavenly-minded and watchful; more patient, laborious and zealous in our Master's service, we but reflect the virtues of her, our beloved sister in the Lord, who has gone before us."

The following is from a letter addressed to Mr. York by Mrs. Arnold.

"*March* 8, 1851.

"You have indeed lost a treasure, one whose whole soul was devoted to the cause of her Saviour, and who was eminently qualified for usefulness in whatever situation she might be placed. Her life of prayer and cheerful piety during the time she was a member of our household, will never be forgotten. Truly this mission has lost one who earnestly, devoutly, and continually, prayed for its prosperity. And the poor Greeks have lost one who felt the deepest interest in their welfare. But she has gone to that land of rest and peace where she will know no more sorrow, nor pain, nor suffering. It is our part to submit to the stroke of our Father's hand, and say, 'Thy will not mine be done.'"

It would have been easy to add to these, many similar testimonials. But it is not our object to eulogize the dead. Such a course would have been most repugnant to the feelings of our dear departed sister. Expressing her own views of such eulogies, she says:—"How differently in many cases would the departed spirit describe his past life, were it permitted him." And could her happy spirit now address us, no doubt she would speak in still stronger language of her own ill desert, and of the fullness and preciousness of that exhaustless treasury, which Jesus has so graciously opened to his people, for the free supply of their every necessity. 'Worthy is the Lamb,' was the song in which she most delighted on earth. But as she now realizes the extent and fullness of that salvation he purchased, the worth of that soul he died to redeem, and the tenderness of that love with which he freely offers salvation to all who repent and believe on him, with what exultation must this language fill her soul as she casts her crown at the Saviour's feet, saying, "Thou, thou alone art worthy." May He, whose rich grace made her what she was, make her example the means of leading many to himself.

"Rest, gentle spirit, rest!
Thy conflicts o'er; thy labors done;
Angels thy friends; thy *home*
The presence of the Holy One."

THE END.

www.ingramcontent.com/pod-product-compliance
Lightning Source LLC
LaVergne TN
LVHW021144110826
845150LV00005B/1120

* 9 7 8 1 4 2 5 5 4 7 4 5 5 *